'This book packs an extraordinary amount of insight into a deceptively small space' Stephanie Flanders, *Financial Times*

'Mr Kay is a brilliant writer.' *Wall Street Journal*

'It will probably be the cheapest and most valuable investment IFAs can make, both for themselves and for their clients.' Russell Taylor, *Money Management*

'Beautifully written and immensely readable.' Jeremy Peat, formerly chief economist, Royal Bank of Scotland.

'I am in awe' Andrew Hilton, Director, CSFI

'John Kay is one of the most engaging and accessible writers on economics in Britain today' *Morning Star*

JOHN KAY is 'both a first-class economist and an excellent writer' (*Financial Times*). He is a visiting professor at the London School of Economics, a Fellow of St John's College, Oxford and director of several public companies. He contributes a weekly column to the *Financial Times*. He chaired the UK government review of Equity Markets which reported in 2012 recommending substantial reforms. He is the author of many books including *Obliquity* [9781846682896] and *Other People's Money* [9781781254455] both published by Profile Books.

the long and the short of it

a guide to finance and
investment for normally
intelligent people who
aren't in the industry

Second Edition

John Kay

P

PROFILE BOOKS

This second edition published in Great Britain in 2016 by
PROFILE BOOKS LTD
3 Holford Yard
Bevin Way
London
WC1X 9HD
www.profilebooks.com

10 9 8 7 6 5 4

Typeset in Minion by MacGuru Ltd
Printed and bound in Great Britain by
CPI Group (UK) Ltd, Croydon CR0 4YY

A CIP catalogue record for this book is available from the British Library.

ISBN 978 1 78125 675 6
eISBN 978 1 78283 268 3

Contents

11: THE INTELLIGENT INVESTOR'S STRATEGY

12: INTELLIGENT INVESTMENT

13: THE CUSTOMERS' YACHTS

Preface

The purpose of this book is to give you the information you need to be your own investment manager. The first edition was written in 2008, as the global financial crisis was unfolding, and published in early 2009. Subsequently, I wrote and published *Other People's Money* (Profile and Public Affairs, 2015), which analyses the process of financialisation that culminated in that crisis and puts forward a programme of reform.

This comprehensively revised and updated version of *The Long and the Short of It* is a natural companion to *Other People's Money*. The critique of the finance sector developed in *Other People's Money* raises two questions: what should be done to protect the public interest, and what should I do to protect my own interests? The concluding chapters of *Other People's Money* attempt to answer the first of these questions. *The Long and the Short of It* attempts to answer the second. In one respect, my task here is easier. To reform the financial sector, we need to persuade politicians, regulators and the public. To reform your financial affairs, the only person I need to persuade is you.

In this book, I'll describe the investment options available, and the institutions that will try to sell them to you. I'll explain the principles of sound investment, and introduce you to the research that supports these principles. Sound investment is based on the returns from productive assets, and in a modern economy these are mostly owned by companies. So I'll describe how businesses succeed, and fail, in generating value for their shareholders, and how to distinguish fact from fiction in what they tell you.

Profitable investment involves risk, and the returns from investment are uncertain. Amateurs and professionals alike are bad at managing investment risks, although for different reasons. I'll discuss why, and explain the theories that try to clarify how we assess risks and the evidence that provides partial, but only partial justification, for these theories. I'll go on to develop a practical investment strategy for the intelligent investor, based on three fundamental principles – pay less, diversify more and resist conventional thinking – and give you the specific information you need to implement that strategy.

I'll describe the sophisticated innovations of the modern financial system. The same innovations that led directly to the global financial crisis of 2008. The world I will describe is complex and sophisticated, but greedy, cynical and self-interested. The only way to cope is to acquire your own knowledge and form your own judgement. You cannot, unfortunately, trust people who offer financial advice. If you can trust me, it is because the only product I am trying to sell you – this book – is one you have already bought. Even so, I need to insert the caveat that I am not offering advice that is specific to your circumstances, that I am not recommending any particular investment or investment product to you and that I accept no liability whatever for the consequences of your investment decisions. When they work out badly – and some of them will – it will be your fault, and when they work out well – and I hope some of them will also – you will certainly take the credit. I will explain that even a decision that works out badly may have been a good decision. But that is not a proposition that ambulance-chasing lawyers, crusading journalists or politicians wise after the event find easy to accept. So I am not going to offer advice, only suggest how you should make your own decisions.

Most investment books advise you how to trade; I suggest you trade as little as possible. Most investment books advise you to get to know the mind of the market; I suggest you think for yourself instead. Most investment books take for granted that your search for new investments is a search for stocks that are likely to go up. While I'm certainly not going to dissuade you from that, I suggest you give equal weight to a different question: is this investment different in character from those I already own?

In this book I shall describe the principles of intelligent investment that lead to these, and other, unconventional conclusions. But you will probably want to begin with a more conventional stance, and I would encourage you to do so. The conventional investor follows the average of what professional investors do. The power of conventional thinking in the City is so pervasive that this is, in reality, what the vast majority of professional investors do themselves. But you can follow that consensus with the aid of publicly available information and the properties of efficient markets. Instead of paying heavily for conventional thinking, you can use conventional thinking for free.

The conventional investor is in awe of those who have a deep understanding of what 'the market thinks'. He should be: he is typically paying enough for the privilege. The education of the conventional investor begins with forming a sceptical view of financial market expertise. The intelligent investor doesn't care what 'the market thinks', save to the extent that its mistakes and irrationalities create opportunities. For the conventional investor, risk is being out of step; for the intelligent investor, risk is losing money.

But it is uncomfortable to be out of step. And the conventional investor will do as well as the average of professional investors, which isn't bad, and better than the vast majority of retail investors. The strategy I recommend is that you begin as a conventional investor, and as you gain experience and confidence, you devote an increasing fraction of your portfolio to intelligent investment. The intelligent investor has a mind of his or her own, can take a sceptical view of market wisdom and make his or her own risk evaluation. Such detachment enables the intelligent investor to earn better returns with less risk of loss.

The term 'intelligent investor' originates with Benjamin Graham, who wrote a book with that title. Graham's modern disciple is Warren Buffett, the most successful investor in history. He has claimed that

> Observing correctly that the market was frequently efficient, they (the academics – and many investment professionals and corporate managers) went on to conclude incorrectly that it was always efficient. The difference between these propositions is night and day. (Cunningham, quoting Buffett, 2002)

I'll paraphrase Buffett's remark by saying that markets are 80 per cent efficient, but the profits from investment are mostly to be found in the 20 per cent that is not.

There is more to this comment – a lot more – than meets the eye. Your immediate, and understandable, reaction might be to ask 'tell me about the 20 per cent'. But I want first to raise the more general philosophical issue. What does it mean to say that a theory is 80 per cent true? We're used to the idea that theories are either true or false. There isn't room for theories that are partly true, or mostly true.

But we have to find room. The world of business and finance is comprehensible only with the aid of theories, such as market efficiency, which are illuminating but not true. It would be easy to pursue this issue into the philosophy of science, but this is intended to be a practical book. I shall simply make the pragmatic assertion that you cannot be an intelligent investor if you believe either that markets are always efficient or that they are not mostly efficient – if you believe that the efficient market hypothesis is true, or if you believe it is false. The same is true of two other theories – the capital asset pricing model and the approach to risk analysis that I describe as 'subjective expected utility' – theories which are central to modern finance theory and to the risk control models widely used in financial institutions.

The 80/20 per cent hypothesis – that the world of business and finance is best understood with the aid of models that are partly true, partly false, is at the heart of this book. You need to understand both the 80 per cent and the 20 per cent. It is necessary both to be familiar with the ideas of efficient markets and subjective expected utility, and yet not to take either notion too seriously. Intelligent laypeople, who approach finance and investment without preconceptions, may find this easier to accept than professionals who have been forced to take one side or another in a debate.

The target readers of this book have to deal with issues of finance and investment because they have been successful in some other, unrelated, activity. These readers expect the same level of intellectual seriousness as from a book of popular science or popular history, and that is the level at which this book is written.

Many issues of finance and investment are, necessarily, technical, and their explanation involves jargon. I've provided at the end of the book a glossary which offers quick definitions of many terms that may be unfamiliar. The jargon is the language of the financial professional. No apology for jargon should be required if the explanation of its meaning needs to be a good deal longer than the word or phrase itself. There is one conspicuous exception to that principle – the use of the term 'high-net-worth' for 'rich'. I hope there is none of the jargon of the management world, in which new terms are coined to conceal emptiness of thought.

But this book is not an academic monograph. I have kept references to a minimum. I give references to enable the reader to check the sources of claims made. In a final section on bookmarks and bookshelves I have indicated some books and web sites that readers can use to pursue issues further. I have not thought it necessary to provide links to the commercial web sites of product providers – these are very easy to locate – but I have included details of some useful web sites that provide information or comparisons useful to intelligent investors.

Acknowledgements

Many people assisted in the preparation of this book. I would like to thank those who have helped me understand the financial services industry over the past twenty-five years. This book is critical of that industry, and of what it offers to small customers. Yet while there are people in the City who are beyond contempt, there are also many who consistently display exceptional intelligence and unquestionable integrity.

I have been privileged to work with, and learn from, some of them.

I am grateful to the people who commented on drafts of the first edition – in particular, Alistair Blair, Tony Boyce, Jonathan Davis, Roman Frydman, Tim Harford, Chris Hughes, Chris Llewellyn Smith, Callum McCarthy, Vaclav Potesil, Jorim Schraven, Robert Tann, Mark White and Martin White – and to the many readers who provided feedback on the first edition. They corrected some of my errors, but I was delighted by the positive tone of their feedback.

The first edition of this book was self-published. I had lost patience with the ineffectiveness of an industry controlled by conglomerate publishers with the short time horizons now characteristic of most public companies – an issue touched on in this book and about which I wrote more extensively in the review of equity markets that I conducted for the British government in 2012. But since then Andrew Franklin and his colleagues at Profile Books have demonstrated that some of the values of a successful book publisher can be sustained outside the framework of public markets. I am pleased to publish this second edition with them.

I am grateful to ThomsonReutersLipper for providing proprietary data and analysis, to Robert Metz and Liz Bates for research assistance on this edition, and to Johanna Vorholz for her work on the first. And especially to Jo Charrington, who has not only organised the process from first draft to finished book but who also, by keeping my life in order, has made the whole venture possible. And an especial thank you to Mika Oldham. She suggested the idea of such a volume in the first place and has been a source of encouragement throughout.

Sense and the City

Can you be your own investment manager?

Many people think that successful investment is about hot tips. If someone rings you with a hot tip, ask yourself, 'Why is he calling me?' and put down the phone. If you act on a hot tip from a friend, you may lose a friend and some money. If you act on a hot tip from a stranger, you will just lose some money.

Books tell you how to become rich from stocks. Software programs and training courses claim to help you trade successfully. Their authors assert that, with their assistance, you can make a comfortable living playing the market. Before you succumb, ask the following question: if I had a system that held the secret of lazy riches, would I publicise it in a book from which I will earn – at most – a few thousand pounds? Writing a book is hard work, believe me.

You may already have asked a similar question: why would anyone who could write a book like this one choose to do so? I am one of a minority, perhaps eccentric, who find the study of financial markets intellectually engaging. And I enjoy writing, and hope that you enjoy reading this book as much as I have enjoyed writing it.

My target reader wants to make good returns on investments without worry. He or she probably thinks that managing money is a chore, and that people obsessed by the stock market are sad. My target reader's financial objective is to have sufficient financial security not to have to worry about money. My target reader would be happy to go on holiday, even for months, and not look at his or her portfolio. My target reader is willing to take risks, but only with small amounts.

My target reader is a retail investor. This is not a technical definition; there are several regulatory classifications of investor provisions that identify high-net-worth investors, sophisticated investors, professional investors. My target reader may be some or all of these things. But by 'retail investor' I simply mean someone who is investing his or her own money. The purpose of this book is to help such a reader become an intelligent investor who can be his or her own investment manager. If you are hesitant about taking on that responsibility, you should, by the end of this book, be able to ask penetrating questions of anyone who offers you financial advice. This book is not for people who want to become professional traders but for those who want to sleep securely, knowing that their portfolio is in the most trustworthy of hands – their own.

A book that told you how to be your own doctor or lawyer would be an irresponsible book. 'The man who is his own lawyer has a fool for a client.' Is it possible to be your own investment manager? The financial services industry attracts many of the smartest people in the country, and certainly includes many of the best-paid people in the country. The City of London is made up of office blocks accommodating thousands of professionals. Traders in the City spend long days dealing in securities, with access to unlimited computing power and extensive data resources. How can you compete with them? You can't, and you shouldn't. But you can hold your own in their world. There are reasons why DIY investing is possible, even necessary, unlike DIY law or DIY medicine.

An obvious and depressing reason for relying on your own

judgement is that most people who offer financial advice to small and medium-size investors aren't much good. A doctor or lawyer may not always get it right, but you can be confident that their opinions are based on extensive knowledge derived from a rigorous training programme with demanding entry requirements. You can also expect that the doctor or lawyer will have real concern for your interests, not just his or her own.

Traditionally, financial advisers were neither expert nor disinterested. People who called themselves financial advisers were salesmen (overwhelmingly they were men) remunerated by commissions and selected for bonhomie and persuasiveness rather than financial acumen. They were financial advisers in the same sense that car dealers are transport consultants. Most of these financial advisers knew little that their customers did not know – except one piece of information which they did not share: how much the adviser would be paid to make a sale.

Things are getting better. Comprehensive regulation of the sale of retail financial services began in Britain only in 1987. As regulators investigated, they found instances of major abuse; the mis-selling of personal pensions and endowment mortgages was followed by the marketing of over-priced and often useless payment insurance (PPI) to millions of customers by salespeople motivated by commissions and targets. Some victims were scammed again by claims management companies which offered to assist in recovering the compensation banks were obliged to pay.

The Retail Distribution Review, implemented from 2013, attempted to clarify the distinction between the independent financial adviser and the sales force, and banned many commission payments, requiring advisers to seek remuneration through clearly disclosed fees. This sits on top of a requirement to 'know your client'; advisers must obtain basic information about their client's situation and needs, and understand key features of the products they sell. Training obligations are more demanding, although there are still many financial advisers whose expertise has been acquired in the school of life, over a drink, or several.

There is still a long way to go. A 'bias to activity' is intrinsic to the processes of financial advice; few people will pay much to be told to do nothing, even though that is often wise counsel. Training is largely concerned with the process of selling and the mechanics of regulation rather than financial economics. After reading this book, you will understand the principles of investment better than most people who offer financial advice to retail investors. You do not have to worry about 'knowing your customer' if you are your own customer. You need not fear that the advice you give yourself will be biased by the prospect of a fat commission.

You can also benefit from the wider set of opportunities that the internet gives the individual investor. Financial services cannot only be bought and sold electronically, but can also be delivered electronically. From home or office you can now obtain a wide range of information, buy and sell securities very cheaply and access many investment products that did not exist two decades ago. Comparison sites enable you to scan a range of providers.

The internet will never replace the truly skilled intermediary, just as it will never replace the doctor or lawyer, though it may change the roles of these intermediaries. But the search engine and the comparison site can now do much of what intermediaries would once have done. Unfortunately, the search engine and the comparison site are also corruptible. Like the salespeople, they are paid by product providers. What these sites display may not be comprehensive; what they highlight is not necessarily what is best for you.

The divergence between your interests and the interests of those who would sell you financial products is pervasive. One of the oldest anecdotes in the financial world tells of a visitor to Newport, Rhode Island, weekend home of American plutocrats, who is shown the symbols of the wealth of financial titans. There is Mr Morgan's yacht, and there is Mr Mellon's yacht. But, he asks, where are the customers' yachts? That question is as pertinent today.

For a time I served on the board of the statutory body that paid compensation to retail investors who had lost money through fraudulent or incompetent financial advisers. One such business was run by a flamboyant and persuasive individual who drove a Rolls-Royce and entertained his customers at lavish parties. In the small town in the north of England where he had lived all his life, his extravagant lifestyle was interpreted as evidence of his financial acumen. In a sense, it was: the money received from customers went directly into his pocket and paid for the chauffeur and champagne.

Crude theft is, fortunately, rare in the financial services industry, although some practices came close to what an ordinary person would describe as robbery. But the lawful earnings of many people in the industry seem ludicrous to an ordinary person, and they are. In the course of this book you will learn how activities of little social value are so profitable for the individuals engaged in them.

No complex analysis is required to see that every penny that people take home from the City is derived from fees, commissions and trading profits obtained from outside the City. This is a simple matter of accounting. You and I, and people like us around the world, pay the large salaries and bonuses of people who work in the financial sector. We do so in our various roles as investors, as prospective pensioners, as customers of financial institutions and as consumers of the products of businesses that use financial services.

There may be consolation for British readers in the knowledge that the City of London is a very large exporter, so that much of what the City takes is paid by foreigners. In Britain, even people who do not work in the City benefit from the foreign exchange earned and the tax paid by City individuals and City institutions, although they also have to compete with City folk to buy houses and hail taxis. This consolation may, however, turn to anger when it emerges that some of the best-rewarded City people pay little or no UK tax – the result of unwisely generous concessions on capital gains tax and liberal interpretation of rules governing residence and domicile.

The massive rewards available in financial services are sometimes defended as the result of competition to attract talented people. The observation is true. The City of London recruits many of the best minds in the country. In my experience, only a few top academics and lawyers rival the best minds in the City for raw intelligence. The mechanism that achieves this result is indirect. Massive rewards attract greedy people. If the number of greedy people is large, then financial services businesses can select the most talented among them. Within the City you find many who are greedy and talented, many who are greedy and untalented, but few who are talented but not greedy. Interest in ideas is generally secondary to interest in money. That is why these people are in the City. So it is, unfortunately, necessary to be suspicious of the motives of everyone who offers you financial advice.

There are people in the financial world whose concerns are primarily intellectual. You will find some in the finance departments of universities and business schools. Others are behind the scenes in banks and financial institutions, where they are described as 'quants' or 'rocket scientists'. Modern financial markets are sufficiently complex, and the relevant analytic tools sufficiently sophisticated, for some people to find observation of these markets interesting for its own sake.

The good news is that the retail investor can take a free ride on all these skills and activities. You can be a beneficiary of the efficiency of financial markets. Efficiency has both a wide and a narrow interpretation. Financial markets, though costly and imperfect, have proved to be a more effective mechanism for promoting economic growth than central direction of production and investment. But in investment circles market efficiency has a specific technical meaning.

That meaning relates to the 'efficient market hypothesis' (EMH), the bedrock of financial economics. Much of this book will be concerned with the implications of that hypothesis and its limitations. The professional expertise of everyone in financial markets is focused on the value of stocks and shares, bonds, currencies and properties, and on advising on when to buy and sell. These market prices reflect a consensus of informed opinions. The information that Vodafone is a successful company or that the economy of Venezuela is in a mess is known to everyone who trades Vodafone stock or Venezuelan bolivars.

The efficient market hypothesis posits that all such information is absorbed in the market-place – it is 'in the price'. The market is a voting machine in which the opinions of all participants about the prospects of companies, the value of currencies and the future of interest rates are registered, and the result is publicly announced. The corollary of the efficient market hypothesis is that the results of the painstaking research of everyone in the City are available to you for free.

If that conclusion seems startling, and it should, then imagine going to an auction – a fine-wine auction, for example – dominated by professionals. At first, you might be intimidated by the assembled expertise. But if you behave prudently, the dominance of professionals ensures you can't go too far wrong, because their bids will be the main influence on the price you pay.

You may not be convinced by this analogy. You may fear that there will be collusion amongst the dealers at the auction, that the market is rigged against the little guy. You may well be right. Fifty years ago you would have been justified in having similar suspicions about securities markets. But, over recent decades, extensive public resources have been devoted to securing the integrity and transparency of financial transactions. This is partly because of popular revulsion at corrupt and fraudulent practice, and also because a reputation for honest dealing, or at least more honest dealing than is found elsewhere, is a real competitive advantage in international markets, in which the City trades so successfully.

These regulatory provisions don't work perfectly, and never will. When you trade, your broker must normally secure 'best execution', which means you get the best price available in the market. The reality is that a bank dealing on its own account will often do better. But not so much better. The edge that the skilled and experienced buyer may have can be more than offset by the advantages you have in trading for yourself. You have greater knowledge of your own needs, you know that you can trust yourself. Best of all, you don't have to pay yourself. Your bonus is already in your pocket.

From gentlemen to players

The efficient market hypothesis describes how the market handles information. Information has always been the lifeblood of markets, but the manner in which information is handled has changed. The old City of London was founded on relationships. Who you knew, who you had been to school with, determined how you did business and especially with whom you did business. The City of London was one of the last areas of English public life in which social class played a major role in career advancement and commercial activity.

For the gentleman stockbroker of yesteryear, information meant gossip. The broker would arrive in the office at nine-thirty or ten in the morning to enjoy leisurely conversations with clients, business contacts and colleagues before the alcoholic lunch that was an essential part of the working day. He

– invariably he – was an agency broker. He would receive orders from an individual investor or a fund manager, and transmit those orders to 'the market'. A jobber on the floor of the stock exchange would seek to match potential buyers and sellers. All brokers charged the same high commissions. These structures disappeared from London as a consequence of a group of regulatory reforms that became effective in 1986 and which are for ever known as 'Big Bang'.

The atmosphere of today's financial markets is very different. The London Stock Exchange no longer has a trading floor where buyers and sellers meet. Now, the large investment banks have their own raucous trading floors, which may contain hundreds of desks, each linked to the market via a screen. The visual display has several parts, designed to convey the impression of an unmanageable flow of new information. Gentlemanly capitalism has given way to the professional City. The modern institution encompasses a mixture of people and approaches: the urbane sophistication of investment bankers who plan new issues and plot mergers and acquisitions; the rocket scientists and the quants – intellectually sophisticated but often lacking in common sense; the traders – some of them graduates of the finest universities and business schools, some with no higher education at all – demonstrating the aggression and ethics of the market stall. The organisations that combine these functions are an explosive mix which frequently does detonate. The overall change is from benign amateurism, based on what would now be called insider trading, to specialised professionalism, based on sophisticated analytic tools.

The development of quantitative techniques in investment analysis goes back more than a century. The first index of stock prices – an average of the prices of twelve leading stocks – was created in the US in 1896 by Charles Dow. A few years later the Frenchman Louis Bachelier presented a thesis, on the mathematics of securities prices, that is generally celebrated as the foundation of mathematical finance. Bachelier encountered resistance, both from practitioners, who ignored his work, and from his examiners, who gave it the modest accolade of 'honorable' – insufficient to enable the author to pursue an academic career. For half a century his work would be ignored.

Other seminal contributors to quantitative finance – such as Harry Markowitz, Fischer Black and Myron Scholes – would also initially encounter negative reactions. I'll describe their theories and these responses in later chapters. Their work, like that of Bachelier, is now fundamental not just to the analysis but also to the operation of modern financial markets. The University of Chicago was where much of this work originated, and Chicago was also where new derivative markets were created. Both the graduates and the techniques were taken up by Wall Street, and subsequently by the City of London. The triumph of players over gentlemen was not confined to banking. The London insurance market would similarly lose much of its competitive position in the face of more professional competitors from continental Europe (southern Germany and Switzerland) and the United States. London would remain a primary location for financial services business even as ownership of the businesses passed out of British hands and the personnel became increasingly cosmopolitan.

While the passing of the old City of London was inevitable, there were losses as well as gains. Much of the old City was characterised by a certain rigid integrity. It wasn't exactly that people wouldn't steal from or cheat each other; rather, that they would do so only in certain well-defined and tolerated ways. This carefully modulated self-regulation – its ultimate sanction, as the saying went, was the devastating rebuke of the raised eyebrows of the Governor of the Bank of England that could end a City career – could not survive the globalisation of financial markets. Globalisation, professionalisation and the rise of financial conglomerates made new and different forms of regulation of financial services inevitable. A wide-ranging, new regulatory regime was introduced in Britain in the 1980s, at the same time as the deregulation of Big Bang. This seemingly paradoxical mixture of regulation and deregulation effectively substituted supervision of behaviour for regulation of the structure of the industry and the incentives of firms and individuals. This shift in regulatory philosophy, which occurred in both Britain and the United States, has proved to be a mistake.

Technology, globalisation and, in London, the erosion of English class distinctions drove this transition. The process of change was mostly handled well, although with results in Britain that no one predicted. Today the City of London is a successful international institution, a major exporter and the country's highest-paying employer. All kinds of financial institution – retail banks, investment banks, insurance companies – have broadened the range of their activities. Retail banks have become financial conglomerates, with a wide range of investment products as well as their traditional roles of providing payment services for large and small customers and lending, mostly to corporate clients. The rationale of such conglomeration lies in cross-subsidy and cross-selling. Cross-subsidy involves selling some products below cost to enhance the sales of other, more profitable lines; cross-selling involves use of the customer list for one group of products to promote others. Both practices generally operate to the long-term, and frequently the immediate, disadvantage of customers. You should take advantage of cross-subsidy when you can, but resist cross-selling.

Many commentators have anticipated the consolidation of retail banks into a smaller number of global firms, and the demise of the bank branch. Both of these developments are happening, but more slowly than has been generally supposed. The emergence of Santander as a new high-street bank, formed by the acquisition of former building societies, is the largest change in industry structure in a century, and there are some fresh challengers, such as Handelsbanken and Metro Bank; but the structure of retail banking, in contrast to wholesale banking, remains largely unchanged.

Still, the manner in which retail banking is conducted has altered radically. The traditional bank manager was an independent financial adviser. He was an active participant in the local community, to which he would usually be attached for many years. He might meet his customer at the golf or Rotary club, and the modern obligation to 'know your customer' would be met implicitly and automatically. The caricature of Captain Mainwaring in *Dad's Army* – self-important, unimaginative, but scrupulously honest and reliable – identifies the qualities that banks sought, and found, in their managers.

Personalised banking is today prohibitively costly for a mass market. While the cost of processing transactions has fallen with the development of information technology, the cost of employing people to handle them has risen. The costs of employing knowledgeable people to handle them has risen particularly rapidly since the growth of the financial services industry enabled people of mediocre abilities to command large salaries. A vestige of relationship-based advice survives in private banking for high-net-worth individuals. But the modern bank branch is a shop, and, like other shops, it is staffed by pleasant sales assistants with limited knowledge and training. The physical environment has been remodelled accordingly.

Despite the efforts of designers, the bank branch is less inviting than most shops. If the goods are money, it is impossible to reconcile security with an attractive display. Few products are more suited to online retailing than financial services, and that is how I suggest you buy them. Still, the branches remain busy, as you discover if you try to visit one at lunchtime. Many people dislike dealing with money and managing financial services, and need personal reassurance when they do. Many readers will continue to feel this need for personal reassurance at the end of this book. Take advice, then, but do not pay much for it. Adopt the same sceptical attitude towards your advisers as you would towards a sales assistant in a shop.

Although regulation of financial services is extensive, even intrusive, regulation has not served well the consumers and citizens who are the readers of this book. The thirty years since Big Bang have seen the mis-selling of personal pensions and endowment mortgages in the 1980s, and the New Economy bubble in the 1990s. Then the promotion of complex packaged securities in the years after 2003 was followed by a near meltdown in the global financial system after the collapse of the market for these products in 2007–8. At the same time, the careless lending of financial institutions in the north of Europe to borrowers in the south has created economic tensions that threaten social stability and the very survival of the European project. The common characteristic of all these episodes has been that the individuals who promoted them became very rich and the public at large – taxpayers and users of financial products – was left poorer.

The fundamental reason for the repeated – and continued – failure of regulation to meet the needs of retail customers is the prevalence of what economists characterise as 'regulatory capture'. Regulation operates, in large part, in the interests of the firms who are regulated rather than the customers of these firms. This is not because the regulators are corrupt – although in the United States, the degradation of the political process by the mechanisms of campaign funding is the primary cause of regulatory failure: in Britain most politicians and administrators engaged in the regulatory process are honest people performing a difficult job to the best of their abilities. We have held, and continue to hold, unrealistic expectations of what regulation might achieve.

Scepticism and wariness are needed in dealing with even the most apparently reputable financial institutions. The intelligent investor needs to develop his or her own strategy. This book is intended to help the intelligent investor do that.

2

Basics of Investment

Before you begin

I'll start with the preliminaries that you should go through before you even think about investment principles or investment options. Compile a list of your financial assets and liabilities. Do it with your spouse or partner. (In Britain the legal status of the relationship matters for some financial issues, though not many.) Whether you manage your financial affairs separately or collectively, plan together. If you subtract your liabilities from your assets, the balance is your net worth. 'High-net-worth' is the new euphemism for 'rich', but what people mean by 'high-net-worth' varies. For purposes of financial regulation, you may be classified as a 'professional client' rather than a retail customer if you have assets of €500,000, but few people in the City will be impressed by your net worth. You are well off, it is often said, if you earn more than your brother-in-law.

Most people will find that their house, with the associated mortgage, dominates the calculation. The regulatory definition of assets excludes your main residence and associated mortgage. I suggest that for most purposes you do the same. But don't put house and mortgage out of your mind altogether. Borrowing on mortgage is the only form of borrowing appropriate for anyone planning an investment portfolio.

In the first edition of this book (published in 2009), I encouraged readers to adopt a 10 per cent target rate of return for their investments. That was an ambitious target – as we will see when we look later in this chapter at the rates that sophisticated investors have actually been able to achieve – but I feared that a more modest aspiration would turn readers away. But recent experience has done a great deal to make expectations more realistic. Aim for 8 per cent. Even if you fall short of this, mortgage borrowing is so cheap that it is realistic to expect to earn more on your investment portfolio than the cost of the mortgage. Many conservative people want to reduce their mortgage as quickly as they can, but such a strategy isn't necessarily wise.

If you have any debts other than a mortgage, repay them before you undertake any investment. In particular, repay outstanding credit card balances. The interest rate on almost all credit cards is well above 8 per cent and certainly above the return you can realistically expect on your investments.

You will pay income tax. Most people with an investment portfolio pay income tax at the higher rate of 40 per cent, which applies to incomes above around £45,000 a year. A still higher rate of 45 per cent is applied to income above £150,000 per year. Income tax in Britain is assessed on an individual basis, so a couple may be able to reduce tax by appropriate allocation of investments and investment income between them.

In most of what follows, I generally assume that you expect to pay tax at 40 per cent. Only a sixth of the population does this, but readers of this book are not average. However, as a result of recent changes in the taxation of savings you need not be paying income tax on the return from your portfolio unless its value exceeds £200,000 or so. With the aid of further tax reliefs for ISAs and pension funds, which I will describe further in Chapter 10, it is now possible to build savings of £1 million or more over a lifetime entirely tax-free. That is a big change even since the first edition of this book. If you can earn 8 per cent, you can keep more or less 8 per cent. And since the tax that is levied on savings is now very complex, there is an additional reason – to simplify your tax return – for trying to keep your savings in tax-exempt vehicles.

Two other taxes may be relevant to an investment portfolio: inheritance tax and capital gains tax. Inheritance tax is payable on estates over £650,000 (for a married couple). Capital gains tax is normally levied at a rate of 20 per cent, but only when you sell assets.* You can deduct losses from gains, and the first £11,100 of gains in any tax year are tax-free.

You need a current bank account, a savings account, a credit card and a mortgage. Most people have been with the same provider for years. This is usually a mistake. Financial institutions rely on inertia and give introductory incentives to buy what later become uncompetitive products. The problem originates with consumers rather than with institutions. Banks or insurers who provide everyday good-value pricing find their customers drift away to the introductory bargains offered by other companies.

If you are willing to be a 'rate tart', sitting regularly at your computer pursuing the best deals, you can benefit permanently from introductory incentives. Most readers have better things to do. I would prefer to find a provider who offers competitive terms and good service, and so, I suspect, would you.

The best buys are often from 'monoliners' – firms that specialise in a single product group – because their future depends on their reputation in these products. Examples of monoliners are Fidelity (funds), Capital One (credit cards) and Direct Line (insurance). Monoliners are often owned by big institutions, but that usually doesn't matter to the consumer because the dedicated business model remains the same.

You need a current account and a savings account.

---

* There is a 28 per cent rate on residential property (other than your main home) and a 10 per cent rate on many business assets.

Internet-only banks are often the most competitive. Stand-alone savings accounts frequently advertise excellent rates, but beware the introductory offer: providers reduce rates once sufficient funds have been attracted to the accounts. Financial services conglomerates, especially the major banks, will try to cross-sell you products. They are not very successful at cross-selling, but they emphasise this business strategy to themselves and the City. The products they cross-sell are rarely competitive, and the sales pitch will waste your time.

Since the modern bank branch is a shop selling products you probably don't want to buy, you do not need to pay fees – in the form of charges or low rates of interest for a branch-based current or savings account – to go there. An internet account will operate on the platforms of the major banks, so that processing of everyday transactions should proceed in exactly the same way. Banks seeking new current accounts now offer services designed to make switching to them easy.

You will usually be offered a choice of a mortgage interest rate fixed for two, three or even five years, or a variable rate that will change with (and may even be linked to) the Bank of England's base rate. A lot of fuss is made about the choice, and you may be asked whether you think interest rates will go up or down over the next two, three or five years. You don't know, and nor does anyone else. These fixed and variable rates reflect underlying market 'swap' rates. (I'll explain swaps in Chapter 9.) If you are persuaded by the metaphor of market as voting machine (although I'll suggest several reasons why you might not be), then you will recognise that the market has voted on the future of interest rates and you probably have nothing to add.

Probably more important – and certainly more under your control – is the up-front fee you are charged. The lender may offer complex combinations of interest rates, fixed fees, percentage fees and valuation and legal costs, so a calculator is needed to work out which combination is best. If these calculations sound tedious, they are not complex and, per minute, may be the best-paid work you ever do. In the first edition of this book I suggested that there was little reason to use a mortgage broker, but conditions have changed. The market has tightened since the financial crisis, and the broker may be able to help you get deals that are not available directly. The regulatory palaver associated with taking out a mortgage is now so extensive that a helpful friend may assist. Be wary, however, of any financial advice offered to you.

The benefits of getting these preliminaries of banking arrangements and mortgages right are so large that anyone who fails to do so isn't serious about managing money. Obtaining a better deal may involve moving away from an established high-street provider (although frequently by moving to a subsidiary of an established high-street provider). You don't need to be a rate tart; a comprehensive review of your arrangements every few years will be enough.

Review financial risks outside your investment portfolio

Households generally cover some risks by insurance – risks such as domestic fire or theft, car accidents, travel disruption. I'll come back to insurance in Chapter 11, after discussing the ways people think about risk. Most people take out insurances they shouldn't, and most people fail to take out insurances they should. Here are a few preliminary pointers.

If you have dependent children, you should consider insurance on the life of both parents. The low take-up of such policies is a legacy of the sale of life assurance, costly savings products with a small element of life insurance, by salespeople on commission. The policyholders could rarely afford the premiums so most policies lapsed, leaving children without protection and creating a well-founded perception that life insurance was expensive.

A more appropriate form of insurance – life insurance that has no savings component but which lasts for the period of the child's dependency – is cheap, since young parents rarely die, although the financial consequences can be extremely serious if they do. Policies that cover costs and loss of earnings from long-term illness or disability are also worth considering, although far from cheap.

Do not buy insurance from someone who offers it when you are buying something else. You will be invited to purchase extended warranties on domestic appliances and to take out travel insurance when you buy a holiday. Because the purchaser has little opportunity to compare prices, or even to consider the purchase carefully, these policies are usually expensive. Payment protection insurance, pressed by banks on customers who took loans from them, was such scandalously bad value that its sale was effectively banned. When you refuse these policies, you are depriving the salesperson of income, since he or she receives large commissions for selling these policies. That is why the policies are expensive and the seller persistent. If you want such insurance – mostly you don't – buy it elsewhere.

Insurance can cover some of the financial risks of everyday life: accidents at home and on the road, theft, sudden death. But the most serious financial risks that the majority of households face come from redundancy and unemployment, old age and chronic illness, and the breakdown of marriage and relationships. Such risks cannot be insured, or only to a limited degree, and can be mitigated only through social institutions, effective money management and successful investment. That's the main subject of this book.

Investment choices

When people discuss investment at clubs and dinner parties, in pubs and lunchrooms, they generally mean investment in securities – stocks and shares, bonds and deposits. But investment finds another meaning in the creation of the physical infrastructure of the economy.

Companies invest in plant and machinery. They must finance inventories and pay for work in progress. They operate from offices and shops. The government invests in schools and hospitals, bridges and roads. People used to make a sharper distinction than they now do between savings – putting money aside for later – and investment – putting that money to use. But, perhaps significantly, these words have lost this differentiated meaning. I'll talk instead about financial investment and productive investment. The return on financial investment must, ultimately, be generated by the return on productive investment. The quest for financial perpetual motion machines is unending, but the basic principle of bookkeeping – money that goes out equals money that comes in – is as immutable as the natural laws of thermodynamics. Financial investments fund physical investments, and the two principal means by which they do so are shares and loans.

A share (an equity) gives you a portion, for better or worse, of earnings and realisations from the productive activities of a company. Secured loans give the lender the right to seize some or all of the company's assets if it fails to pay agreed interest and the original money lent.* Unsecured loans give the lender a legal claim against the borrower for payment, which will be met

---

* A mortgage – the loan most familiar to many readers – allows the unpaid lender to repossess the mortgaged house if certain conditions are met. In Britain – and in most European countries, but not the United States – if the sale of the house does not realise enough money to pay the debt, the bank remains an unsecured creditor for the balance.

only after secured creditors have realised the value of the assets pledged to them.*

Physical objects, such as offices and machinery, are not the only productive assets. Many of the assets of modern companies are intangible. Companies own brands, and build reputations. They acquire licences and intellectual property, and they build internal systems and structures. These assets earn a return, just as plant and buildings earn a return; many such assets can be bought and sold, and can even provide security for loans.

Some financial assets are not directly associated with productive assets. Governments discovered – hundreds, even thousands, of years ago – that they could borrow to finance wars and profligate consumption because lenders knew that states could raise taxes to repay the loans. (This did not always mean that they would, as lenders continue to rediscover.) Individuals can, more modestly, borrow to spend now on the strength of their ability to earn income in future. So some investments are backed by what economists coyly call 'time preference' – the premium that impatient or hard-pressed people will pay to spend now rather than later.

Lending to government, or to a credit card borrower, must compete with lending to a company. So the returns you can earn on these financial investments are ultimately governed by what productive investments can earn. None of the complexity of modern financial markets, which package and repackage securities in ever more elaborate ways, can alter that essential truth. A loan that is tradable is called a bond.

---

* The distinctions between shares, equities and secured and unsecured loans have become much less clear-cut than formerly as a result of financial innovation. A non-recourse loan gives the lender rights over the asset on which the borrowing is secured, but not over the other assets of the borrower. Junior, mezzanine or subordinated debt will be paid only after other lenders have been repaid. Such debt may, in recompense, enjoy some share of the profits.

While investors mostly own indirect claims on productive assets, through shares and loans or bonds, investors can also own a direct claim on the productive activities of businesses, governments and households. They sometimes do so by owning the buildings – shops, offices, warehouses, factories and houses – from which businesses, governments and households operate. Or they may lease equipment to them.

Shares, bonds and property are the main investment options. I will discuss 'alternative investments' – which have become increasingly popular – in Chapter 9. Most investors will also require some cash for immediate needs, and to exploit investment opportunities as they become available. In gloomy economic circumstances, cash may be an investment class in its own right.

What choices should you make? The strategy I will propose in Chapters 10 to 12 is that you should begin as a conventional investor – relying on efficient markets to provide you with the assembled wisdom of the financial services industry. Recognising that this efficient market theory is only illuminating, not true, you will want, over time, to become an intelligent investor, employing your own judgement to pay less, diversify more and take contrarian stances.

Realistic expectations through conventional investment strategies

The conventional investor follows the average of other professional investors. The power of conventional thinking in the City is so pervasive that this is what the vast majority of professional investors do themselves; there is a self-referential consensus. You can follow that consensus with the aid of publicly available information and the properties of efficient markets. Instead of paying heavily for conventional thinking, you can use conventional thinking for free.

What do conventional investors do? The largest investors in Britain are pension funds. UK pension funds hold total assets of around £1,500 billion, and dominate the British investment scene. These funds are required to keep detailed accounts of their activities. Most of them provide reports in standardised form to The Pensions Regulator, to their trade body, the Pensions and Lifetime Savings Association, and to private companies, which provide performance-monitoring services to their subscribers.

Local authority pension funds offer a benchmark for the conventional investor. This sounds unadventurous; it is meant to be. Local authority pension funds are meticulous in obtaining the best and widest range of advice, and in acting on it. They pay close attention to their own performance, and that of other similar funds. They are long-term investors; local authorities know that they will still be around in ten, twenty, even fifty years' time, and that they will be responsible then for the consequences of their actions today.

I have chosen local authority pension funds, rather than pension funds as a whole, because many private-sector pension funds have closed their schemes to new entrants and are beginning to run down their activities. In many cases, the sponsoring company is now mainly concerned with minimising its involvement and its liabilities. As a result, private-sector funds hold many more bonds than they once did. Or than municipal funds, with a long-term perspective, do. According to State Street Investment Analytics, British local authority pension funds held (at the end of March 2014) 63 per cent of their assets in shares, 17 per cent in bonds and 8 per cent in property. The remaining 12 per cent was mainly in cash and 'alternative assets'. (I'll discuss these alternative options in Chapter 9.)

What have they been able to earn on these assets? Pension funds are encouraged to 'think total return', and I encourage you to do the same. An earlier generation of investors was taught (in some cases compelled) to limit their spending to their income

– the interest and dividends they received each year from their portfolio. When interest rates rose to 15 per cent or more in the 1970s, and inflation was running at 27 per cent, anyone spending their income was wildly imprudent. Conversely, if your investments have a low yield but continue to generate capital gains – as with many investments in the last two decades – then it may be sensible to anticipate the value of some of that growth.

'Thinking total return' means treating both income and capital gain as part of the yield on your investment. A report in 2014 by pensions consultancy Hymans Robertson showed that over the five years to 2013 the median local authority scheme (within the Local Government Pension Scheme) made a total return of 6.4 per cent per year. There was some dispersion around this figure, but more than half of all schemes earned within plus or minus 1 per cent of it. To describe 6.4 per cent as the median return means that half of all the schemes did better than 6.4 per cent, and half did worse. The median is also known as the 50th percentile of the distribution of outcomes, and I will come back to this important statistical concept in Chapter 7. With inflation at 3.1 per cent, a 6.4 per cent median return meant that the typical fund increased the purchasing power of its assets by an average of 3.3 per cent per year. But 2008–13 was not a good time for investors, who suffered the impact of the global financial crisis in 2008–9, especially if they were heavily exposed to shares and property. Returns were somewhat better over most earlier and later five-year periods. Over the twenty-five years to 2011, these local authority funds made, according to calculations from State Street analytics, an average return of 8.6 per cent, equivalent to a real return of 5.0 per cent after inflation of 3.6 per cent.

Charitable endowments, managed for the long term, provide another benchmark. In Britain there are funds established centuries ago whose investments yield public benefit today; for forty years I have been involved with the endowment of St John's College, Oxford, which still holds some property bequeathed more than 450 years ago by the founder, Sir Thomas White. But one British endowment dwarfs all others. The Wellcome Trust is the legacy of Sir Henry Wellcome, who bequeathed to it the pharmaceutical company he built. When the Wellcome business was sold to the company that is now GlaxoSmithKline, the trustees invested in a diversified portfolio and now control assets of around £18 billion. The returns on that endowment are a major source of funding for British science. Wellcome has a strong investment record. Over ten years, its total return is 8.6 per cent per annum (6.0 per cent in real terms), and over twenty years 8.9 per cent (5.2 per cent in real terms).

Table 1 show the distribution of the assets of the Wellcome endowment. I have included for comparison three funds from outside the UK, each among the largest investors in the world. CALPERS is the pension scheme for employees of the State of California; ABP, the scheme for public employees in the

Table 1: **Distribution of assets by long-horizon funds, 2015**

	Wellcome Trust (UK)	CALPERS (State of California)	ABP (Netherlands)	NBIM (Norway)
Shares	48	51	28	61
Bonds	0	26	43	36
Property	13	9	10	3
Hedge funds	12	0	6	0
Private equity	24	9	5	9
Cash	4	3	0.2	0
Other	0	2	8	0

Source: Wellcome Trust Annual Report and Accounts (at 30 September, figure 6); CalPERS Comprehensive Annual Report (at 30 June, pp. 55 and 101), ABP Quarterly Report (at end-Q3) and NBIM Government Pension Fund Global Annual Report (at 31 December, Table 8)

Note: Numbers may not add up to 100 due to rounding.

Netherlands, is the largest pension scheme in Europe; while Norges Bank Investment Management (NBIM) manages the oil fund established by the government of Norway for the long-term benefit of the country's population. All these funds, like those of British municipalities and Wellcome, have time horizons stretching into the indefinite future.

I anticipate two different types of reaction to this discussion. Some readers may feel dispirited by the size and scale of the resources available to these professional investors. The funds of NBIM exceed £100,000 for every man, woman and child in Norway; your own portfolio may well be smaller than that. The answer is that you can mimic at very low cost what these large conventional investors do – and in Chapter 10 I will explain how to do just that.

Other readers may think that the returns reported by local government pension schemes and by Wellcome – between 8 and 9 per cent in the long run – are disappointing. They have heard stories about people who have made a killing on the stock market through hot tips and inspired timing. If you click on internet bulletin boards, you will read about the search for 'ten and twenty baggers' – stocks that will rise, or have risen, to ten and twenty times their initial value.

If you open an online stockbroking account – and you should – you will soon be seduced by bulletin boards and offered hot tips. Often these tips are for 'penny shares', priced so low that any movement seems to have a large effect on the wealth of the holders. When you begin investing, you may be inclined to back some of these tips, and I wouldn't discourage new investors from doing so with a very small proportion of their available funds. It is a cheap way of beginning to learn about the mechanics and the psychology of the market. A few people, possessed of ill-founded self-confidence or books or courses on how to trade, set out to make a fortune in this way. The New Economy bubble in the late 1990s saw the emergence of 'day traders', who bought and sold stocks several times a day. Stockbrokers established offices to service them.

As with many forms of professional gambling, there do seem to be small numbers of people who are good at it. To good luck they add exceptional psychological insight and rigorous self-control. But surveys of day traders show that after a few months most give up, or are obliged to do so by their families. Not all. Besides the few who develop successful careers, a larger group of people become addicts, whose financial stability and family lives may be destroyed by their obsession.

Financial innovations, especially in derivative markets, have greatly increased the opportunities and risks of market-related gambling for both amateurs and professionals. In securities markets, many people are in a position to gamble, legally, with their employers' money. Some become hooked; a few corporate and municipal treasurers have lost large sums; and a personal tragedy has become an expensive disaster for shareholders or taxpayers. The most sophisticated punters are managers of hedge funds and operators in the proprietary trading operations – 'prop desks' – of investment banks. Even here, there is a heady mix of real skill, addiction, obsession and self-delusion on the part of both individuals and organisations. In 2008 the hubris of sophisticated financial professionals brought some of the largest and longest-established financial institutions in the world – Royal Bank of Scotland, Union Bank of Switzerland and Citigroup – to the point of collapse. If you are tempted to make a living from stock market speculation, this is not the book for you. There are many other books aimed at the seekers after twenty baggers. The target reader of this book is concerned – as are local authorities and the Wellcome Trust, the cautious trustees of the pensions of the public employees of California and the Netherlands, and the guardians of Norway's oil wealth – with the careful and responsible stewardship of assets. In your case, the assets of which you are the careful and responsible steward are your own.

That Hyman Robertson report on the Local Government Pension Scheme offers an insight into why some funds did better than others.*

Characteristics of funds in the top 10 (by performance):

They use a limited number of managers (typically 1–3 managers with balanced mandates focused on equities and bonds);

They retain their managers for the long term, even through inevitable periods of underperformance;

They adopt a simple structure focused on equities, bonds and property;

They make limited use of alternatives;

Some use internal management; and

There is evidence they rebalanced assets back to benchmark over 2008/09 as equity markets collapsed; this enabled full participation in the equity market rebound in 2009/10.

Source: Hymans Robertson

There is good advice here for all investors. Keep it simple, take a long-term view, do not chase either asset classes or managers that have recently performed well, or ditch those that have recently performed badly. If you do employ investment managers, put your trust in a few, do not pay too much and stick with them. But consider carefully whether you need them at all.

The evidence that you have much to gain by taking control of your own affairs is compelling. Retail investors like you and

---

* Selman, L., and Wright, J., (Hymans Robertson), 2014, LGPS structure analysis: December 2013, Department for Communities and Local Government, available at: https://www.gov.uk/government/uploads/system/uploads/attachment_data/file/307926/Hymans_Robertson_report.pdf

me don't have the same opportunity as these pension funds and endowments to measure and compare performance. The return on the average balanced fund managed for retail investors is below the average return on local authority pension funds (Table 2). This is not surprising, since the same people manage both types of fund and the charges on funds managed for retail investors are higher – sometimes much higher.

Table 2: **Average returns to retail investors, 1995–2015***

Total return to 1 February 2015 (% p.a.)	10 years	20 years
Mixed Investment (based on Association of British Insurers classification, 40–85% in company shares)	7.0	6.6
Life insurance policy	2.2	6.1
Instant access account	0.3	0.9

Source: *Money Management*

Table 3: **Performance of UK retail funds 2005–15**

Total return to 31 December 2015 (% p.a.)	5 years	10 years
Median UK equity fund	7.3	11.7
Median Sterling corporate bond	5.6	7.4
Median Sterling gilt	4.3	8.4
Median UK real estate fund	6.4	4.4

Source: ThomsonReutersLipper

The return on with-profits life assurance policies, the most common balanced investment held by retail investors, has over the last ten years been a shocking 2.2 per cent. Although the twenty-year return is higher, it is difficult to understand why anyone would want to pay substantial fees, or anything at all, to the people who achieved this result.

---

* Based on premium/savings of £50 per month; income reinvested.

Perhaps retail investors, who make their own choices, do better. Perhaps. Hindsight and selective memory play a large role in anecdotal accounts of investment successes, and the evidence points to the need for stern discipline in investment decisions. The US investment research house Dalbar has for many years measured the average return earned by investors in mutual funds, the main vehicle for attracting the long-term savings of the American public. Over twenty years (to end-2014), the annual return to those who invested in equity funds has been 5.2 per cent. Not unsatisfactory, you may think – until you are told that the total return on the S&P 500 index, the principal US stock market index, has been 9.9 per cent over the same period. The average return to holders of bond funds has been a miserable 0.8 per cent against 6.2 per cent for the equivalent bond index. This underperformance – averaging 5 per cent per year – has persisted, year in year out, in the Dalbar analysis.

Why do retail investors do so badly? Charges are part of the explanation. Mutual fund investors pay not only management fees but also the trading costs within the funds they hold and further trading costs when they themselves buy and sell, which they do too often. But the principal explanation is bad timing. Retail investors buy high, and sell low. They are late into fashionable sectors, and late out of unfashionable ones. There is probably no worse investment strategy than following the conventional wisdom with a time-lag, and that is precisely what many small investors do – often with the encouragement of their advisers.

You may want to close the book at this point, and either continue, alone, the search for the twenty bagger or decide you might as well leave your money in the bank. Both decisions would be mistakes. Intelligent investment is rewarding over the long run. Albert Einstein is reported as having said that compound interest is the most powerful force in the universe. There is no evidence that Einstein said this, and it is unlikely that he did, but the intelligent investor should recognise the force of the axiom. The reinvestment of returns over a long period has dramatic consequences. Over ten years, £100 invested at the average instant access rate of that decade, 1 per cent, would become £110. At the 8 per cent return exceeded by Wellcome and achieved over the long term by local authority pension funds, £100 becomes £216. Over forty years, the difference between a 1 per cent return and one of 8 per cent is the difference between £149 and £2,172. While many amateur investors tend to be attracted by capital gains and attach little weight to dividends, reinvested dividends play a large role in long-term capital accumulation. If your target 8 per cent return were made up of 3 per cent dividends and 5 per cent capital gain, your £100 would accumulate to £2,172 with reinvested dividends and £704 without them.

An average return of 8 per cent per annum before inflation is a demanding, but not impossible, target for the intelligent investor. The Bank of England's inflation target (which has mostly been undershot) is 2 per cent,* so that a corresponding real return is between above 6 per cent. An 8 per cent return will turn £100 into £215 in ten years, and a 6 per cent real return will add 80 per cent to the purchasing power of your savings in a decade. Although 8 per cent may seem a disappointing rate of return to locker-room braggarts, it appears high when viewed as a return on productive investment, rather than on financial investment. While businesses often target higher returns on investment than this, they rarely achieve them.†

---

* There are several different measures of inflation. Two that are relevant to intelligent investors are the Retail Prices Index (RPI) – used to determine the returns on index-linked bonds – and the Harmonised Index of Consumer Prices (HICP) – the basis of the Bank of England's inflation target. The RPI, which has more extensive coverage of housing costs and differs in technical details of construction, has generally risen faster.

† The return on equity they say they earn is often much higher. After reading Chapter 6, you should understand why.

Look at it in another way. The return on secure assets such as cash and government bonds is today between zero and 3 per cent depending on the length of time for which you are willing to invest your cash. If you succeed in earning an 8 per cent rate of return, that means you are receiving an additional 5 per cent – 8 per cent per annum for taking on risk – the risk premium. This is a handsome reward, and an achievable one.

This generous level of return for risk has been sustained over very long periods – a century or more. The question of why the risk premium is so high has puzzled financial economists, who call it the 'equity premium paradox'. I'll come back to the equity premium paradox in Chapters 7 and 8. The size of the premium is a reason why most investment institutions allocate very little to cash. You should do the same. (There are stronger reasons for making allocations to indexed bonds.)

If you set yourself a target rate of return of 8 per cent, you are already differentiating yourself from many conventional and most professional investors. Asset managers are mostly judged relative to the performance of their peers, and therefore focus not on absolute return but on relative return. It is not enough to have earned 20 per cent if the benchmark index has returned 25 per cent (as it often will, over a short period, and as it did over longer periods in the 1990s). It is defensible (even if uncomfortable) to have lost 15 per cent if the benchmark has lost 20 per cent. The manager can blame 'the market' for his poor performance.

When you become your own investment manager, the incentives and consequences are different. The money you manage is your own, and there is no one else to blame. Relative performance may pay the salary and bonus of a fund manager, but relative performance doesn't pay the bills of the investor. What pays bills, in the long run, is total return in absolute terms after tax and expenses; and by focusing on absolute rather than relative return you can immediately give yourself an advantage over the conventional investor. In the next chapter, I'll review the ways in which shares, bonds and property can contribute to that objective.

3

Investment Options

Sense about shares

You might buy a share in an initial public offering (IPO), when a company raises capital by selling its shares to the public. It is much more likely that you will buy a share on a market that trades shares in established businesses. Businesses like Vodafone, the mobile phone company, which has for many years been the most popular share among small investors.

Vodafone shares are quoted on the London Stock Exchange, and, like many large British companies, Vodafone makes its shares more accessible to American investors through a New York listing for American Depository Receipts (ADRs).* Vodafone's share price varies every minute of the trading day.

You can find the price from a wide variety of internet sources (possibly the price as it was fifteen or twenty minutes ago). The real-time price is considered valuable information and is typically available only to people who pay for the information or are clients of stockbrokers. As I write, the price to buy Vodafone is 221.10p and the price to sell is 221.00p. The average of the two, 221.05p, is called the mid-market price. In the course of the day,

---

* A tradable certificate, denominated in dollars, issued by a US bank which holds a corresponding number of Vodafone shares.

the mid-market price has varied between a low of 217p and a high of 222p. Because Vodafone shares are so actively traded, the difference between buying and selling prices is very small. That difference – the spread – will be much wider for small companies, perhaps as large as 5 per cent of the value of the share.

What do you get for 221.10p? People often say that shareholders 'own' the company. They don't, at least in Britain, as you will find out if you turn up at Vodafone's head office in Newbury to assert your 'ownership'. In 2003 the House of Lords reaffirmed its 1948 ruling that 'shareholders are not, in the eyes of the law, part owners of the company'.* As the court explained, what shareholders own is their shares, and ownership of shares confers a variety of rights. The value of a share is the value of these rights.

In 2015 Vodafone made a profit after tax of about 22p per share, from which it paid dividends amounting in total to just over 11p. The directors of the company decide how much will be paid to shareholders in dividends and how much will be retained for investment. The company doesn't have to pay the shareholders anything. What the directors decide to pay can be, and generally is, varied in line with the performance of the business. But if the company does declare a dividend, all shareholders have an equal right to receive it. If the company is wound up, the shareholders are entitled to whatever is left – normally very little – when all the liabilities of the company have been met. Most companies are worth more as a going concern than the realisable value of their assets, and the usual reason a company is wound up is that the business is failing. But the possibility that the value of the business could be distributed to the shareholders influences the value of the stock, even if such a distribution rarely happens in practice.

Another right conferred by a share is the right to vote. At annual general meetings of companies, shareholders elect directors and can pass resolutions to determine the policy of the

---

* Evershed LJ in *Short v. Treasury Commissioners* [1948] 1 KB 116 122.

company. In practice, these meetings are agreeable but insignificant occasions attended by professional advisers and a few, mostly retired, small shareholders. All nominations and resolutions are put forward by incumbent management and approved by overwhelming majorities. The process resembles elections in totalitarian states.

These shareholder powers to elect and remove directors are important, even if rarely exercised. Someone – typically another company – who acquires a controlling block of shares in a company can appoint the senior managers of that company and take control of the direction of the business and of its assets and earnings. The threat of such a takeover means that the value of the stock is influenced not only by what the directors decide to pay – the dividend policy – but also by the value of these underlying assets and earnings.

Let's look at the assets, earnings, dividends and assets of Vodafone. When you think of a phone company like Vodafone, you think of the masts and cables and radio equipment that make it possible to run a telecommunications network. The accounts of Vodafone put the value of this equipment at around £27 billion. Since there are around 26 billion Vodafone shares in issue, these assets work out at only around £1 per share, as against a market price of 221p per share. The gap between the value of the operating assets in the accounts and the total value of the company is large, but a difference of this magnitude is common in modern companies. In 2015 Vodafone made a profit of around £5.8 billion after interest and tax, consistent with earnings per share of 22p. With a share price of 221p, the PE ratio – the ratio of price to earnings – is 10. Dividends of 11p per share imply a dividend yield – the annual income as a percentage of the share price – of 5 per cent on an investment of 221p. These ratios – the price:earnings ratio and the dividend yield – are key numbers for all investors. The return on a stock like Vodafone will depend partly on the dividend yield but also on the capital gain, or loss, that shareholders make as a result of changes in the market's valuation of the business. Together these make up the total return.

The 5 per cent yield compares with the 0.1 per cent you could currently expect to earn on cash, or the 3 per cent you might earn on the long-dated government bonds I shall describe below. In other words, if you expect Vodafone to maintain its dividend and the capital value of its shares – not to increase its earnings or its assets, but simply to maintain their value – Vodafone would be a good buy and certainly a much better buy than a government bond.

Clearly, many people fear that competitive pressure in the telecommunications market will leave Vodafone unable to maintain its earnings, or that new technologies will leave the company behind. Holders and potential holders of Vodafone shares are more optimistic; that is why they are shareholders. But they are endlessly jittery. So the share price is constantly changing.

Even for a stable, well-established company like Vodafone, the share price may rise, or fall, by more than the 11p annual dividend in a single month – or even sometimes in a single day. People in markets offer *post hoc* explanations for these constant fluctuations – the release of new economic data, or a Delphic utterance from the chairman of the Federal Reserve Board. The idea that these events can add or subtract £5 billion to or from the value of Vodafone's assets and earnings makes no sense. These share price fluctuations are what natural scientists call 'noise', random interference in physical processes. Developing this analogy, financial economists describe people who trade on hunch and gossip, with little skill or knowledge of what they are doing, as 'noise traders'. Most tip sheets, and many of the books on how to trade the market, are written for noise traders.

As the relevant time horizon extends beyond a few days, the rise and fall of the Vodafone share price will reflect perceptions of the prospects of the company. These assessments will, in turn, depend on the outlook for the telecommunications sector and Vodafone's performance relative to other phone companies, and on market sentiment towards Vodafone. Do analysts rate the management team highly? Is a large institution attempting to buy, or sell, a large block of shares? How does Vodafone stand in the competitive world of telecommunications?

Behind statistics there is always a story. Although now one of Britain's largest companies, Vodafone was founded only in the 1980s. Racal Electronics, a manufacturer of military radios, won one of the two licences to introduce mobile phone service in the UK. Vodafone was the more successful of the two licensees. An IPO followed in 1989, with the shares then valued at the equivalent of about 20p. As mobile phones were transformed from clunky instruments for businessmen into fashion accessories for teenagers, Vodafone's revenues, profits and share price climbed steadily. In the second half of the 1990s the boundlessly ambitious Chris Gent became chief executive and the 'new economy' bubble was under way. At the peak of the market the price of Vodafone shares reached nearly £5 and the company then accounted for 15 per cent of the total market value of all British listed companies, well ahead of great and long-established businesses such as Shell and BP. This absurd overvaluation of the shares enabled Gent to embark on a global acquisition spree, in which the company acquired mobile phone operators all round the world.

The bubble burst. But unlike most heroes of the 'new economy', Gent and Vodafone were left with a solid business, albeit one worth only a fraction of what they had paid for it. Today Vodafone is still the world's largest mobile network operator, although the current management have taken steps to rationalise its sprawling activities. But those who invested at the top of the market have today a holding worth less than half what they paid for it fifteen years ago (although this calculation is complicated by the distributions shareholders received when the company sold its share in its US business to its partner Verizon). Once the darling of the market, Vodafone is today languishing out of favour, recommended to investors not for its growth prospects but for its yield.

Each company has its own history; its fortunes wax and wane, in ways few anticipate, and investors must live with these fluctuations. In the first edition of this book I chose to illustrate the mechanics of stocks with what was then Britain's largest company, the oil giant BP. Like Vodafone, BP was acquisitive in the 1990s. In 1911, John D. Rockefeller's Standard Oil had been broken up by the US courts and through the twentieth century the world oil industry was dominated by seven companies often called 'the seven sisters'; in the 1990s investment bankers began to put together what anti-trust legislation had taken apart. John Browne, BP's then chief executive, masterminded bids for two large American companies, launched a 'Beyond Petroleum' initiative to position his business as environmentally friendly and socially aware, and produced rapid earnings growth by a vigorous cost-cutting programme. With these moves, Browne was seen as having outflanked both Shell and the company's largest American competitor, Exxon. For the best part of a decade Browne was Britain's most admired businessman.

Then it all went wrong. An explosion in 2005 at BP's Texas City refinery killed fifteen people, and the following year maintenance failures forced the closure of the pipeline to the company's huge Alaskan reserves at Prudhoe Bay. Cost-cutting seemed to have had insufficient regard for long-term consequences. From 2003 to 2007 BP shares substantially underperformed the market. Browne fell victim to an internal power struggle, and announced his retirement date. Then he resigned abruptly after revelations of a gay relationship and false statements in court documents.

As a result, BP was out of favour when I described it in 2008, struggling on a dividend yield of 3.8 per cent – still a better rating than Vodafone today – and a PE ratio of 9.5 – a worse rating than Vodafone. But things were to go from bad to worse. Much worse. In 2010 the company's North American operations suffered a still bigger disaster when the Deepwater Horizon rig spilled oil into the Gulf of Mexico. The incident cost BP $50 billion in fines and damages – around one-third of the company's market value – and more in reputation.

This discussion of 'poor performance' and being 'out of favour' is based on an idea of relative valuation of these and other companies – in particular, on a comparison between Vodafone and BP and the overall market index. Ever since Charles Dow published the first share price index over a century ago, investors and market professionals have given constant attention to the indices. When they ask 'What is happening in the market?', they will begin by looking at what has happened to 'the index'.

The earliest indices were simply averages of share prices, but the calculation has become more refined. In Britain today, the two main indices are the FTSE (pronounced 'footsie') 100-share and the FTSE all-share indices. The first is an index of the prices of the 100 largest companies. The composition is revised quarterly, so that every three months some of the smaller constituents that have performed poorly are ejected and newcomers admitted. The all-share index includes all companies quoted on the London Stock Exchange. However, in both indices the constituents are weighted by their size, so that the 100 largest companies typically account for about 80 per cent of the value of the all-share index.

The value of shares in Vodafone, BP and other companies depends partly on the fundamentals of the company – assets, earnings, cash flow and dividends, brand, competitive position and management strengths – and partly on market sentiment. Returns from shares are the result of the interacting influences of the company's fundamentals and 'the mind of the market'. These issues will be the subject of the next three chapters.

Basics of bonds

Treasury 4.25 per cent 2055 is possibly the most boring investment you could own. If you buy £100 of these bonds, the British government will pay you £4.25, in two half-yearly instalments, every year till 2055 and will then give you back your £100 (the principal).

If you are happy to sit in your armchair for forty years, you can do so with absolute security. Well, almost absolute security. There is a risk that the British government will not be able or willing to meet these obligations. This is not a very big risk, but it exists – and if the government were that of Argentina or Zimbabwe, it would be a serious risk. The risk that the issuer will not pay is the *credit risk* of the bond.

Another risk is that you might stir from your chair and want your £100 back before the redemption date of 7 December 2055. The government not only need not, but may not, repay you a day earlier or a day later than the redemption date. If you want to realise your investment before 2055, you will have to sell your bond to someone else. This is easy to do, but the price you will get for it may be more or less than £100. Today it is much more: £145. Because interest rates are unprecedentedly low, most bonds today sell at prices above those at which they were issued.

Treasury 8 per cent 2021, which was issued at around £100 between 1995 and 1997 and will be repaid in 2021 at £100, currently sells for £134. Price fluctuations such as this are the result of *interest rate risk* associated with the bond. Interest rate risk may work in the investor's favour – as it has done for initial holders of this bond – or against it. The longer the life of the bond, the greater the interest rate risk.

In 1888, in the heyday of Queen Victoria's reign, her government issued 2.5 per cent Consols. These bonds paid interest, but the government accepted no obligation to redeem them, though it retained the right to do so. Such irredeemable bonds carried the greatest interest rate risk of all. By the time of Victoria's jubilee in 1897, the price of Consols was above £100, and it would reach this level again in 1947, when the post-war Labour government pursued a policy of very low interest rates under Hugh Dalton, a distinguished economist but an incompetent Chancellor of the Exchequer. By December 1974, with rapid inflation and economic and political crisis, the value of Consols had fallen to £15. But as interest rates fell, the price rose steadily, and in July 2015 the government finally repaid holders the £100 it had borrowed 127 years earlier. At today's interest rates it could borrow even more cheaply than Queen Victoria had been able to do.

Treasury 4.25 per cent 2055, whose current price is £145, leaves you exposed to inflation until 2055. Inflation almost wiped out the savings of people who invested in Consols. In 1888 you could have bought a house with £100; in 1974 you might have paid more than £15 to replace the lock to the front door, and the £100 you received when Consols were repaid in 2015 would still not have been enough to buy the door itself.

Since 1981 you have been able to protect yourself against inflation risk through index-linked government bonds, an even more boring investment. Both the amount of interest and repayment of capital on Treasury 1.25 per cent 2055 are linked to the Retail Prices Index (RPI). The guarantee comes at a price – the much lower interest rate of 1.25 per cent. If inflation is more than 3 per cent, the total return from the indexed bond will be greater than that on Treasury 4.25 per cent 2055; if inflation is less than 3 per cent, you will get a better return from the conventional security.

Indexed bonds remove inflation risk, but all bonds are subject to interest rate and credit risks. Most British government bonds currently sell above their issue price, because interest rates have fallen over the last thirty years. Treasury 8 per cent 2021 pays £8 per year, an 8 per cent yield to someone who bought it at its £100 issue price. But for someone who pays £134 today, the annual income is only 6 per cent of their investment. This return is called the 'running yield'. And then you must factor in the inevitable and considerable capital loss of £34 between today and 2021. The price of the bond will decline, until it reaches £100 at maturity. The total return on such a bond, including both running yield and capital loss, is known as the gross redemption yield (GRY), and for Treasury 8 per cent 2021 the GRY is only 1.4 per cent.

Treasury 8 per cent 2021 was issued when interest rates were high, but there is a much more recent issue of Treasury 1½ per cent 2021. Plainly, the 8 per cent stock must sell at a higher price than the 1½ per cent stock. The market moves so that the gross redemption yields are much the same on all bonds with the same maturity, old and new. This is 'arbitrage', a process in which investors look at similar securities and buy those that are relatively cheap and sell those that are relatively expensive. It is such arbitrage which has pushed up the price of Treasury 8 per cent 2021 to £134.

I have written as though there were a single interest rate, but there isn't. As I write, the gross redemption yield on five-year government bonds is around 1.4 per cent. For a ten-year bond the GRY is around 1.8 per cent and for a twenty-year bond you can get 2.5 per cent. This relationship between return and maturity is known as the 'yield curve'.

Conventional wisdom holds that the 'normal' shape of the yield curve has this upward slope, because longer bonds carry more interest rate risk. But although this is frequently true, it is not necessarily true. The main influence on bonds with short maturities (the short end) is the Bank of England's interest rate policy, and the main influence on bonds with long maturities (the long end) is expectations of future inflation. Sometimes, when the Bank's Monetary Policy Committee reacts to worries about inflation by raising interest rates, yields rise at the short end and fall at the long end. Even Treasury index-linked 1.25 per cent 2055 carries interest rate risk. The government will guarantee the purchasing power of your £100 only if you hold the bond through to 2055. As with a conventional bond, you can realise the value of your bond earlier only by selling it to another holder. The price of an indexed bond will vary with real interest rates, rather than with nominal interest rates.

You might expect that real interest rates on indexed bonds would not vary much, but they do. In 1998, during the New Economy bubble, conventional investors, expecting to become rich from their dot.com stocks, were not interested in securities that did little more than guarantee their holders against inflation. The price of index-linked stocks fell, and the real gross redemption yield on them rose above 4 per cent.

After the bubble burst, more realistic expectations set in. The price of index-linked stocks rose and yields fell. Long-term investors were attracted to these assets. During the global financial crisis, Treasury index-linked 1.25 per cent 2055 proved a racy investment. Pension funds looking for long-term security pushed the price of these bonds up by 30 per cent in just a few months. Today, the real yield on short-dated British government-indexed bonds is actually negative – the government guarantees that the value of what you get back will be less than the value of what you put in. The price of Treasury 1.25 per cent 2055 is currently £193, which implies a negative real redemption yield of -0.7 per cent.

Before 2008, people occasionally worried about Argentina or Zimbabwe but did not take seriously the idea that there was credit risk associated with the bonds of countries in North America or the European Union. Now they do. In 2007 the Greek government could borrow at rates only marginally higher than those charged to Germany, but within five years Greece was unable to borrow at all. The contagion spread to Portugal and then to Ireland, Italy and Spain.

As members of Congress grandstand over the legal authority of the US government to meet its obligations, it is timely to remember that people who bought Russian and Chinese bonds a century ago did not worry about credit risk. After all, Russia and

China would always have a government. And indeed Russia and China did always have a government. But they did not always have a government that was willing to pay the debts incurred by its predecessors, and there was nothing foreigners could do about it.

Still, even now the most soundly financed governments, such as the German, have as low a credit risk as can be imagined. The signature rates are those of the ten- and thirty-year 'bund', and in early 2016 these bonds have GRYs of around 0.25 per cent and 1 per cent respectively. The security of the debt of other Western countries and of international agencies is not far behind that of Germany. Next come the biggest and best industrial companies, such as Nestlé and Shell. Banks were once regarded as the soundest risks of all – houses like Rothschild prospered because their banks were more creditworthy than kings – but there have been too many instances in modern history of banks letting down their customers, bondholders and shareholders. The security you are right to feel when dealing with major banks comes mainly from the knowledge that governments will not allow such institutions to fail.

The downside of this implicit guarantee – more disturbing, therefore, to taxpayers than to investors – is that large retail banks use their deposit base to support complex speculative transactions that their senior management may not understand. The successive collapses of financial institutions in 2008, and the costs of guarantees and bail-outs to avert losses on further collapses, illustrated just how expensive the consequences might be. This concern is the rationale behind America's 'Volcker Rule', designed to prohibit proprietary trading, and Britain's plan to ring-fence the retail activities of conglomerate banks.

Credit rating agencies, such as Moody's and Standard & Poor's, make influential judgements about the quality of borrowers and their bonds. The very best corporate borrowers, along with the governments of rich countries in Europe and North

America, enjoy credit ratings of AAA (often called 'triple-A'). Sensationally, Standard & Poor's downgraded the debt of the United States after the debt ceiling dispute in July 2011. And, to the surprise of some and the ultimate disillusionment of others, many of the structured products, which I'll describe in Chapter 9, also qualified for high ratings from these agencies. The top four credit ratings are described as 'investment-grade', and many institutions will only buy investment-grade bonds. Ratings below investment-grade are known as 'junk'.

The initial yield on a bond reflects the credit risk when the bond is issued, but a bond that is prime investment-grade when issued may deteriorate over its lifetime. Ford and General Motors were once among the most respected companies in the world. But by 2006, fears over these companies' obligations and their then weak trading meant their bonds were rated as junk. In 2009 General Motors filed for bankruptcy, and its bondholders were forced to accept a writedown of the value of their holdings.

There is no such thing as an absolutely safe long-term investment. If you know that you want to buy something in 2055, Treasury index-linked 1.25 per cent 2055 is about as good as you can get, though the price you pay for that certainty is high. But not many of us are certain about our future plans, and certainly not about what we will be doing in 2055. In Chapter 7 I'll discuss more systematically what is meant by security and by risk. And in Chapters 10 to 12 how you should construct your portfolio to protect yourself from risk.

Pillars of property

If you own a property, you own both the building and the land on which it stands. The insurance value of your house is its rebuilding cost. In Britain today that rebuilding cost is generally less, and sometimes much less, than the market value of the house. My London house, for example, is worth more than five times its insurance value. The site is a great deal more valuable than the building itself.

Sometimes, however, the replacement cost is greater than the market value. This implies that, if the building did not exist, no one would plan to construct it. Most stately homes are impractical for modern living and their rebuilding cost exceeds their market value. At the other end of the spectrum, a small terraced house in northern England may also be worth less than its rebuilding cost. Population has moved away, and demand for property is weak. There is not much new construction, and what is built today is constructed to much higher standards.

If you draw up a personal balance sheet in the way a company would, you are very likely to find that your most valuable asset is your house. Yet your house is not quite like your other investments. You bought your house in order to live in it, and for the rest of your life you have to live somewhere. That doesn't mean you are indifferent to its value, as you will learn from the interminable dinner party bores who celebrate the rising value of their house with too much Sauvignon Blanc.

As a homeowner, you are both an investor in housing and a consumer of housing services. When you are young, your investment in housing is probably modest, and your prospective consumption of housing services extensive. As you age, your investment in housing is greater and the date draws closer at which the graveyard caters inexpensively for your accommodation needs. Young people want housing to be cheap; older owner-occupiers benefit from it being expensive. People in middle age may intend to move to a smaller property when their children leave the nest. Retirees may use equity release schemes to realise some of the value in their houses.

Much of the value of their house will accrue to their heirs. Only you can decide how you view that legacy. Providing a nest egg for your children may be one of your investment goals; or their good fortune may simply be an unavoidable consequence of your inability to realise the whole value of your assets for your own benefit in your own lifetime. For all these reasons your house, and the associated mortgage, cannot be treated in the same way as the assets you own for purely investment motives. And housing and house prices are inevitably a politically charged issue.

Most people first encounter the magic of leverage when they take out a mortgage. Leverage allows you to have assets that exceed your net worth. Suppose you own a house today worth £300,000 with a mortgage of £100,000. You might have begun by putting down a deposit of £50,000 to buy that house for £150,000. The value of the house has doubled – from £150,000 to £300,000. But your equity in the house – the difference between the value of the property and the debt – has increased fourfold, from £50,000 to £200,000.

If leverage sounds too good to be true, it is, because it works in both directions. In the late 1980s many young professionals in London were desperate to find a place on the housing ladder. They might have bought a £100,000 flat with a loan of £95,000. Their finances went spinning out of control when interest rates rose and house prices fell. If their flat would realise only £85,000, their savings of £5,000 had become a *debit* of £10,000, an outcome described as 'negative equity'. If these individuals had been companies, they would have been required to declare themselves insolvent. As matters were, they were unable to move from their property because they could not repay the outstanding mortgage.

Folk wisdom has it that house prices always go up, at least in the long run. In Germany and Japan, however, many houses are worth less today than twenty-five years ago. In Britain, as in the United States, prices have risen over time, but with considerable short-term volatility. Britain's major housing crash was in the early 1990s: in 1995 house prices were, in real terms, 35 per cent below the level of 1989. House prices fell again after 2007 but soon recovered, and the Halifax national house price index is today at an all-time high. The British experience in the global financial crisis is different from that of the United States: there was little subprime mortgage lending in the UK, and fewer repossessions followed the global financial crisis than had been seen in the 1990s. American house prices fell by around 30 per cent after 2007, and although they have since recovered, they are still below their peak levels. The falls in some areas, such as Florida and Las Vegas, have been much larger.

Like shares, property values go up and down. The history of the property market is full of stories of well-known names who have discovered to their considerable cost that leverage can work both ways. Donald Trump has been to the bankruptcy court four times – three times in failed casino ventures and once after his highly leveraged acquisition of New York's grandest old hotel, the Plaza. The Canary Wharf development, an ambitious scheme of the Canadian Reichmann brothers to establish a new financial services centre in London's docklands, was taken over in 1992 by banks who had lent too much. The venture was ultimately a success, but under different ownership.

'Safe as houses' is true only if you plan to live in one. The positive experience of owner-occupiers has encouraged many individuals to buy houses and flats to let. Although an investment property of reasonable quality is likely to cost £100,000 or more, gearing means that such a property can be bought with a deposit of £30,000–£40,000. While residential property is less volatile than most other asset classes, leverage multiplies the risk. Buy-to-let is a low-risk strategy only for someone rich enough to make it a modest part of a larger portfolio.

While individuals have recently been active in buy-to-let investment properties, there has been little new institutional investment in residential property. Insurance companies and pension funds prefer shops, offices and industrial premises which only rich individuals can hold directly. Small investors can access these properties through funds, and they generally should.

Ownership of property was once bound up with power and status – landed estates were associated with aristocratic titles. The capitalist owned the premises – the mill, the shop, the factory – where the workers laboured. Today, great estates are liabilities, not assets, and businesses rarely own the premises they occupy. Financial markets have become more sophisticated, and premises have become less specialised. Once, a textile business or a steel company would build a mill or a plant to its own particular requirement. Today's companies will often rent space on an industrial estate, in a unit adaptable to many alternative uses.

On the main streets of provincial towns, shops and offices are little changed. You will pass the premises of solicitors and other small businesses, and shops occupied by chain retailers. The professional firms (or the pension funds of their partners) may own their offices; the retailers generally will not. If you pass to the side-streets or even visit some of the less desirable high-street sites – secondary locations – you will see charity shops, a familiar indicator of a location in decline. Trade has moved out of town, and retailers to warehouses on the outskirts.

In the City of London, office blocks built only twenty to thirty years ago are pulled down to make way for modern replacements with cabling and air conditioning and the style of internal layout that today's office workers require. Yesterday's office, like yesterday's shop, is outdated, and the implication for the investor is that, even if the property does not physically decay, its economic value does. In the most valuable locations – such as prime sites in the City – the value of the property lies mostly in the land, rather than the building, and that is why constant renewal of the building makes sense. For the unit on the outskirts of a northern town, however, the proportions are reversed – the property value lies mostly in the cost of the building.

Commercial property is leased from its owner to a tenant. A typical English lease has a fixed initial term with five-yearly rent reviews – twenty-five years used to be the norm, but lengths have been shortening. At each five-year period the rent is reset in line with the rent of comparable local properties, with arbitration if the parties cannot agree. A property for which the actual rent is below the market rent is called 'reversionary', while if the actual rent is above the market level the building is described as 'over-rented'.

A tenant who signs a twenty-five-year lease does not have to occupy the property for twenty-five years. The lease may be assigned to a different tenant, but the rent remains payable to the landlord. A tenant may be able to assign a reversionary property at a premium, but would have to pay someone to take over a lease on an over-rented property. These specifics of the terms of leases, the conventions of the property market and the legal framework are vital to property investors and vary substantially from country to country. For these reasons – and because of tax complications – it is much more difficult to buy overseas property than overseas shares. But funds allow individuals with small sums to invest in foreign property.

Facts about funds

The conventional retail investor usually holds securities indirectly, through investment funds. Funds may be open-ended or closed-end. Open-ended investment companies (OEICs) used to be known as unit trusts in the UK (and often still are), and are called mutual funds in the US. Hedge funds and insurance bonds are also open-ended funds. Investment trusts, investment companies and real estate investment trusts are closed-end funds.

The manager of an open-ended fund computes the value

of the portfolio regularly and will buy or sell shares at a price that reflects that underlying value. These funds are called open-ended because the fund grows or shrinks as the fund attracts new investors, or existing investors redeem their units. The size of the closed-end fund is determined by the amount the original shareholders subscribed. Some funds that are open-ended, especially hedge funds, may nevertheless be closed to new investors. They will redeem shares from their existing holders, but will not expand the fund to accommodate new ones.

You can dispose of your share of the portfolio in a closed-end fund only by selling it to someone else. Traditionally, this meant a closed-end fund could be more adventurous – it could borrow, or invest in assets that were not easily realisable, without having to worry about savers withdrawing their subscriptions. But open-ended hedge funds have recently been far more adventurous than any closed-end fund. Hedge funds deal with the potential problem of realising illiquid assets by imposing conditions that allow them to delay pay-outs to their investors. Sometimes they exercise such conditions. When the credit crunch hit, many hedge funds chose to refuse or delay redemption.

The value of your share in a closed-end fund can be more or less than the value of your share of the underlying assets in the portfolio. The possibility of variability in this premium or discount to asset value compounds the investment risk. If property is currently a fashionable investment, real estate investment trust shares may sell at a premium to their asset value – the value of the shares is greater than the value of the properties the company owns. If emerging market stocks are unfashionable, it may be possible to buy shares at a large discount in investment companies specialising in emerging market stocks. You can sometimes buy out-of-favour funds at discounts of 20 per cent or more. Closed-end funds involve extra risks, but also extra opportunities.

In practice, most closed-end funds sell at discounts to their asset value. If the fund is at a premium, the manager can issue more shares to satisfy demand, and often does, since fees can be earned from the new issue and from managing the additional assets. If the shares are at a discount, then there might be a potential gain to the holders in winding up the fund and giving them back their money. The managers of the fund are usually not keen to do this.

Some people – arbitrageurs – try to make a profit by taking control of companies with discounts to asset value. Alliance Trust, one of the largest closed-end funds in Britain but one with a lacklustre record of performance, has recently been under attack from US hedge funds, beating off Laxey Partners only to confront a more determined assault from Elliott Advisors. But the costs of taking control may be large, and there may be taxes and other costs to pay in realising the portfolio. The prospect of liquidation limits the size of the discount, but not by much. Buying shares in closed-end funds at a discount may sometimes be an attractive way of investing in out-of-favour assets. There is rarely a case for buying a closed-end fund at a premium.

Most funds, open- or closed-ended, are actively managed, which means that the portfolio manager selects assets he or she thinks will do well and trades in and out of them as their prices and his or her views change. Passive funds simply replicate the performance of an index. A computer buys and sells shares to minimise the tracking error – the difference between the index and the value of the assets the fund holds. A more recent innovation is the exchange-traded fund (ETF). The mechanics of ETFs are more complex, but the objective is that the investor can buy or sell a share that will reproduce almost exactly the performance of an index – the FT all-share index, an index of Brazilian stocks or a basket of commodities.

In the first edition of this book I strongly recommended exchange-traded funds as a tool for intelligent investors. But, as so often, the greed of financial innovators messed things up.

Promoters launched complex ETFs and created synthetic funds based on derivatives and supported by collateral drawn from the dustbins of the sponsoring banks. While many transparent and honest ETFs remain, it is not easy for the intelligent investor to separate the wheat from the chaff, and my recommendation of these instruments must now be muted. I will make more specific suggestions in the final part of this book.

In this chapter I've described the three main asset categories available and the choice of direct or indirect investment. In the next three I will review the relationship between prices and values – the fundamental issue of intelligent investment. In Chapters 10 to 12 I'll explain how to build these different assets into an investment portfolio.

4

Efficient Markets

Efficient markets and asset values

Few of the many jokes about economists are funny. One tells of the finance professor walking down the street with his wife. 'There's a ten pound note on the pavement,' she says. 'Don't be silly,' he replies, 'if there was, someone would already have picked it up.'

The joke refers to the efficient market hypothesis (EMH), but the joke is on the teller. There are few £10 notes on the street, for the reason the professor elucidates. People rarely drop £10 notes, and when they do, the notes are quickly picked up. Most pieces of litter that look like £10 notes are, indeed, litter. The professor's theory of why there are no £10 notes on the pavement is illuminating. It will save considerable time for anyone who plans to make a living searching for £10 notes on the streets of London. The theory is not, however, true. There are occasional discarded £10 notes. There are also people who make profits by picking them up. Otherwise, it would be easier to find £10 notes in the street.

In a securities market, the £10 note is the difference between the price and the value of an asset. Since the efficient market hypothesis is illuminating but not true, such differences occur, but rarely, and they are hard to identify with confidence. So what determines the relationship between price and value?

An economist, another joke goes (following a remark of Oscar Wilde's), knows the price of everything and the value of nothing. The relationship between price and value is a subject with a long history – particularly among accountants. There are two basic approaches:

- the value of an asset is what someone is willing to pay for it;
- the value of an asset is the cash it will generate over its life.

I'll call these the 'mark to market' principle and the 'fundamental-value' principle. Almost all valuation methods are based on one or both of these principles. If you are appraising a property, you might call in a valuer to mark it to market. The valuer will have experience of transactions in similar properties in the area and should have a good idea of what the building will fetch. The mark to market principle is easy to apply in this case.

The fundamental value principle looks instead at the cash generated over the life of the asset. Begin with the flow of quarterly rents from a property, taking account of possible increases at future rent reviews, then deduct any expenses you might need to incur to preserve the value of the property. Perhaps the building has a finite life, like an industrial warehouse or modern office block; you will need to consider what the property will be worth when the structure needs to be replaced. Other buildings can, with some attention, maintain a satisfactory flow of rental income for ever.

The fundamental value of a company is calculated in a similar way. Look at either the path of dividends or the stream of earnings. If you focus on dividends, observe the current dividend level and speculate on how rapidly the company will increase that dividend in future years. If you focus on earnings, you need to estimate their probable growth, bearing in mind the growth rate of the economy, the industry and the specific prospects of the business.

The mark to market principle and fundamental value principle are certainly different, and seem incompatible. They involve different styles of thinking and lead to different approaches to investment. The mark to market principle is easier, and less speculative. But it is a common mistake to emphasise what you can measure at the expense of more important things that you can't measure. It is generally better to be approximately right than precisely wrong.

Which of these principles should be applied? Market prices can't be independent of fundamental value because opinions about fundamental value influence market prices. This is the metaphor of markets as 'voting machine'. Everyone who trades registers an opinion. The results of this survey of opinion are reported in the financial papers every day. The metaphor contains a possible reconciliation of the mark to market and fundamental value principles: the market price is the result of a plebiscite on fundamental value.

The market is democratic in the sense that everyone is allowed to vote, but it is not a fair election. The weight given to your opinion depends on the amount of money you can put behind your vote. The votes of a large fund management group such as BlackRock or an investment bank such as Goldman Sachs count more than the votes of you and me. Perhaps this is as it should be. If you are really confident of your opinion, you can make that opinion count by putting a lot of money behind it. I shall describe how George Soros pulled a spectacular coup by doing exactly that.

The concept of the market as a voting machine provides a justification for my claim that every investor can access, without charge, all the expertise that the financial services industry can bring to bear. That idea leads to the efficient market hypothesis. If the market price were an average of informed estimates of fundamental value, markets would be efficient, not only in the narrow technical sense that all available information is in the price but also in a broader sense – that market prices provide signals that guide the efficient allocation of investment funds.

In this chapter I'll focus on the narrower interpretation of market efficiency, the one relevant to investors. But there are three sub-interpretations, because there are three variants of the efficient market hypothesis, involving progressively more demanding assumptions:

- the weak form – past movements of prices convey no information about future price movements;
- the semi-strong form – all public information about securities is already reflected in their price; and
- the strong form – everything that could be known about securities is already reflected in their price.

Louis Bachelier, the little-honoured Frenchman whose PhD thesis on 'The Theory of Speculation' proved to be the foundation of finance theory, discovered that his data resembled the observations of natural processes, such as the movement of small particles suspended in a fluid. Physicists call this behaviour Brownian motion. Financial economists, more engagingly, employ the term 'random walk'. A random walk is directionless. Every step is independent of every previous step and just as likely to be in one direction as in another. All three versions of the efficient market hypothesis claim that securities prices will follow a random walk. The random walk is a mathematical concept inseparable from the EMH.

Most of the evidence observed by early researchers was favourable to the random walk theory. The earliest evaluations were undertaken by statisticians – until the 1950s, Wall Street and the City of London were innumerate, and there was no serious finance theory in business schools. At Stanford

University, Holbrook Working showed that commodity prices also seemed to follow a random walk. The British statistician Maurice Kendall analysed long series of stock prices, and more than a hundred years of cotton price data. He concluded that 'The Stock Exchange, it would appear, has a memory lasting less than a week.' While none of the three versions of the efficient market hypothesis is true, each offers its own shafts of illumination. Markets may have no memory, but commentators on markets do, and the random walk theory suggests that most of the commentators' observations and analysis are of little use. 'Shares are 20 per cent lower than a year ago – this is a buying opportunity.' 'The market needs to pause for breath after its recent rise.' 'The dollar is experiencing a technical correction, which will continue.'

You regularly hear statements like these in popular discussion. The weak form of the efficient market hypothesis claims that no such statement can ever be justified because prices move independently of their history. The probability that they will rise next year, or next month, or today, is unaffected by whether prices rose yesterday afternoon, or last week, or in the first quarter of 2016.

The weak EMH is a blow for people who rely on projections of historical trends, or identification of recurrent patterns, to make their investment decisions – most of all for chartists, whom I'll describe in the next chapter. But the weak version does nothing to discourage people from looking at fundamental values. Rather the opposite – the weak EMH encourages you to believe that you might make money at the expense of noise traders by close attention to fundamentals.

Thus there is a considerable practical difference between weak and strong EMH. Strong EMH – that everything that could be known about securities is already in their price – essentially rules out any possibility of investment skill. Legendary investors such as Buffett have simply been lucky. No research or analysis can be useful, because its results will already be reflected in the market. Put like this, the theory seems absurd.

Indeed, the strong version of EMH contains an inherent contradiction. If it were the case that research and analysis could never be profitable, because the result of that research and analysis would always be 'in the price', why would anyone undertake such research and analysis? If markets were always efficient, what could be the process by which they become efficient?

The semi-strong version of the efficient market hypothesis is less extreme, claiming only that information is 'in the price' if publicly available. Thus the semi-strong version does not exclude the possibility that insightful new analysis, unpublished or not yet widely circulated, might be valuable to those who possess it. It certainly permits possibilities of profit from trading on private information. The investment banker who knows of a planned takeover, the corporate executive who knows that the coming results will be worse than those generally expected, can both deal advantageously on the basis of this inside information.

Such insider trading was once the daily practice of brokers and fund managers, and put small investors at a substantial disadvantage. But most countries, including Britain, have made it illegal for people who have inside knowledge to deal. These laws do not cover all forms of trading on private information, nor can they ever be perfectly effective, but they have probably reduced the incidence of these practices. Few people are convicted of insider trading. This is because evidence is hard to obtain, not because the activity is rare. The cases that have come to court show that criminal insiders often made little profit from their unlawful activities because their actions moved market prices against them. Information held by insiders does not have to be announced to percolate into the market-place.

So intelligent investors should be wary of sustained individual price movements that seem to have no explanation. A falling share price may be the result of inside knowledge; a rise that cannot be accounted for may herald a possible takeover. Perhaps information the investor does not know, and may never know, is already reflected in the market. Be suspicious of advisers whose predictions are based on extrapolations from past price movements, or who claim to see patterns in data.

Illuminating but not true

The efficient market hypothesis has a sufficiently strong hold on the investment world – particularly among finance academics – for deviations still to be described as 'anomalies'. Over the last two decades, evidence of anomalies has accumulated steadily. One collection of essays is provocatively titled *A Non-Random Walk down Wall Street* (Lo and MacKinlay, 1999), in deliberate contrast to Burton Malkiel's popular introduction to efficient market theory in *A Random Walk down Wall Street* (Malkiel, 1973). Robert Shiller, who achieved wide attention by publishing *Irrational Exuberance* (Shiller, 2000) at the peak of the New Economy boom, has become the intellectual leader of the sceptics. In a bizarre conjunction, the 2013 Nobel Prize in economics was shared between Eugene Fama, for his work in developing the efficient market hypothesis, and Shiller, for his work in refuting it.

There are many investment maxims, mechanical rules that promise superior returns. 'Sell in May and go away.' Benefit from 'the small company effect' – consistently higher returns on smaller companies that may be the subject of less intensive research. Buy 'the dogs of the Dow' – the worst performing large companies of the previous year. These ideas rarely work. There are several problems. It is always possible to find some such pattern by studying the past; that doesn't mean that the same pattern will persist in future. Even if the scheme appears profitable, profits may be inadequate to offset the costs of turning over a portfolio. And the very fact of publishing these seemingly attractive investment ideas may lead others to desist from the behaviour that gave rise to the so-called anomalies. The efficient market hypothesis strikes back.

So, is the empirical claim that prices follow a random walk correct? You may still be puzzled by the equivalence of the weak EMH and the random walk theory. Why does the assumption that all information is 'in the price' imply that prices follow a random walk? Bachelier's empirical observation of the random walk, and Kendall's supporting data, long preceded a comprehensive explanation of the relationship.

The definitive account of why price movements in an efficient market would appear random came in 1953 from the Nobel Prize-winning economist Paul Samuelson, whose introductory textbook is familiar to everyone who has taken a basic economics course. Return to that metaphor of markets as voting machine. The result of every election depends on the question you put to the voters. The question that is put to the voters here is not 'What do you think the Federal Reserve should do?' It is not even 'What do you think the Federal Reserve will do?' The question is 'How do you think the bond market and the currency market will react to what the Federal Reserve will do?'

Suppose people think that the Federal Reserve Board will raise American interest rates or that Vodafone will announce good results. These expectations lead these people to sell American bonds and buy dollars, or to buy Vodafone shares. Views about the future are therefore built into the level of prices we see in the market today. If the Federal Reserve Board is expected to act, bond yields and currencies will already reflect this, and will move only if these expectations change. If Vodafone's business is improving, the market price will already acknowledge the improvement. The price will move only if people think that outcomes will be better still, or that these outcomes will not, after all, be as good as previously expected. Traders are not voting on what Vodafone's results will be, or whether Vodafone is a good business; they are voting on what they think will happen to Vodafone's share price. They vote 'up' when they buy, and 'down' when they sell. John Maynard Keynes described this process through the analogy of a newspaper beauty contest. Competitors were asked to choose the most beautiful faces, and those who selected the most popular faces, according to the majority choices of all competitors, were the competition winners. As Keynes explained, what thoughtful entrants are trying to do is not to choose the most beautiful, but to decide what they think others will find most beautiful, or even what they think people will think other people will find most beautiful – and so on.

Samuelson elaborated on this idea. Everyone in the market knows that prices will change in future as sentiment changes. If more people are expecting favourable changes in opinion than unfavourable, they will buy. If they think these yet unknown market events are more likely to be adverse, they will sell. So at any time, prices will be bid up or down until the expected impact of future changes is equally likely to increase values as to reduce them. That is why, Samuelson claimed, properly anticipated prices fluctuate randomly.

Market reactions to events and to changes in the trading environment are not easy to predict and may seem disproportionate to the events that trigger them. Certainly they may be larger than can possibly be explained by reference to assessments of fundamental value. The worst day in the history of modern stock markets was 19 October 1987, when the Dow Jones Industrial Average, the most widely followed US stock index, dropped 22 per cent. The Brady Commission, established by the government to investigate, concluded that the fall was triggered by a higher than expected trade deficit and a rumour of higher taxes, magnified by the use of portfolio insurance – computerised trading systems that sold large quantities of stocks when markets fell.

Perhaps. In any event, none of these factors was directly

relevant to the British stock market, which fell by almost as much. Within a few days, and for no obvious reasons, market sentiment switched from sanguine optimism to unreasonable pessimism. On days like 19 October 1987 market movements can be explained only by reference to market psychology; attempts to explain them by reference to changes in fundamental value are simply false rationalisations. Prices rise or fall in the short run on ephemeral changes in sentiment, with little, if any, basis in fundamental value.

In some markets, such as that for Old Master paintings, concepts of fundamental value are themselves elusive. These market prices are the result of the whims of a small number of very rich men. The principle that an asset is worth what someone will pay remains dominant in this market. But it is implausible that the prices of bonds, shares or properties can for ever remain unrelated to fundamental value. Prices move around fundamental value – sometimes violently so, as on 19 October 1987 or in the New Economy bubble. Constantly changing, prices are influenced, but not determined, by a fundamental value that is itself unknown and constantly changing.

From time to time, the path of market prices strays far from the path of fundamental value, but these divergences are ultimately corrected. Prices display 'short-term positive serial correlation' – if you examine prices over a day, a week or a month, then upward price movements are slightly more likely to be followed by further upward price movements. Downward price movements are also more likely to lead to further downward price movements. This feature of short-term price change is called 'momentum'.

There is also evidence of 'long-term negative serial correlation'. If you look at prices over much longer periods – three or five years – upward movements are more than averagely likely to be followed by downward movements, while periods of underperformance of this length are more than averagely likely to be followed by periods of outperformance. This feature of long-term price movements is called mean reversion. Like the efficient market hypothesis, with which it is closely associated, the random walk model is illuminating but not true.

Information asymmetry

Market prices measure prevailing market sentiment, incorporating all the analysis, prejudice, skills and irrationality of market players, and the efficient market hypothesis, even if not true, is illuminating. Ten pound notes in the street are not easy to find. What is general knowledge will normally be 'in the price' and of little value to investors. Information such as 'Vodafone is a well-managed company', 'oil and mining are going through a difficult time' or 'utilities are a sound business' does not provide a reason to trade related stocks, even though all these things are true. This information is in the market.

'General knowledge' includes such knowledge as we have of the future as well as knowledge of the present and past. The term 'consensus forecast' is used to describe the common expectations of City people about economic prospects. There usually isn't a very wide spread of opinions. The canard that economists always disagree is much exaggerated. (Although there are many other, well-founded, criticisms of economists, especially of zealots who embrace the EMH with fundamentalist fervour.) You don't have to pay for the consensus forecast, or spend time reading about it – it's already 'in the market'.

The glossy descriptions of economic prospects that financial advisers, investment managers and banks circulate to clients may be illuminating (I rarely find them so), but not as a guide to investment decisions. You don't have any valuable insight into the future – and nor do they. I've sometimes asked people in business and finance, who crave accurate economic forecasts, 'If

I gave you the exact figure for national income three years from now, what would you do with the information?' Useful economic knowledge is usually specific rather than general.

This central role of information, and the dependence of trade on differential information, distinguishes securities markets from other markets. Trade in modern economies is mostly the result of specialisation. I grow apples, you grow pears, and each of us gains by swapping one for the other. We call on the plumber for his specialist skills. We buy from Ford because the company is organised to produce cars, and we are not. America sells computers in return for Saudi oil. All these exchanges normally benefit both parties to the trade.

Sometimes trade in financial markets has a similar character. An importer buys foreign currency because he and his customers are based in the UK, and his supplier is based in China. The commercial transaction requires a foreign exchange transaction. But most trade in securities markets – even in foreign currency markets – is not like that. Both parties to the transaction have the same need – to make as much money as possible; they just have different ideas about how to do it. I think the dollar will rise in value; you think it will fall. I think Vodafone shares are underpriced; you think they are overvalued. In each of these trades, one of us will be proved right, the other wrong.

In any market in which there is wide and irresolvable uncertainty, in any market where participants have different information and beliefs, many trades will be the result of mistakes. And in financial markets uncertainty and differential information are endemic. A brilliant exposition of the problems that this would create for market efficiency – in both a narrow and a wide sense – was provided in 1970 by George Akerlof, who would receive the Nobel Prize for his analysis. Akerlof used the metaphor of the market for lemons. Some cars are 'lemons', prone to faults. The seller knows whether the car is a lemon; the buyer does not. If the price of the used car reflects the average probability that the car is a lemon, that is a good price for owners of lemons and a bad price for everyone else. Sellers will be inclined to sell lemons, but not good cars. The proportion of cars on used car lots that are lemons will be much greater than the proportion of lemons in the population as a whole. As buyers realise this, the price they will pay for any second-hand car, lemon or not, will fall. The result of this will be to reduce still further the proportion of good cars on sale. The outcome is a market characterised by mutual mistrust, low prices, low-quality products and buyer dissatisfaction.

If you fail to understand the problem of imperfect information, you may fall victim to the 'winner's curse': you think you have won, only to discover subsequently that you wish you hadn't. This problem was first identified when the US government auctioned offshore oil blocks. The bidders in all cases were the same large oil companies. Both the government and the companies quickly realised that the successful bids were higher than had been expected, or than were justified. All the companies wanted the oil and had similar access to funds. Their preferences and resources were the same, but their assessments of the potential differed. All judgements were to some degree in error, but the successful bidder was – by the nature of the auction – the one who bid highest. The most likely reason that estimate was higher than the rest was that the winning company's geologists had made a mistake.

You might think that the inevitable errors made by market participants with imperfect information would tend to cancel out. They don't. Assets will always tend to be bought by people who are too optimistic about their value rather than people who are too pessimistic, and sold by people who understand what they are selling better than those who are buying.

This combination of the lemons problem and the winner's curse, along with the herd instincts of so many financial market participants, gives rise to systematic, and destabilising, asset mispricing. The growing complexity of the products that are sold in financial markets means that mispricing originating in information asymmetry occurs with increasing frequency. In Chapter 9 I will look at some of the consequences – and at how information asymmetry has been central to the recent recurrent financial crises.

Strategic trading, moral hazard and market manipulation

The winner's curse and the lemons problem would exist even if people made no attempt to take advantage of market inefficiencies arising from imperfect information. But of course they do, and nowhere more so than in financial markets. This is known as the problem of moral hazard. Wherever there are imperfections of information, people with superior information can use that knowledge to sell products for more than they are worth, or to rid themselves of risks that others underestimate. As the lemons example illustrates, the result is a decline in the average quality of products and risks. Moral hazard has always been evident in insurance and credit markets (there is no divorce insurance because only unhappy couples would pay the premium), and it is widespread in financial services.

In an experiment, Professor Joe Stiglitz would invite a class to bid for the money contained in his wallet. Of course, there was no obligation on him to accept the highest, or any, bid. It would be a mistake to participate at all in such an auction. If a bidder offers less than the amount in the wallet, the professor will refuse to trade. If the bid is more than that sum, it will be accepted. If the seller is willing to sell, the buyer is foolish to buy. Why do I want to buy what they want to sell? In a market to which information asymmetry is so fundamental, you never do. Anyone tempted to purchase a complex financial product should ponder the lesson of the wallet auction.

Sellers of securities usually have the advantage over buyers. The people who run a company know more about it than the people who plan to invest in it. The people who promote a bond know more about the issuer than the buyer does. The people who construct a complex derivative understand its characteristics better than the people who buy these securities. Some of the derivatives and structured products of modern finance can only be valued – if at all – using the models created by the banks that devised them. This not only leaves the purchasers vulnerable but also leaves the banks themselves at the mercy of the few employees who understand the models. You can never know what information the seller has, or, in many cases, who the seller is.

Once oil companies understood the winner's curse, they adjusted their bids downwards. Markets characterised by differential information are reflexive, because prices reveal information about the behaviour and the expectations of other parties, and these may in turn affect assessments of fundamental values. If offers to buy or sell reveal what other people think, then there are opportunities for strategic behaviour; traders may deal with a view to influencing the expectations of others, and hence creating profit opportunities in future.

In 2006 the hedge fund manager John Paulson recognised that the marketing of subprime mortgages to indigent house buyers in the United States would end in tears. He persuaded the investment bank Goldman Sachs to put together securities whose value was based on the performance of particularly egregious subprime mortgages, and to find buyers for these products. The transaction had no underlying purpose other than to enable Paulson and his investors to benefit from the inevitable defaults on the mortgages. When the market did indeed collapse in 2007, the outcome for Paulson was described, with some exaggeration, as 'the greatest trade ever' (Zuckerman, 2009). Although Paulson was not sufficiently communicative to be featured in Michael Lewis's *The Big Short*, and hence escaped being played by Brad

Pitt, his was almost certainly the largest of the bets against the US housing market that that film described. Goldman Sachs would pay a fine of $550 million, without admitting legal liability, for its part in the affair.

The most entertaining form of market manipulation is 'the corner', in which a bidder attempts to dominate the whole of the available supply and force buyers (especially) to pay whatever price the bidder chooses. In 2008–9 there was a battle for control of Volkswagen within the Porsche and Piëch families (descended respectively from the son and daughter of Ferdinand Porsche). Some hedge funds believed (correctly as it turned out) that Wolfgang Porsche and Wendelin Wiedeking, his chief executive at the eponymous luxury car maker, would not succeed in taking over the much larger VW company. The funds acted as 'short sellers', vendors of shares they did not own (I'll explain this more fully in Chapter 9), in the hope of making profits when the bid failed and VW shares fell. But they misunderstood the complex shareholding structure of Volkswagen; almost all the voting stock was controlled either by Porsche or by the state of Lower Saxony. When VW shares rose in value, the short sellers discovered that there were no shares available in the market. Obliged to buy to meet their obligations to return the stock they had sold, they found themselves having to bid for VW stock at any price. The stock has typically sold for between €100 and €200; as a result of the 'corner', some shares were sold at prices around €1000.

This is a rare instance of a successful corner. The experience of the Hunt family, Texas oil billionaires who tried to corner the world silver market in 1980, is more typical. As the price of silver soared, individuals rooted through their attics to find silver to add to the Hunts' hoard, but in the end the oil fortune was inadequate to achieve the corner, and the price (and the fortune) collapsed. An outrageous case of market manipulation at the expense of retail investors was the practice by which some US mutual fund managers allowed friends and associates to trade in the funds on a favoured basis, making profits at the expense of fund investors. As with insider dealing, extensive regulation seeks to protect you – and market professionals – from abuses that involve the fraudulent exploitation – or creation – of differential information. This regulation is less than perfectly effective. Necessarily so – the financial services industry exists because of differential information.

Investment strategies for imperfectly efficient markets

Momentum rules in the short run, mean reversion in the long run. A day is short run, five years is long run. If there were a means of telling just when the short run becomes the long run, there would be a sure-fire route to making money: ride the wave, jump off before it breaks.

This isn't possible. The two phenomena of momentum (short-run positive serial correlation) and mean reversion (long-run negative serial correlation) map into two basic investment techniques. One is achieving insight into the vagaries of market sentiment; the other is analysing the sources of fundamental value.

Recognition of information asymmetry – that market participants have different levels of knowledge and understanding and will seek to use these differences to take advantage of those with less knowledge and understanding – leads to the same conclusion. You can succeed in markets either by having a deeper appreciation of the behaviour of other market participants or by ignoring them and making your own assessment of the underlying determinants of value and cash generation.

The first strategy seeks to understand the mind of the market and the psychology of its participants – exploit momentum, buy into market rises, sell ahead of market falls. The alternative approach ignores these fluctuations, focuses attention on fundamental value and anticipates that, in the long run, truth will out through mean reversion. The first of these strategies can be associated with George Soros, the second with Warren Buffett. These two men are the best-known and most successful investors of recent decades. Both are now over eighty years old, having begun their public investment careers in the 1960s.

Soros left Eastern Europe as a child refugee. A devotee of Karl Popper, he would prefer to be remembered for his philosophy rather than for his fortune. But Soros will go down in history as the man who broke the Bank of England in 1992. His massive bet against sterling on 'Black Wednesday' – another contender for the title of 'the greatest trade ever' – proved decisive in forcing Britain out of the European Monetary System. Soros's Open Society network has made large philanthropic contributions to the promotion of education and democracy in post-Communist Eastern Europe, and the Institute for New Economic Thinking, which he founded, has led the process of taking academic finance theory beyond the efficient market hypothesis. His Quantum Fund – an early example of what is now known as a hedge fund – returned an average of 30 per cent per annum to its investors over the period from 1970 to 2000. The Quantum Fund traded actively, buying currencies or commodities and any other assets that appealed to Soros and his colleagues, and selling those which failed to appeal.

Buffett's investment vehicle is Berkshire Hathaway, an American corporation. Anyone can buy shares in it, although a single share will set you back over $200,000.* Berkshire Hathaway was a textile company when Buffett took control, but insurance is now its largest business. Insurance premiums are received well before claims are paid, so insurance generates a large float of

---

* The company's non-voting B shares allow small investors an opportunity to buy.

investable cash. Berkshire has used this money to buy large stakes in businesses such as Procter & Gamble and Heinz. Buffett's investment success has taken him from modest beginnings to matching Bill Gates (to whose foundation he plans to donate most of his fortune) among the world's richest men. Despite that, Buffett still lives in the bungalow in Omaha that he bought fifty years ago, and regularly enjoys a meal, washed down with a glass of Cherry Coke, at a local steak house (he switched brands after buying a 10 per cent stake in the Coca-Cola Corporation).

There will always be individuals who have outperformed the market – just as there will always be winners of the lottery. I'll observe in Chapter 8 how exceptional investment performance rarely persists. Most people who do well are lucky rather than clever. But Buffett and Soros not only established outstanding records; they continued to demonstrate remarkable performance even after they had been widely recognised as the most talented managers of their generation. To win the lottery once may be evidence of either luck or skill; to win it repeatedly is evidence of skill.

You might think that the strategies of the folksy Buffett and the philosophical Soros would be the subject of intense study by students of finance and investment professionals. You would be wrong. These individuals receive a lot of journalistic attention but no academic attention. Since Buffett and Soros cannot exist, according to the strong efficient market hypothesis, they are treated as if they don't. A lot of ink has been spilt on the proposition that what plainly exists in practice can't exist in theory.

In turn, Buffett and Soros are open in their contempt for most academic work in finance. They can afford that contempt. But their contempt is not simply the practical man's disdain for the intellectual – they are both clever and well-read people. They simply believe that much of this academic work is misdirected, engaged in obsessive pursuit of narrow ideas of limited application. The distinction between the market as a mechanism for voting on events and the market as a mechanism for voting on market reactions to events was understood and expressed generations ago by Keynes and Samuelson – and by Benjamin Graham, the original intelligent investor. But the distinction is not understood by many commentators, who regard market judgements as a repository of wisdom, not just about the market judgements of other market participants but about the real economy.

The distinction between the anticipation of events and the anticipation of beliefs about events is elided by most finance academics. They understand that there might be such a distinction, but have developed a group of arguments – known, in extreme form, as 'rational expectations' – to suggest that the difference does not matter. The rational expectations school is associated with the strong form of the efficient market hypothesis – all information that is capable of being known is already incorporated in prices.

But the distinction between market judgements and underlying realities, the distinction between prices and values, and the distinction between the mind of the market and economic and business fundamentals manifestly do matter. By exploiting divergences between them, Buffett and Soros have made billions of dollars. Both individuals recognise that such divergences are the basis of their success. Buffett shouts from the rooftops that markets are only imperfectly efficient. Soros, quoting Keynes's metaphor of the beauty contest, writes that 'The fact that a theory is flawed does not mean that we should not invest in it as long as other people believe in it and there is a large group of people left to be convinced ... we are ahead of the game because we can limit our losses when the market also discovers what we already know' (Soros, 2003, p. 25).

The essence of Soros's investment strategy is to read, and anticipate, the changing mind of the market more successfully than other traders. The essence of Buffett's investment strategy is to emphasise fundamental values and use the volatile mind of the market as an opportunity to buy assets that are underpriced relative to their fundamental value. I'll discuss these two broad approaches in the two chapters that follow.

5

The Mind of the Market

Market psychology

People in the City use phrases such as 'The market thinks', 'The view of the market is' or even, if the person is more senior, 'We could ask the market'. Of course, the market does not think; only people can think. But the anthropomorphic view, which treats 'the market' as if it were a person, is so pervasive that the metaphor is part of everyday language. Benjamin Graham formulated the anthropomorphic analogy when he wrote of the moody, volatile Mr Market (Graham, 1985). Mr Market has grown in influence in subsequent decades. Mr Market features regularly in Warren Buffett's homilies.

This metaphor contrasts with the metaphor of the market as a voting machine, which aggregates and weighs the different views of different players. Although there is some similarity between the two, there is also a fundamental difference. The market as voting machine is democratic – the analogy supposes a diversity of views, in which all judgements are relevant (if not necessarily equal). The personal analogy is hierarchical – the market view can be ascertained and interpreted, but not questioned. City players talk of 'confidence', by which they mean the standing of an individual, organisation or opinion in the eyes of the market – in much the same way as commentators identify the confidants at the court of an autocratic politician or chief executive. This confidence needs to be earned, and can easily be forfeited.

And yet the person who inspires such deference, whom it is perilous to defy, has no tangible existence. There is no Mr Market. 'The mind of the market' is what people believe the mind of the market to be, and the evolution of what 'the market thinks' is a process of convergence of these common beliefs. Understanding 'the mind of the market' – a deep appreciation of the psychology of Mr Market – is a potentially rewarding investment strategy, and some people are good at it. Not, however, as many as those who think they are good at it.

Trading once took place in physical markets, where buyers and sellers would meet to exchange securities and to exchange information. Some of the information might have been true, other parts of it false; some information would be contained in what participants said, some of it contained in the way they behaved. In the crudest versions of face-to-face market making, such as the 'pit' of the Chicago Mercantile Exchange, the physical capacity of traders to elbow aside their colleagues would contribute to their success. This short-term trading environment was a testosterone-laden world. Technology transferred trading from meeting places to screens.

Most traders are now employees of major investment banks, financial conglomerates such as Goldman Sachs and J. P. Morgan. These traders sit beside each other in dealing rooms and make electronic contact with their competitors at other firms. The atmosphere is still frenzied – and still very masculine, even though there are now some women traders. You will still hear frequent obscenities on trading floors; many City firms have faced claims of sex discrimination and harassment; and lap-dancing clubs can be found around the fringes of the City.

As well as trading on their own account, the institutions that make markets manage assets for investment clients, execute deals for fund managers and provide advice to major corporations.

Banks are required to maintain 'Chinese walls' in order to prevent people in these different departments communicating with each other. There are differing views on the effectiveness of the Chinese walls. Within these institutions are assembled expertise and information, unparalleled elsewhere, in and about all aspects of securities markets and, indeed, about wider economic and geopolitical events.

It is difficult, even for the banks themselves, to judge the long-run profitability of their trading activities. Nor is it clear where these profits come from. While most trades are made on behalf of clients, the bank is itself acting as principal in these transactions – the intermediary is more like the used car dealer, who buys and sells vehicles from his own stock, than the real estate broker, who facilitates a meeting between a buyer and a seller. When the 'Volcker rule' limiting the scale of proprietary trading – dealing purely on the banks' own account – was introduced in the United States after the 2008 crash, banks claimed that proprietary trading constituted only a small part of their overall activities. However, trading profits account for most of the reported revenues of investment banks such as Goldman Sachs and a significant part of the revenues even of organisations that are principally commercial banks.

Traders use the capital, credit and reputation of their employers. They also take a significant share of the profits from their activities, but not the losses. The penalty for making large losses is being fired. This asymmetric structure of incentives artificially encourages risk-taking. In particular, there is an attraction to trading strategies and styles that return regular profits while incurring the likelihood of occasional exceptional losses which may, over time, swamp the profits. These structures – which I will call tail-gating plays or Taleb distributions – have a central role in modern finance, and I'll come back to them in Chapter 8.

If markets are characterised by weak positive short-term serial correlation – momentum – and weak negative long-term serial correlation – mean reversion – then it ought to be possible to analyse the processes that give rise to these 'anomalies'. George Soros describes the boom-and-bust process associated with momentum and mean reversion. A momentum-driven boom creates the seeds of its own destruction and leads to an inevitable downturn. Soros illustrates this with reference to a variety of markets, from acquisition activity by conglomerates to the progress of real estate investment trusts.

But accurately describing the cycle is not at all the same as picking accurately the turning point of the cycle. Soros did, indeed, identify correctly the broad shape of some large swings in behaviour during the 1970s and 1980s to profit both on the upswing – following the momentum-driven herd – and on the downswing – benefiting by anticipating a period of mean reversion. These judgements proved very profitable. But such success became harder to achieve.

Can mathematical techniques help with understanding past and future cycles? Many amateur speculators rely on charts or other forms of what is known as technical analysis. This approach to investment analysis involves the identification of recurrent patterns in price series. The technical analyst looks at a chart of recent prices and identifies trends, believing that it is possible to identify buy and sell signals from inspection of the chart.

Purists among chartists do not care what the chart records – whether it is the stock price of Vodafone, the exchange value of the dollar or the price of an index-linked bond. Chartists look for pictures in the data – the 'head and shoulders' is an especially popular image. They draw trend lines through market rises and declines and horizontal resistance levels across more stationary ones. They see recurrent cycles. The Kondratieff fifty-year cycle has been discussed since the 1920s, and there is just enough evidence of long-term fluctuation to make continued attention to it plausible. The Elliott 'long wave', the discovery of an accountant and amateur investor, is a favourite of many chartists. Among the community of finance academics in universities, technical analysis has a terrible reputation. Most textbooks simply refuse even to acknowledge that the technique exists. But Chartism continues to have a cult-like following, and market prognostications based on technical analysis are regularly found in the financial press and business journals.

There are good reasons for professional disdain. Many of the statements made by chartists resemble those of astrologers. The analytic component is a-scientific and, as with the readings of astrologers, the predictions are often sufficiently ambiguous not to be falsified by any likely events. Chartists make use of the natural human inclination to see patterns in data – the same tendency that leads us to see images in ink blots and to interpret rocks as sculptures.

Technical analysts are often associated with investment gurus, more common in the United States, where there are many published investment newsletters, or tip sheets. The guru makes an outlandish prediction. Sometimes the prediction comes true, so the newsletter attracts subscriptions, the seminars are oversubscribed. The guru continues to make predictions – often the same prediction – but when these are proved to be false, both audience and reputation gradually drift away.

Chartists, gurus and people with proprietary and secret systems are, overwhelmingly, charlatans. But the story is not quite so simple. A central tenet of this book is that the efficient market hypothesis, although illuminating, is not true. And so it is not enough to assert that since the EMH is true, no claim made by chartists, gurus or for mechanical rules or trading systems can ever be valid. At most, what can be said is that there is little evidence that any individuals or systems use these methods with sustained success.

Still, perhaps there are patterns in historic price series and we lack techniques sufficiently powerful to identify them. At some level this must be correct. No one really believes that price movements are truly random – the most that might be claimed is that explanations of price movements are so complex and so varied that we can never do better than to describe them as a random process.

Much of this book describes the theory of finance that originated in Chicago around fifty years ago and has been developed by economists since. Today that body of analysis is subject to a pincer movement, pressured from one side by behavioural economics – the applied psychology that emphasises the ways in which the beliefs of traders influence the determination of prices – and from the other side by higher-powered mathematics and the computers used by high-frequency traders that analyse 'the mind of the market' by constantly offering to buy and sell. (Most of the offers to buy and sell which these computers make do not result in trades.)

Techniques brought to bear on financial markets more recently push towards, even beyond, the frontiers of applied mathematics. These approaches use models to reproduce what the most skilled traders may be able to do instinctively. In what is superficially a paradox, soft revisions from psychology and hard revisions from mathematics turn out to be two sides of the same coin. The mathematics of complex systems may help to explain the formation of expectations and the dissemination of beliefs in markets. If it does, then the ways in which expectations are formed and beliefs disseminated will change.

In the first edition of this book I exhorted readers to 'watch this space'. And speculated that there would be more on this mix of psychology and mathematics in subsequent editions – even that the chartists might have the last laugh. Since then behavioural finance has become the subject of widespread attention among financial analysts. And high-frequency trading now accounts for most of the volume of business on the London and New York stock exchanges. Keep watching this space.

In Chapter 1 I suggested that the intelligent investor could fend for him- or herself in a world populated by financial professionals. But in the world I have described in this chapter, the intelligent but amateur investor cannot fend for him- or herself. A minority of successful traders in hedge funds and investment banks have an intuitive feel for market psychology. These few individuals have honed their skills over years of experience and are exposed to a wide range of market information every minute of the trading day.

The mathematicians who build trading systems have access to the best brains and most powerful computing resources available. Successfully riding market momentum involves frequent trading, and investment banks have much lower trading costs than retail investors. Even with all these advantages it is not at all clear that over the long run the activity is profitable for investment banks. You need to set the losses from supposedly unforeseeable events and allegedly unauthorised trading against the profits. We simply don't know whether over a period of years banks make money out of these market judgements (as distinct from making money out of their customers' transactions), and nor do they. Most people who are described as successful traders blow up after a – possibly lengthy – lucky run.

The David and Goliath notion that with a home computer, a proprietary software package and a book of trading rules you are likely to succeed where the best-resourced institutions in the world have largely failed, is laughable. Most people who claim to trade successfully in this way are themselves on a lucky run in a rising market, or engaged in self-delusion, or both.

The intelligent investor cannot match the professionals in understanding market psychology. But he or she does have advantages when it comes to fundamental value. In the remainder of this chapter and the next one, I'll explain why and how.

When the market loses its mind

There have been asset bubbles for as long as there have been financial markets. In the Dutch tulip mania of 1636–7 a single prized bulb was supposedly valued at the price of twelve acres of land, or ten times the annual earnings of a skilled craftsman.

In the preceding chapter I described the two enduring general principles of asset valuation: an asset is worth what someone is willing to pay for it; and the value of an asset is the cash it will generate over its life. The characteristic of a bubble is that the first of these principles overwhelms the second. Assets are bought with little or no regard for their fundamental value in the hope that soon someone else will pay more for them. That was why a tulip bulb was, briefly, equal in value to twelve acres of land.

Most bubbles have their origins in some real economic, technological or geopolitical event that changes the fundamental determinants, though not the fundamental principles, of asset valuation. The spread of the railways, the establishment of market economies in the developing world, the exploitation of the internet – whenever there is such a change, there is a human tendency to enthusiasm and to exaggeration of the pace and significance of that change. A tendency that is increased if the enthusiasm is profitable as well as fashionable.

The effects spill into asset markets. Early spotters make profits, and the herd follows. And as bubbles expand, the belief that however elevated the price, someone else will offer more, seems to be borne out by events. Those who point to the absurdity of prices unrelated to fundamental value are exposed as fools who have passed up the opportunity of an easy profit. Many of them will finally join the party. That was the fate of the scientist Isaac Newton, who was more than intelligent enough to see that the South Sea bubble was a fraud. But after watching on the sidelines, he could not bear to miss out and was finally persuaded to invest. 'I can predict the motion of heavenly bodies, but not the madness of crowds,' he (allegedly) lamented as he counted his losses when the bubble burst.

When I was a student, I read J. K. Galbraith's account of *The Great Crash, 1929*, the speculative bubble of that era. The crash and the depression that followed had been followed by fifty years of historically exceptional stability in financial markets. 'How could people have been so stupid?', I wondered. One chapter of that book was entitled 'In Goldman Sachs We Trust'. 'Why would anyone ever do so again?', I mused, as I learned of the leveraged piles of junk that Goldman and other investment banks of that era had put together, and their customers had rushed to buy.

I was soon to learn how little human nature had changed. The first great modern bubble occurred in Japan in the 1980s. Japan's post-war economic development had transformed the country from a primitive society to a new industrial state in two generations. The growth rate achieved during this explosive development, projected into the future, suggested that Japan would soon dominate the economic world. Growing demand for Japanese assets from foreign investors and the excitement this engendered among domestic speculators reinforced each other, and the share prices of Japanese companies and the value of Japanese property exploded, as did prices. At the peak it was widely claimed that the grounds of the Imperial Palace in Tokyo were worth more than the entire state of California. The Nikkei index of Japanese share prices peaked at 38,957. Almost thirty years later, it is still less than half of that level.

The New Economy bubble began to inflate in 1995, with the initial public offering of Netscape, a company whose internet browser made access to the worldwide web widely available. A report by Mary Meeker, 'the internet goddess', pointed to other companies that might attract similar enthusiasm. Many other stock analysts became heroic figures, such as Henry Blodget, who presciently urged his clients to support one of the few genuinely successful internet businesses – Amazon – but was disgraced when, after the bubble burst, emails were released giving his private opinion of the stocks he was recommending: one was 'a piece of shit'.

Meeker worked for, and Blodget was recruited by a financial conglomerate (Morgan Stanley and Merrill Lynch respectively). As a result of the structural changes in the financial services industry that created these conglomerates, the companies sought banking and issuing business from the corporations on which their analysts did research. With stockbrokers now owned by banks, the brokers' new bosses feared that research critical of customers might jeopardise other, more lucrative, relationships between banks and large corporations.

The language of the City distinguishes the 'buy side' – investment managers – from the 'sell side' – the provision of financial advice to companies and the issuance of securities. Integrated banks combined the buy side and the sell side. These banks generally concluded that the sell side mattered more to their revenues. Certainly the representatives of the sell side – the investment bankers – were usually decisive in the politics of these institutions. So the analyst became part of the sales force of investment banking business. The expectation of enthusiastic promotion of a company's virtues through 'research' provided to prospective investors would attract lucrative corporate deals to the banks.

The conflict between buy side and sell side has a long history. America's Glass–Steagall Act, passed in 1933, required the separation of investment and commercial banking operations, following the excesses of the 1920s and the crash of 1929. Senators Glass and Steagall argued, with considerable justification, that banks had pleased their corporate clients by plying their retail customers with worthless stock.

The Glass–Steagall Act was successively relaxed in the face of industry lobbying. In 1998 the legislation was the last remaining obstacle to the achievement of the well-connected and ambitious Sandy Weill's aspiration to become chief executive of Citibank.

Weill's telecoms analyst, Jack Grubman, maintained that what had once been a conflict of interest was now a synergy – investors were able to benefit from the exceptional insights derived from Grubman's close contact with corporate clients. This privileged knowledge enabled Grubman to maintain his enthusiastic recommendation of WorldCom and admiration for its then chairman, former basketball coach and future convict Bernie Ebbers, until the day the company went bust.

The disgraced former Governor of New York, Eliot Spitzer, made his once stellar reputation by exposing these New Economy deceptions. Spitzer uncovered details of how the Citigroup analyst's insights had pleased Michael Armstrong, a Citigroup board member who was also CEO of AT&T, and whose support was needed to secure Weill's elevation over rival John Reed. Grubman had been unenthusiastic about America's oldest and dullest telecommunications company, but he suddenly became persuaded not only of its solid virtues but also of its exciting growth opportunities. Contemporaneously, the bank's generous donation to the 92nd Street Y school helped secure the admission of Grubman's twin daughters to a Manhattan nursery rumoured to be more selective than Harvard.

Britain had no Spitzer; its internet boom came later, and prosecutions not at all. Few European internet companies made it through to their IPO before fundamental values reasserted themselves. In the spring of 2000 the bubble burst. Across the world.

Bubbles should be distinguished from asset mispricing. Asset mispricing occurs when market participants, faced with imperfect information and an uncertain future, get values wrong. Such mispricing occurs all the time and provides opportunities for intelligent investors. In bubbles, few traders are concerned with fundamental values, and they generally hope to sell on their securities, soon, at a higher price. Intelligent investors can do little in bubbles except watch from the side-lines.

In Chapters 9 and 10 I will describe how another bubble, in parts of the US housing market, contributed to the financial crisis of 2007–8. That bubble was promoted by brokers who encouraged borrowers to take out mortgages they could not afford in the expectation that the brokers would be able to refinance the mortgages for a higher value, and further commission, within a year or two. The structure was predicated on the assumption that house prices would rise continuously, so that even a pause would bring that structure crashing down. That pause eventually happened.

As a student, I had wondered how the markets of 1929 could have accommodated such folly. In 1999–2000 I had learned how people could indeed be so foolish; in 2007–8 I learned that such foolishness was ineradicable in modern financial services markets. The origins of these events lie not so much in innate stupidity as in the capacity of clever people, especially when blinded by the prospect of financial gain, to fall victim to the power of conventional thinking. And to suffer, and foster, information asymmetry and moral hazard.

The power of conventional thinking

In the New Economy bubble, and again in the credit expansion of the new millennium, conventional, yet magical, thinking created its own reality. It is hard to overstate the power of group thinking in business and finance. People repeat to each other the same transitorily fashionable views in mutual reinforcement. What matters is not to have a well-informed opinion of one's own, but to have a good knowledge of currently prevailing opinion, of 'what the market thinks'. For most investment professionals that is the only thing that matters. That is the force of Keynes's metaphor of the beauty contest. The market judgement that emerges from this process need have no foundation in objective reality. Both truths and falsehoods spread contagiously, forming what Galbraith called 'the conventional wisdom'.

Such processes of contagion can lead people to believe absurd things – that Salem was besieged by witches, that the US was endangered by Communist subversion, that the internet would within a few years put paid to conventional retailing and shopping malls, that house prices could only go up and that you could create a completely safe asset by bundling a package of mortgages all of which were likely to default. It is not only common, but reasonable, to believe what is widely believed, especially among business and political leaders, who have little time for reflection. I believe the world is round, not because I have myself verified it, but because the general belief is that the world is round. If I had lived a thousand years ago, I would have believed the earth was flat, and for the same reasons.

In the complex and uncertain world of modern finance such behaviour takes us far away from market efficiency and fundamental value. In all market bubbles – tulips or the South Sea, the New Economy or the credit bubble – distortions are supported by commercial interests that benefit from their promotion. There was always a kernel of truth in the exaggerated propositions. Speculators in the South Sea bubble were on the verge of an industrial revolution and an explosion of world trade. Railways, electricity and modern information technology were indeed transformational discoveries. Financial innovation did create opportunities for better risk management. The people who lost money in these bubbles were not mistaken in their basic thesis, but they greatly overestimated both the pace of change and the extent to which individual companies would benefit from it.

Beliefs – true or false – affect prices and may even affect fundamental values themselves. George Soros describes this phenomenon as 'reflexivity'. Although the development of the internet was not an event of great significance for Tesco and Walmart, the belief that it was a significant event had a large influence on their businesses. There was an even larger effect on the investment climate within which these companies operated. The New Economy bubble led to large overinvestment in telecommunications capacity, which itself made nemesis more likely. The massive overpayments by European telecoms companies for mobile phone licences were the result of misperceptions of reality generated by the New Economy bubble.

The senior executives of these businesses were captured by these misconceptions and could not have escaped them even if they had been more thoughtful people. Five years later the senior executives of banks were in the same position. In the distorting mirror provided by ostensibly sophisticated risk management models, they saw irresistible profit opportunities. There was a new paradigm for banks, as there had been a new paradigm for retailers and phone companies, and the winners would be the ones to pursue their fantastic vision most vigorously. And even if some of these senior executives were sceptical, they could not stand in the way of the crowds of colleagues rushing to benefit from these profit opportunities. The price of contradicting the mind of the market was to lose one's job.

The price of going along with the market would also be to lose one's job, but at a later date. Some bank and telecoms executives were left with more time to spend with their families (though they were also left with a great deal more money to spend on their families). After the New Economy bubble a few participants, such as Enron's Skilling and WorldCom's Ebbers, were thrown to the wolves. Men such as Blodget and Grubman, leaders among the analysts who puffed hopeless shares, and Frank Quattrone – the leading investment banker of the technology sector – were barred from the financial services industry. But they were nailed by regulators for specific misconduct, not fired by their employers for professional incompetence. (Sir) Fred Goodwin of Royal Bank of Scotland was hounded into comfortable retirement after his bank failed in 2008, while the merely naïve – people like

Mary Meeker, with more enthusiasm than judgement – continued in similar well-paid employment. After every crisis there is a determined attempt to pretend that a system that was inherently sound was damaged by the actions of a very few individuals.

The mind of the market is its own reality. Investors sought insight into 'the mind of the market', and that was what they received – and continued to receive. What was true was what was believed, and what was believed was true. And when the bubbles burst, what had once been believed and was therefore true was no longer believed and therefore no longer true. The dot.com shares that were once stars were now dogs; there was nothing more to be said. Practical men of the financial world, who would be appalled at the suggestion that they might be influenced by French philosophy, are the most determined of postmodernists. In financial centres across the world, truth is in the eye of the observer. Jean Baudrillard notoriously remarked that 'the (first) Gulf War took place only on television'; in much the same sense, the New Economy was observed only on Wall Street.

Not everyone was deceived. But risk for a fund manager is not volatility, but underperformance relative to an index. It is, as Keynes observed, better for a career to be conventionally wrong than unconventionally right, and disastrous to be unconventionally wrong. So although the fund manager is paid for stock selection, the composition of his fund mirrors closely the composition of the index. Most fund managers receive daily reports of their overweight and underweight positions, relative to the benchmark index. The successful fund manager is one who can stay close to his benchmark index but be consistently slightly ahead of it. You might think that this could be achieved by close attention to fundamental value. If performance were measured every five years, when mean reversion would have asserted itself, this would probably be true. But performance isn't measured every five years, but much more often – commonly every three months, often even more frequently. Over such short periods momentum dominates mean reversion – this quarter's outperforming stocks are more than averagely likely to have been last quarter's outperforming stocks. For the fund manager, knowing the mind of the market trumps fundamental value. As a result, many allegedly 'actively managed' funds virtually replicate an index, a practice known as closet indexation.

The pressure to follow the herd is hard for professionals to resist. If an asset manager had made the – good – call that shares were overvalued in 1996, he would almost certainly have been fired, and some were. From 1996 to 2000 shares rose steadily. If you are managing other people's money, three years is a long time – too long to be, or to appear to be, wrong.

Managers who are doing markedly worse than their peers for as long as three years will find their jobs in jeopardy. All the great investors were out of favour in 1999. 'Where have all the geniuses gone?' *Fortune* asked. Warren Buffett 'didn't get it', and shares in Berkshire Hathaway fell by almost 50 per cent in that year. George Soros failed to read the timing of boom and bust correctly, and retired from active involvement in managing other people's money, content to devote himself to the philanthropic management of his own.

Keynes reportedly said (there is no evidence he did) that the market can be wrong for longer than you can stay solvent, warning of the risks associated with ignoring the mind of the market in favour of fundamental value. Writing today, he would say that the market can be wrong for longer than a contrarian fund manager can hold his or her job. And so it proved.

While three years is a long time-scale for an investment manager, it isn't a long time-scale for the intelligent investor. This difference in the time-scale on which you are judged gives a big advantage to the DIY portfolio manager. Patience pays. The emphasis by institutional investors on quarterly figures has led analysts and fund managers into a symbiotic relationship with corporate executives known as 'earnings guidance'. In pre-war days the great figures who headed large companies, such as Harry McGowan of ICI or Alfred Sloan of General Motors, had virtually no contact with shareholders. The emergence of the hostile takeover was probably the most important single factor in changing this behaviour. Senior managers of large companies began to pay closer attention to the share price – their jobs depended on it. The growth of stock options as a means of payment reinforced the trend. It provided an additional reason for executives to pay close attention to the share price – their wealth depended on it.

Now, most large companies have an investor relations department, or employ a specialist firm to handle these issues. The chairman, chief executive and chief financial officer will expect to devote a substantial proportion of their time to investor relations. They promote the company to analysts, and talk to the investment managers who are the principal shareholders. Analysts may benefit from lavish hospitality in the course of learning about the company's affairs, even though insider trading rules preclude the company from supplying information not available to the general public and prohibit the analysts from making use of such information if it is inadvertently disclosed.

The market responds not to good and bad news from companies but to news that is better or worse than market expectations. Therefore many businesses want to manage both outcome and expectation themselves. They seek steady earnings growth just a little faster than the market is anticipating, and manage their quarterly reporting in order to achieve this goal. I will describe in the next chapter how much scope finance directors have for keeping their reported earnings on a steady path. Often the main criterion by which analysts judge the quality of management is whether executives do the things they say they will do. This mutually rewarding process of earnings guidance has only the loosest of connections with how the business is actually performing.

Occasionally fund managers have developed such a strong reputation with investors that they can ignore these pressures. While Buffett was criticised for refusing to participate in the New Economy bubble, he could laugh all the way to the bank, and the steak house. Eventually, of course, fundamental value breaks through. There is a stock-exchange-regulated process – the profit warning – by which companies abandon informal earnings guidance and confirm that things are not as everyone would like them to be. Profit warnings are often followed by second, and even third, profit warnings.

A major part – in many cases much the largest part – of the remuneration of senior executives is now related to movements in the company's share price. That makes it inevitable that the mind of the market takes precedence over fundamental value. In tribute to the power of Mr Market, many companies display the constantly fluctuating share price in their reception area. Some chief executives have it on their desks, and it is not unknown for them to check it several times a day. Their business plans are heavily influenced by the conventional wisdom of their peers, analysts and bankers, rather than their own judgement. Success, as measured by the market, is being able to anticipate the new fashion slightly more quickly than other people. Advance insight into the conventional wisdom is the commodity that many consultants, business gurus, journalists and investment analysts now sell.

Boards appoint non-executive directors with 'appropriate experience', which in practice means the directors seek out people with backgrounds and opinions indistinguishable from their own. Closer links between politics and business mean that the statements of politicians and leaders of business and finance increasingly echo each other. In the New Economy bubble, politicians and business leaders, journalists and investment professionals vied with each other in talking nonsense. In the years before the 2008 credit crisis, central bankers and financial titans congratulated each other on how financial innovation had made the system more resilient, which proved to be the exact opposite of the truth. The power of conventional thinking asserts itself in the reiteration of banal opinions on fashionable issues. Today these opinions include excitement and paranoia over China's economic development, an obsession with climate change and a new wave of indiscriminate enthusiasm for new technology.

The unproductive contact between finance directors and analysts provides an opportunity for the individual investor – the rewarding opportunity to ignore it. You aren't party to earnings guidance, but it doesn't matter, because the information such guidance provides has little to do with the substance of the business. You don't have to remain popular with company management to do your job. You don't have to worry that you will be fired if you underperform the market in one quarter, or several. Being close to the market is not necessarily an advantage. Remember that Warren Buffett lives in Omaha.

Best of all, you can emphasise absolute, rather than relative, returns. That emphasis enables the intelligent investor to focus on the analysis of fundamental value, rather than on the mind of the market. For the intelligent – and therefore patient – investor, there is a simple reconciliation between the mark to market and fundamental value principles: an asset is worth the higher of its fundamental value and its market price.

If the market price is above fundamental value, an intelligent investor can sell for the market price and look for something else. If the market price is below fundamental value, an intelligent investor can continue to hold and enjoy the benefit of the projected stream of cash returns.

This freedom gives the intelligent investor an immediate advantage over the majority of professional fund managers, bound by the routine of quarterly performance measurement. For the professional fund manager, the mark to market principle rules – an asset is worth what someone is willing to pay for it. Being able to take a detached view of fundamental value is a big advantage. But it is not easy. Estimating fundamental value requires a view on the long-term future prospects of the company. The information you need is extensive, difficult to obtain and changes constantly. The analysis of fundamental value is speculative, and different people are likely to come up with different answers. In the next chapter I'll look at what is required.

6

In Search of Fundamental Value

Accounting for earnings

Fundamental analysis of a company begins from its profits. With earnings of around 22p per share, and a share price of 221p, Vodafone's price:earnings ratio in 2015 was 10. This is a low figure for a sound business. In the long run a normal PE ratio is between 10 and 20. Sometimes, when investors are optimistic and economic conditions are thought to remain favourable, the average PE ratio for the market is above 20. Sometimes, in gloom and recession, the market average is below 10. Such fluctuations are usually followed by long-term mean reversion – either earnings catch up or prices adjust. At the height of the bubble in 2000, the FTSE all-share price:earnings ratio was 27, but today the figure is close to a more normal 16.

Just as price:earnings ratios vary across companies and business sectors, so they vary also over time. The cyclically adjusted price:earnings ratio (CAPE) is a measure popularised by Nobel Prize-winner Robert Shiller (of *Irrational Exuberance* fame). This measure looks at the ratio of the current market price to average earnings (adjusted for inflation) over the previous ten years. For the US, Shiller has calculated the long-run historical average CAPE (over more than a century) for the market as a whole as 16.5.

Not only does the price:earnings ratio also vary considerably across countries but it varies considerably and persistently between countries. Table 4 shows how at July 2015 CAPE is low in many European markets, while the US figure is close to the top of its historical range.

Table 4: **CAPE (Cyclically Adjusted Price:Earnings) ratio in different equity markets (July 2015)**

Spain	9.4	France	15.3
Austria	9.8	Germany	18.0
Italy	11.0	Japan	24.2
UK	12.1	US	24.4

Source: Wellershoff and Partners

You would have been better off over most subsequent ten-year periods buying at the low end of the range rather than at the top: and on the three occasions when the US market has broken through the top end of this range – the late 1920s, the mid-1960s and the late 1990s – the high rating has been followed by a major stock market decline. (The crashes of 1929 and 2000–01 are well known: there was no 'crash' in 1966, but the Dow Jones index did not regain its 1966 level until 1982.) While no reader should conclude from this that CAPE provides is a method of timing the market, its predictive value, resulting from the power of long-run mean reversion, is relevant to the patient investor.

But less relevant to the herd. Whenever the price:earnings ratio moves outside its conventional range, analysts opine that historical experience is no longer relevant. When Japanese share prices soared in the 1980s, they advised that Japanese companies should not be looked at in the same way as companies elsewhere. A decade later many financial commentators argued that the New Economy and the business-friendly economic and political environment that followed the end of the Cold War had changed the basic principles of stock valuation. New tools of risk management had tamed financial risk, and a 'great moderation' was in progress.

Once again, the world had not changed, only opinion. Long-term mean reversion struck, and PE ratios returned to more normal levels. There is a saying that the most expensive words in investment are 'It's different this time'. Sceptics who were reluctant to believe the rules had changed avoided the bubbles in Japan, the New Economy and the credit boom, to their ultimate benefit.

These broad market averages conceal large variations between industries and firms. Generally, high PE ratios indicate industries or individual companies thought to have better than average growth prospects; low PE ratios attach to sectors or businesses thought to have worse than average growth prospects. A high PE ratio may mean either that investors are optimistic about the growth prospects for the company or sector – as I write, the PE ratio for the UK technology sector is 35. Or it may mean that earnings are thought to be cyclically depressed – as I write, the PE ratio for the oil, gas and mining sector is over 60.

Some people look at the ratio between the price:earnings ratio and the growth rate or earnings ratio (the PEG ratio). Their reasoning is that a low PEG ratio suggests that future growth can be bought at a relatively modest price. It's not that easy: measures such as PEG are only ways of beginning to frame questions about the fundamentals of a company. The PEG ratio is a simple screen for identifying companies whose fundamentals deserve further examination.

For a stock such as Vodafone with a PE ratio of 10, the earnings of 22p attributable to each share are equal to 10 per cent of the share price. This ratio, the inverse of the PE ratio, is known as the earnings yield. If a normal PE ratio is between 10 and 20, a normal earnings yield lies between 5 and 10 per cent.

Since shareholders do not receive the company's earnings,

the earnings yield is not directly relevant to the shareholder. However, earnings determine the capacity of the company to pay dividends, and the earnings yield is a guide to the long-run rate of return that it is reasonable to expect from owning shares.

Creative accounting

But the value of these numbers depends on their integrity. The collapse of Enron brought to the attention of a wider public what market professionals and companies have always known: companies have a lot of scope to make their reported earnings and assets what they want them to be. What is the profit of a company? It all depends on the meaning of 'is', as Bill Clinton explained to the Grand Jury. Creative accounting is the quantitative equivalent of the modern politician's lie – a statement that is in some narrow technical sense true, but is substantively false.

The jury decided that the practices at Enron constituted fraud, and the former chief executive, Jeff Skilling, and former chief financial officer, Andy Fastow, went to jail for their part in one of America's most spectacular corporate collapses. Yet the methods Skilling and Fastow employed were only aggressive versions of financial techniques used by the most respectable companies. Wall Street wanted companies to report a steady stream of increased earnings (part of the process of managing investor expectations that I described in the previous chapter). So that is what companies reported. How were companies such as Enron able to manage, not their businesses, but their declared earnings, in this way?

Most large businesses are, from a legal perspective, a group of companies under common ownership. Consolidated accounts aggregate the individual accounts of all these companies and report the overall result as if the business were a single entity.

Since shareholders are, indirectly, shareholders in all the companies within the group, this is the only sensible way to present the figures in a manageable, comprehensible form.

But companies often give stakes in associated businesses to outsiders. In a joint venture between two or more companies, each cooperating company will usually have a share of the legal entity that conducts the business. A firm establishing a new business venture may want to give shares to key individuals. Or a company may simply own shares in another business as a strategic investment.

The general principle – and it is a sensible one – is that if a company manages and controls a subsidiary or associate company, the consolidated accounts of the parent should include the relevant share of assets and earnings of the subsidiary or associate. If the parent does not manage and control the other company, then its interest should be treated as if it were an investment. The asset is the value of the shares, and the income is the dividend.

So far so good, if not so simple. But what exactly is meant by management and control? Accounting standards try to pin this down. There are two sets of international accounting rules; International Financial Reporting Standards (IFRS), promulgated by the London-based International Accounting Standards Board, and Generally Accepted Accounting Principles (GAAP), imposed by America's Securities and Exchange Commission. But whenever standards try to pin down a concept, the creature flies away. Creating subsidiaries that you do, in reality, manage and control, but that you do not manage and control for the purposes of generally accepted accounting principles, has many advantages for the creative accountant. You can use transactions between the parent and subsidiary to create profits, or to make them disappear. As with most creative accounting techniques, this doesn't work for ever; sooner or later these manoeuvres will have to be reversed. But you can make it later rather than sooner.

And remember, in the long run we are all dead. Or, in the case of Enron, in the federal penitentiary.

Enron created hundreds of these subsidiaries. If you went through the detail of the company's accounting filings, you would discover all this. But to do so would involve burying yourself in thousands of pages of figures. Some analysts did figure it out. I'll come back to them in Chapter 9. But most analysts were employed by investment banks that earned, or hoped to earn, large fees from Enron's hyperactive transactions.

It is generally easier and more rewarding to be impressed by a company's slick presentation and generous hospitality than it is to immerse yourself in the detail of company accounts and incur the hostility of corporate executives. Another fraudster, Bernie Ebbers, of WorldCom, reduced the slick presentation to bare essentials. He would arrive at meetings and simply point to a graph of the company's rising share price before inviting questions. Any more extensive account of what the company was doing might have taxed his business knowledge and financial expertise. The accountants of both Enron and WorldCom, encouraged to support that rising share price, made extensive use of two other common devices – 'revenue recognition' and 'acquisition accounting'.

A long-term contract or project will incur costs and accrue revenues over several years. A conservative approach recognises the profit when the books have closed and the money is banked, acknowledging only the bird in the hand. An optimistic frame of mind takes credit for the anticipated profit on the deal the moment it is signed, chalking up many birds in the bush as soon as the hunter's gun is primed.

A true and fair view would strike a position somewhere in between. The right balance requires careful, and subjective, judgement. But the exercise of careful judgement was not the activity in which self-aggrandising executives were engaged. Some companies of the New Economy era would simply exchange long-term contracts to supply each other with the same thing, enabling both to credit turnover and profits even though no real transaction had taken place – or ever would.

The issue of revenue recognition is an aspect of a much larger problem. Managers given a target of finding 5 or 10 per cent cost savings, a frequent corporate practice, can usually deliver. Sometimes this cost saving can be achieved with little effect on the efficiency of the business or the quality of its product. But we have all encountered people who reduce, rather than increase, the effectiveness of the organisation that employs them. You can always spend less on maintenance, or on customer service, or press employees to work harder. These actions will have an impact on future profits, but the consequences will be some time ahead, and may prove to be more or less expensive than the initial cost savings.

Most large companies have engaged in successive rounds of these cost savings in the last decade, either to enhance measured efficiency or to produce the 'synergies' that justify their merger activity. Such savings are the main reason why corporate earnings have grown faster than revenues or than the economy as a whole. Some of the cost reductions represent real efficiency gains; others enhance current profits at the expense of future profits. Often, only time will tell.

BP took cost-cutting too far, with disastrous long-term consequences both for profits and corporate reputation. Through the 1990s Marks & Spencer steadily increased margins at the expense of the company's famous value for money until, in 1998, the business earned record profits. Then sales dropped sharply. Within a period of only a few months the iconic reputation had evaporated. The privatised Railtrack penny-pinched on maintenance until, following serious accidents, the inept company threw money at its problems in a desperate, and unsuccessful, attempt to restore the confidence of passengers and government.

Banks sold their customers payment protection insurance

(PPI) on which many of the policyholders stood no chance of a successful claim, until regulators forced them to return billions in compensation to their customers. Pharmaceutical companies stressed marketing and cost reduction and spent their ample profits on buying each other rather than on new research, leaving empty their pipelines of new drugs and endangering the fragile implicit contract between the industry and the public.

Despite these regrettable examples, there are many British businesses that are far better and more tightly run today than two decades ago. Almost every company can reduce cost at the expense of future revenues, and if analysts project this short-term growth of earnings into the future, the stock price gets a double bonus. The key issue in every case – BP, Marks & Spencer, Railtrack and the banks that sold PPI – is to look at the sustainability of the business strategy and, above all, the sustainability of the firm's competitive advantage: the reputation of BP and of the pharmaceutical industry; the relationship between Marks & Spencer and the banks that mis-sold protection, and the customers of those businesses; Railtrack's franchise. Competitive advantage can only be understood by going behind the earnings statement.

A prudent business that acquires another will take a careful look at the assets it has acquired. So will an imprudent one. The imprudent one writes down the value of these assets to low levels and then attributes to its own superior management skills the gains made when these undervalued assets are sold or used in the business. The 'restoration' of value can be used to enhance profits for many years. This practice is called 'acquisition accounting'.

In the 1980s several companies – such as BTR, which bought businesses as diverse as Dunlop's sports goods and Hawker Siddeley's aviation activities – presented a consistent picture of growing earnings to pave the way for the next large acquisition. Every takeover had to be larger still to maintain the momentum. Eventually, the music stopped.

Advisers and accountants connived in these schemes. It is impossible to believe that sophisticated, intelligent investment bankers did not realise that Kenneth Lay, Enron's chairman, was an affable, skilful political operator with little grasp of business detail; that Jeff Skilling, the chief executive, was as corrupt as he was brilliant; or that Bernie Ebbers had none of the attributes needed to run a global telecoms company. But Enron's complex financial transactions and WorldCom's constant acquisitions generated large fees.

Accountants were once the butt of jokes – stuffy people with a rigid professional ethic. In the 1980s the large global firms that audit virtually all major corporations in Britain and the United States consolidated, a process that ended with the emergence of 'the big four': KPMG, PwC, EY and Deloitte. Their partners became hungry for consulting revenue as fee levels from their traditional audit business came under pressure.

Pleasing corporate clients received greater emphasis and the ethos of the profession less. 'Eat what you kill' – partners taking home the revenues they have personally earned rather than a share of the collective profits – was an increasingly common slogan in law and accountancy firms. The characterisation of clients as prey is revealing. Arthur Andersen, always the most commercial of the major firms, would pursue new clients most aggressively – and would be destroyed by its acquiescence in Enron's frauds.

The main counteracting force to the effect of competitive pressures in reducing standards is public regulation of accounting standards through bodies such as the International Accounting Standards Board and the Securities and Exchange Commission. These organisations have done much to rein in abuses, and, as a result, formal accounting statements now contain much less rubbish than they did even a decade ago. Still, the presentation of company accounts remains confusing. Many companies highlight partial or misleading information, and commercial pressures on analysts to join in corporate self-congratulation and facilitate the process of earnings guidance remain strong. Beware of pro forma earnings or any numbers that are adjusted to reflect supposedly non-recurring items. The figures that company executives present are sometimes described as 'earnings before bad stuff'.

Also be wary of EBITDA (Earnings Before Interest, Tax, Depreciation, Amortisation), now widely and misleadingly used to appraise companies; the concept was invented in the heady 1990s to flatter the accounts of unprofitable technology businesses, and interest, tax and depreciation are all real costs which must be covered before a company can properly make distributions to shareholders or employees.

One clear pointer to the problems at Enron was that the company, while supposedly very profitable, was not generating the cash that matched its reported earnings. Cash is a good reality check. If the people at Barings ostensibly supervising rogue trader Nick Leeson had stopped to ask themselves why his trading successes needed to be financed by repeated injections of money from the rest of the group, Barings might still be in business today. A common feature of all the accounting wheezes described above – dubious transactions between the company and its subsidiaries, premature revenue recognition, inappropriate writing down of acquired assets – is that increases in reported earnings have no cash counterpart. Tax is also a clue to what is really going on. Revenue authorities have many faults, but they do not often levy tax on profits that do not exist. High profits and a low tax charge may be explained by clever tax planning, or by extensive investment programmes that produce large deductions. Another possible explanation is that profits are not what they seem.

There are ways of penetrating the fog created by earnings reports. One method is to focus on the ability of a business to generate cash. Another is to look in a more qualitative way at the inherent capabilities of a company's business. I'll look at each of these approaches in turn.

Cash is king

Most thoughtful analysts look at cash flow and assets rather than reported earnings when they wish to assess the fundamental value of a business. The two general principles of asset valuation apply just as much to a company, and to the assets of a company, as to a security:

- an asset is worth what someone is willing to pay for it; and
- the value of an asset is the cash it will generate for its owner over its life.

Applying the second of these principles requires a process for translating a stream of cash that accrues continuously over time into a value at a particular point in time. The cash flow will come from the dividends on a share or on the earnings of a company. The standard method is called 'discounted cash flow' (DCF), the first and indispensable tool for any quantitative investment analyst.

Compound interest at 8 per cent per year means that £100 now will be worth £108 a year from now, £117 in two years' time and so on. If £100 is worth £108 a year from now, then £100 a year from now is today worth £93 (£100 ÷ 1.08). A similar calculation would make £100 two years from now worth £86 today (£100 ÷ 1.17). In this way the method of discounted cash flow derives a set of conversion factors which, like exchange rates, can be used to convert cash at any future date into an equivalent value of cash today. (£100 in 2018 corresponds to £86 in 2016.) A promise to pay £300 in three equal annual instalments, starting now, is worth not £300 but £100 + £93 +£86, or £279. All you need do is choose an appropriate discount rate. The choice of an appropriate discount rate is not a minor problem, as we shall see.

The method of DCF valuation of a company can be applied either to the cash flow accruing to the shareholder – the dividends to be paid – or to the cash accruing to the business itself. I'll look at each of these approaches in turn.

Suppose a company, like Vodafone, is paying a dividend of 11p per share. We need to estimate the likely growth of that dividend. If dividends grow at 2.5 per cent, next year's dividend might be 11.3p, rising to 11.6p the year after and so on. All we need to do is write down that stream of cash flows and discount it at, say, 8 per cent. In this way we can calculate a discounted cash flow valuation of the dividends the shareholder can expect to receive and treat this as the fundamental value of a share.

If 2.5 per cent growth is the long-term average, there is a simplifying trick. Subtract 2.5 per cent, the growth rate, from 8 per cent, the discount rate. The difference, 5.5 per cent, should be the dividend yield on the share. It is easy to work through the mathematics, but you may prefer just to believe the result. The fundamental value that emerges from this calculation is 220p, which happens to be the current share price.

The DCF approach requires knowledge of the appropriate discount rate and of the appropriate cash flows. The usual approach is to say that future cash flows should be discounted at the rate the company has to pay to raise money – the cost of capital. In the calculation above I used an arbitrary 8 per cent – the target rate of return of Chapter 2 – as discount rate (a common procedure), but if the technique is to have scientific value, the number requires a more scientific basis.

The gross redemption yields on those long-dated Treasury 2055 stocks might be a good starting point. Payments of interest and principal by the British government are secure. But since the future dividends of Vodafone are speculative, it is common practice to use a much higher discount rate to reflect the greater risk associated with investment in shares. This allowance for business risk is called the 'equity risk premium'. The simplest and commonest way of measuring the equity risk premium is the average historical difference between returns on shares and the return on safe assets. The data on long-term returns in Chapter 2 might justify a figure of about 5 per cent for the equity risk premium. This is roughly consistent with an 8 per cent figure for the cost of equity capital if long-term nominal interest rates are around 3 per cent, and is aligned with the intelligent investor's target rate of return. I'll come back to the calculation of this risk element of the cost of capital in the next chapter.

The alternative approach to DCF appraisal for a company like Vodafone is to look at cash flows generated within the business itself. The free cash flow approach subtracts necessary investment in productive assets from the cash generated by a company's operations. The balance – the free cash flow – is the relevant amount for the DCF calculation. If we had a sufficiently long series of future free cash flows, the DCF technique would enable us to calculate the fundamental value of the business as a whole. But that is a big if.

A rapidly growing business may have negative free cash flow, because the company is spending more building the business than it is currently earning. Most new companies are in this position. Only after several years will projected cash flows become positive. Many years of data are therefore required before any clear assessment of fundamental value can be made.

But there is a further difficulty, which is common to both the dividend growth model and the free cash flow valuation. As illustration, go back to the DCF valuation of Vodafone and use the dividend growth approach. Over the next five years the DCF value generated from dividends will be around 40p, which is less than 20 per cent of the hypothetical value of the share. Most of the projected cash flow lies in a far distant future – and this for a company whose shares yield well above the market average.

Worse still, the result of the calculation is extremely sensitive to the assumptions. Suppose the dividend growth projection is 5 per cent rather than 2.5 per cent, and that the discount rate is 6 per cent rather than 8 per cent. These aren't large adjustments – just a move from a weak growth assumption to a fairly good one, and a slightly lower allowance for business risk in a more benign economic scenario. But such adjustments raise the projected share price from 220p to £11. Or suppose you are more pessimistic. Put dividend growth at zero and the discount rate at 10 per cent: then the shares are worth only 110p.

At this point you may be inclined to give up on the use of DCF measures of fundamental value. Yet the DCF technique doesn't create the problem – it reveals it. Most of the value of today's major businesses really does lie in a future beyond the five or ten years that seem reasonably foreseeable. Small changes in assumptions, compounded far into the future, have large effects on current values. DCF calculations are illuminating, but don't make the mistake of believing that any particular DCF calculation is true.

There is a partial solution to these problems, which is to cut off the cash flow analysis after a period – five years is a common choice – and make an assumption about the value of the business at that date. This is not a very satisfactory answer. It resolves the difficult question posed initially – what is the fundamental value of the business now? – by requiring an answer to a still more difficult question – what will be the fundamental value of the business five years from now? At this point the first principle of asset valuation – an asset is worth what someone is willing to pay for it – becomes confounded with the second – the value of an asset is the cash it generates for its owner.

That emphasis on asset value suggests another approach to valuing a business. Look not at the earnings but at the assets the business owns. Every company you might invest in produces a balance sheet, a statement of the value of the assets it owns. Traditional accounting practice was conservative: the balance sheet should report the lower of the amount the company paid for an asset and its current value, which might be either the amount for which it could now be sold or its DCF valuation – the present value of the cash the asset will generate over its life. While this formulation closely mirrors the general principles of asset valuation, it does so in a deliberately cautious way. This caution arose, first, from insisting that the lower of the possible answers was used, and second, by substituting the amount the company paid for the asset for the amount someone else would be willing to pay for it.

Both IFRS and GAAP have, however, been moving in the direction of what is known as 'fair value' accounting. Fair value is what you could expect to get for an asset if you sold it in an orderly market. Most financial assets and some others must now be treated in this way. While this basis seems more realistic, if less conservative, it raises a number of issues. If there is an active market, then valuations will be buffeted by the noise created by moody, volatile Mr Market; these fluctuations may have little relevance to underlying business realities. If there is not an active market, then the numbers used will be estimates – 'mark to model' is a process with obvious scope for abuse, and such opportunities for abuse were widely adopted in the years before the global financial crisis.

Fundamental analysis

The pioneers of securities analysis, such as Benjamin Graham and David Dodd, operated successfully by simply having the skills and energy to penetrate accounting statements when such skills and energy were rare. Since the assets reported in the balance sheet were generally estimated conservatively, shares whose prices were below the reported asset value were generally good buys. Some investors became rich by identifying companies where the value of the assets the company owned – shops or land – was greater than the value of the company as a trading entity.

Charles Clore became Britain's largest shoe retailer not because he was interested in shoes but because he was interested in the shops in which shoes were sold. Jim Slater enjoyed a meteoric career as the whiz-kid of the late 1960s before his sprawling business empire collapsed in the economic crisis that followed the 1973 oil shock. Slater looked at the business not as a trading concern but as a collection of assets. The term 'asset stripper', coined for him, remains a term of abuse today.

Those days of easy returns have gone. Today most companies have stripped their own assets. When assets have a value separable from the company that uses them, companies have generally realised that value. I have already explained that modern businesses rarely own the premises from which they operate and usually don't own the computers and the vehicles that their employees use.

The important assets of modern businesses are no longer their buildings, plant and machinery, but their intangible property – their reputation with customers, their relationships with suppliers. When pompous executives proclaim, 'Our people are our greatest asset', what they say is often true. Most other assets are owned by, or pledged to, the financial sector.

Financial companies directly or indirectly own much of the plant or the property occupied by other industrial and commercial businesses. It is important to understand the structure of the assets of property and investment companies, and important, but rarely possible, to understand the assets of banks and insurance companies. There are a few sectors, such as oil and house-building, where the market position of the company will depend on its control of future reserves of petroleum or of land.

But while all company accounts report a figure for the net assets of the company, the asset value is usually now a poor guide to the value of its shares.

Investment analysts used to distinguish between value and growth investing. Broadly speaking, value investing focused on companies with strong tangible assets, growth investing on companies with strong intangible assets. Nowadays these categories have become too blurred to be useful. Some people think that more systematic attempts should be made to include the value of intangible assets in company accounts. But I am sceptical.

Accounting theorists want to revive the balance sheet for a modern era; creative finance directors want to present the most favourable impression of the company's affairs. In any event, you will be bewildered by studying Vodafone's balance sheet, which includes over £65 billion of intangible assets, almost three times the value of its physical property. Over £20 billion of assets are 'goodwill' – which the company helpfully explains is the difference between what it paid for acquisitions and the fair value of the related assets, a value that it attributes to the synergies it hopes to realise in future. This figure is calculated after writedowns of much larger figures it reported in the past on this account. Another £15 billion or so is the value of spectrum, the amounts Vodafone or the businesses it has acquired paid to governments for licences to operate mobile services – amounts that it hopes to recover from future customers.

Most startlingly, the company records over £30 billion of deferred tax assets. These are accumulated tax losses which it plans to offset against future profits. This is a modest fraction of the actual tax losses the company claims to have incurred; tax losses arising in Luxembourg alone (a country with a population of around half a million) exceed £70 billion (*sic*). This is not because mobile phone provision in Luxembourg is massively unprofitable; Vodafone does not in fact provide a mobile phone service in Luxembourg. In common with many large multinationals, Vodafone has a complex web of companies designed to minimise the tax it pays. Although the company is headquartered in Newbury, Berkshire, and is the UK's largest mobile phone provider, Vodafone pays virtually no corporation tax to the UK government.

Competitive advantage

These balance sheet numbers should be disregarded. Corporate accounts reveal imperfectly, or not at all, the most important determinant of a company's fundamental value – its competitive advantage. In the nineteenth-century businesses that Karl Marx described, the capitalist owned the factory and the plant in which workers produced the goods, and that state of affairs defined both the economic and the political relationship between them. The analytic framework of that era lingers, although the modern business environment is quite different. The bosses of large corporations have authority because of their job titles, not their wealth (though they are increasingly inclined to use the former to secure the latter). They don't own the place where they work, and nor, as a rule, does the company that employs them.

The modern company is best viewed as a collection of capabilities. It is defined by its brands and its products, through its internal systems and its relationships with customers and suppliers, by the resources to which it has access and the operating licences it holds, and by its reputation with the public, governments and prospective employees. We have capitalism without capital.

When the company's most valuable assets leave the building at the end of the month, they take their pay cheques with them. The ability of the company to generate returns for shareholders depends on its ability to add value to its employees through its own capabilities. In a competitive market-place, a business can add such value only if there is something distinctive about these capabilities that yields a competitive advantage.

A distinctive capability becomes valuable when it yields a sustainable competitive advantage. That is what Warren Buffett understood when he bought stakes in Coca-Cola, Gillette and Heinz. He didn't think he was buying a bottling plant, a razor blade manufacturing line, or a manufacturer of 57 varieties of processed foods. He was buying powerful brands and irreproducible market positions.

The largest of Britain's companies by market capitalisation (the blue chips) are Shell, HSBC, BAT, GlaxoSmithKline, BP and Vodafone. The two oil companies, Shell and BP, are similar in many respects. They are integrated businesses with activities that include: exploration and production; trading, transportation and refining; and selling petrol, heating oil, aviation fuel and other petroleum products to final consumers. Historically, BP's strengths have been more upstream – closer to production – and Shell's more downstream – closer to consumers. BP seemed to have established a lead over its rival when it took a central role in the restructuring of the world oil industry in the 1990s. It consistently impressed the mind of the market with vigorous cost reduction and repeated earnings gains, while Shell's standing with the public was diminished by environmental and political controversies, and its standing with investors diminished by its conservative business strategy and a scandal over mis-statement of its oil reserves. But in the last five years these rankings have been sharply reversed as BP has encountered problem after problem while Shell has moved ahead. The mind of the market was, as always, too ready to project the present into the future.

The sustainability of the competitive advantages of BP and Shell is demonstrated by the way in which these businesses have, for decades, been not just the leading European oil companies but among the leading European companies of any kind. It is hard to imagine that any firms outside the small group of established oil majors could replicate their integrated systems or their ability to attract and develop strong teams of managers and engineers. The well-resourced national oil companies of major producing states such as Norway and Saudi Arabia have not really tried, while Russia's predatory Gazprom continues to depend on Western expertise and distribution systems. The distinctive capabilities of these businesses extend from privileged access to oil reserves through their integrated production and distribution systems to their retail brands.

HSBC has an even longer history, although its emergence as a major international bank is recent. As the Hong Kong and Shanghai Banking Corporation, the company facilitated trade and investment in the Far East in the heyday of the British empire. In 1980, with China still emerging from the rule of Mao and the status of Hong Kong uncertain, the future of the business seemed in doubt. But the company's fortunes have since been transformed by a programme of acquisitions around the world and the emergence of China as an economic powerhouse. Well-established banks have a series of competitive advantages: a name that others trust, a customer base of corporate and private accounts, and branch networks. The company has attempted to develop HSBC as a global retail brand, rebadging the local banks it has bought in many countries.

Glaxo was a small British drug company that discovered and developed an anti-ulcerant, Zantac, one of the most commercially successful products in the history of the pharmaceutical industry. By reinvesting these profits in research, and taking over two rivals, Wellcome and SmithKline, the company became one of the world's leading pharmaceutical businesses. The acquisition of Wellcome – and the decision of the trustees to diversify away from the shareholding in Glaxo they acquired as a result – is the origin of the Wellcome Trust's investment portfolio. Today, Glaxo's sales are heavily biased towards the United States, as is its management.

Glaxo's competitive advantage depends in significant part on the intellectual property it derives from drug patents. Even though these patents have limited life, drugs such as Zantac continue to have brand value in the face of the generic competition that emerges when such protection expires. As the leading British pharmaceutical company, Glaxo enjoys a privileged position in association with Britain's strong academic science base.

But original research in pharmacology is moving from large pharmaceutical businesses towards a mixture of publicly funded basic research and smaller specialist businesses financed by venture capital. The era of blockbuster drugs such as Zantac, which alleviate but do not cure the chronic illnesses of the well-to-do, is coming to an end. Companies like Glaxo are organisations focused on marketing and the management of the complex processes of regulatory approval.

Vodafone's competitive advantage is based on its operating licences and ownership of the physical networks, which are hard to reproduce, and the customer base it has accumulated. Many of these assets – such as the Mannesmann acquisition and the 3G licences obtained in Britain and Germany – are worth much less than the company paid for them. That is part of the explanation of the company's bewildering balance sheet and eye-watering tax losses. Much shareholder wealth has been destroyed; the company's share price is well below the level at which most holders acquired or received their shares. But the underlying competitive advantages of the businesses based on infrastructure and customer base remain, although they are less valuable than the company or its shareholders once supposed.

These firms illustrate common types of competitive advantage. Generally, the distinctive capabilities that create competitive advantages fall into four broad categories:

- Brands and reputation – important for BP and Shell, both for the retail brands that attract their customers

and the reputation that encourages governments to select these firms as partners in exploiting oil reserves (brand and reputation are also important to HSBC);
- Strategic assets – exclusive access to specific resources, such as Vodafone's licences and the reserves controlled by BP and Shell;
- Proprietary architecture – systems and structures, such as those of the oil companies and banks;
- Innovation and intellectual property – vital to Glaxo.

The value of competitive advantages depends on the extent to which these competitive advantages are appropriable and sustainable. A competitive advantage is appropriable only if the company can defend it against suppliers and customers. An asset is not appropriable if it can go down in the lift – much of the value created by City firms is paid out in bonuses to employees. A competitive advantage has continuing value only if it is hard to replicate.

Primark's brand of cheap retailing, for example, has recently been so attractive to customers that police had to be called to keep order when the company (a subsidiary of Associated British Foods) opened its Oxford Street store. But in retailing almost every successful new formula, including Primark's, can be quickly reproduced. Other stores can see what is being done and can buy products from the same or similar suppliers. Competitive advantages based on market positioning – successfully identifying unfilled product niches – are rarely sustainable.

The competitive advantage created by a strong retail brand, such as those of John Lewis (owned by an employee trust, and not available for equity investment) or Marks & Spencer, is much harder to reproduce. The same is true of the (depreciating) competitive advantage that Tesco and Sainsbury enjoy by controlling a network of well-positioned out-of-town sites. Planning restrictions now ensure that, even if similar sites are identified, they are hard to develop.

In a slow-moving industry such as soft drinks, a brand like Coca-Cola can, with appropriate management, be sustained indefinitely. If the market can be developed through geographical expansion – introducing Coke to China – or product extension – such as the sale of Diet Coke – the value of this competitive advantage may continue to grow.

In a fast-moving market, such as consumer electronic goods, a brand can maintain its value only if the name can be attached to a stream of innovative products. Apple has enjoyed astonishing success in this regard. The company's technology is not, in itself, remarkable – the underlying electronics is available to everyone. But the company has repeatedly shown itself able to package these capabilities in products that meet consumer needs – often consumer needs that the consumers did not previously know they had. Apple's first breakthrough was the graphical user interface (GUI), which allowed small computers to be used by people who understood nothing of DOS or programming. But this innovation – which had in fact been pioneered by Xerox – was soon imitated by Microsoft with Windows. The idea of a GUI could not be protected by patent or copyright, while the computer code of the Microsoft operating system did enjoy such protection. But Apple could repeat its innovative achievement with its music and video player, the iPod, and then with the iPhone and iPad. And could do so more sustainably by linking the innovation to a music library and operating systems which could, unlike the idea of smartphone or tablet, be protected intellectual property. The market leadership that these products delivered proved sustainable. Although the concept of the smartphone could be imitated – and was – the operating systems, linked to Apple computers, were intellectual property. (These various contrasts raise questions about the economic effectiveness of such legislation.)

The value of such innovations depends critically on the timing and presentation of such innovations. The tablet computer had been invented several times before – even by Apple itself. But only when the range of mobile services had reached a certain stage of development did this idea appear irresistible to customers. Innovation is not only, or primarily, about the application of advanced science. Commercial success in innovation is largely about marketing and timing. While Glaxo's Zantac was a success that made the company's shares spectacular outperformers for twenty years, EMI's path-breaking CAT scanner – a more original innovation – proved bad news for EMI shareholders in the long run. America's General Electric was able to manufacture similar machines but brought enduring competitive advantages in marketing expertise and political networking to their sale in the massive US healthcare market.

Glaxo benefited because its innovation was supported by a patent. (Although there were numerous patents around EMI's scanner, the central breakthrough – the concept of computer-assisted tomography – could not be protected.) Pharmaceuticals is one of relatively few industries in which intellectual property protection is sufficiently powerful to make innovation appropriable. Even here the issue is more complex. Zantac was a me-too drug – the pharmacological principle was pioneered by Tagamet, a similar drug marketed by SmithKline (not then part of the GlaxoSmithKline conglomerate). Glaxo's primary achievement was to market its product more effectively. Innovation – especially, but not uniquely, among sources of competitive advantage – is most effective when supported by complementary, but perhaps less distinctive, capabilities.

Strategic assets such as those of BP or Vodafone are powerful and valuable capabilities. But these depend on governments, and what governments give they can also take away. The Russian government expropriated part of BP's assets in that country. Western governments rarely expropriate but can, and do, set and alter the terms on which monopoly franchises are offered, as demonstrated in the regular *ad hoc* modifications to North Sea oil taxation, or in the US government response to BP's American disasters. Regulatory authorities can reduce the value of existing franchises by issuing more of them, as with airline liberalisation. More sustainable strategic assets are found where the monopoly is intrinsic rather than government-conferred, as with Heathrow Airport (owned by BAA, now a subsidiary of the Spanish company Ferrovial), or the *Financial Times* (recently sold by Pearson to the Japanese media company Nikkei). The pink paper operates in a niche profitable for one newspaper but unlikely to be profitable for two.

Valuable competitive advantages are sustainable over time, appropriable by the firm that holds them and defensible against pressure from competitors, suppliers and customers. Is it possible to use these principles to compute, numerically, the fundamental value of a business? It is certainly possible to sketch the outlines of a calculation. Such an exercise may have value as reality check – could these competitive advantages equal, or be much more or less than, the value implied by the current market price?

But you should treat such calculations as illuminating rather than true. I'll discuss bogus quantification further in Chapter 8. The analytic framework described here, like many others, is better used as a set of questions. What are the sources of competitive advantage? Are they replicable, sustainable, defensible, appropriable? The calculations are a better guide to relative valuations than to absolute ones.

Value investing was once the purchase of tangible assets at levels below their market value. Value investing today is buying sustainable competitive advantages at a good price. The opportunity to do so arises most often because the mind of the market is distracted by essentially short-term considerations – a poor economic outlook for the industry, a strategic mistake by the business, weak management or simply negative momentum. These are the signals for the intelligent investor to make contrarian purchases. I will return to contrarianism in Chapter 11.

7

Risk and Reward

Risk and uncertainty

The first share I bought was in a small shipyard called Robb Caledon. It was a decidedly contrarian purchase because the yard was bankrupt. Yet the experience was both a rewarding investment and a rewarding lesson in investment.

You might naturally begin to establish an investment portfolio with a selection of blue chip stocks, such as BP, HSBC, Glaxo and Vodafone. Such a strategy sounds much less risky than a stake in Robb Caledon. But when I bought Robb Caledon, I was learning about the capital asset pricing model (CAPM), the dominant theory of modern financial economics. That theory suggests the opposite conclusion.

Fast-forward more than two decades. I am attending a meeting of government economists and senior executives from major defence contractors. The largest defence contractor, BAE Systems, had recently suffered huge losses from cost overruns on a major project. Its business was in turmoil, its shares depressed, and loss of confidence and aversion to risk had affected the whole sector.

The government economists, who had recently learned the CAPM at the best graduate schools, explained that the cost of capital to these companies was very low – on a par, in fact, with the government bond rate. They repeated themselves several times. They needed to – the business people reacted as they would have reacted to aliens describing life on another planet. The two sides meant completely different things when they talked about risk. In this chapter I'll explain the CAPM and illustrate the different interpretations attached to the term 'risk' by business people and financial professionals.

During the New Economy bubble, stocks carried large risk for investors. Speculators hoped for – and sometimes made – large profits, and ultimately suffered very large losses. The principal risk faced by investment managers, confronting the same opportunities, was that they would lose the support of their customers by failing to match the performance of their rivals. The risk perceived by the fund manager was different from the risk faced by the customer.

Common sense tells us that flying is risky. Travelling in a metal tube at high speed and an altitude of 10,000 metres is intrinsically dangerous. But precisely because flying is potentially dangerous, planes are scrupulously maintained, pilots are rigorously trained, and safety precautions are extensive. Fewer than 1,000 people per year die in commercial plane crashes (and in 2014 and 2015 the four most serious air accidents were all caused by criminal activity, either by air crew or from the ground, rather than pilot error or equipment failure). More people died in England and Wales alone from falling down the stairs.

Worldwide, 1.2 million people die each year in road accidents. But the probability that you will die in a motor accident in Britain or Sweden is less than one-fifth the global average, despite high levels of vehicle ownership and use in these countries. Fewer children are killed on the roads in Britain today than in the 1920s. The roads are more dangerous, but, because parents recognise this, their children are safer. The statistics do not lie, nor do our assessments of risk. The dangers that risks pose to our health – and our financial well-being – are the product both of the intrinsic riskiness of an activity and the measures, both social and individual, that we take to counteract them. The figures showing that flying is safe, and the intuition that flying is risky, are both correct. It all depends on what you mean by risk.

Until recently, households found security in large families. In many parts of the world they still do. Infant mortality was high, and only in a big family was it probable that some children would live to become providers and homemakers. Few people in rich countries now think in this way. Large families are more exposed financially and run more serious risk of grief through accident or serious illness. What is risky in one context may be provident in a different context, and vice versa.

The government economists who thought some risks could be completely diversified used a different frame of thought from the business people who worried that a risky project might bankrupt their companies. The investor who worried about losing his shirt and the fund manager who worried about losing his job had different perceptions of risk. The nervous passenger and the student of accident statistics see flight risk differently. Some parents think it would be imprudent to have a large family; others think it would be imprudent not to.

The antithesis of risk is security. Much of the ambiguity in the meaning of risk results from different concepts of security. Do not confuse security with certainty. Certainty is knowing what is going to happen, but perhaps what is going to happen is not very satisfactory. The man who knows he is going to be executed tomorrow has certainty but not security. More generally, low aspirations give a degree of certainty but rarely security. People who crave certainty frequently achieve its appearance by relinquishing control over their lives, only to find that there are no certainties. People who sought careers which offered lifetime employment only to see their employers renege on the implicit promise. People thought that giving most of their retirement savings to Equitable Life offered safety and diversification but found that their investment was almost worthless. People make career and retirement plans but are then suddenly diagnosed with a grave illness. The lowest percentiles of the risk distribution are generally the consequence of wholly unanticipated events.

The citizens of East Germany functioned in a predictable environment at the price of a dull life and a modest standard of living. Many were willing to accept that offer, only to witness the collapse of the regime that had made the deal. To take control of one's own life or financial affairs may seem to create uncertainty, but it is a prerequisite of security in a world that is inescapably uncertain. The most attractive financial goal for most people is to have enough money not to worry about money.

Security is a high degree of confidence that one's reasonable expectations will be met. Not 100 per cent confidence, because in a real world – as distinct from a model – there can be no such thing. For the prudent investor, security means confidence that investment performance will enable him or her to achieve realistic goals, and risk is failure to achieve these goals; for the investment manager, security means earning a large bonus for outperforming the market or attracting new business, and risk means being fired. All these perceptions are subjectively valid. What is risky depends on who you are and the situation in which you find yourself.

These multiple perspectives lead to confusion in the ways people describe and interpret risk, and to ambiguity in their use of the word 'risk'. And the differences of definition mean that misunderstandings and errors are frequent. There are consequent opportunities to gain, and to lose, substantial amounts of money. Much financial services activity relies for its profitability on confusions and inconsistencies in attitudes to risk and interpretations of risk.

Subjective expected utility

Yet among academics who teach students the theory of finance – and I have been both student and teacher – there is one, and only one, correct way of thinking about risk: the approach I had in mind when I bought Robb Caledon.

The scheme of thought that I will call the theory of 'subjective expected utility' (SEU) is so universally accepted in financial economics that any other behaviour is described as 'irrational'. SEU is the basis of virtually all the sophisticated models and quantitative techniques used in financial markets today. These models are both normative and positive – their proponents claim that people should think about risk in SEU ways, and they derive conclusions about market behaviour from the assumption that they actually do.

Although this SEU approach dominates today, it was not always so. Early in the twentieth century alternative ways of describing risk vied for supremacy. On both sides were an urbane Englishman from Cambridge and an assertive American from Chicago. The winners of this intellectual competition were Frank Ramsey and Jimmie Savage.

Ramsey was a Cambridge philosopher who made important contributions to economics in his spare time. He died at the age of twenty-six, but his brother, perhaps the less talented sibling, went on to become Archbishop of Canterbury. Savage was labelled Jimmie by a nurse since his parents, not expecting him to live, did not bother to name him. (He survived another fifty-three years.) Ramsey and Savage, the founders of SEU, proposed a means of taking the mathematical tools of probability theory far beyond their initial field of application – the gaming saloon – into the boardroom and on to the trading floor. They are the founders of modern risk management techniques.

On the other side of the debate were John Maynard Keynes and Frank Knight. Keynes's fellowship thesis – in effect, his doctorate – was not an essay in economics. (Keynes, one of the great polymaths of the twentieth century, had taken a degree in mathematics.) His subject was probability theory, and his work was eventually published in 1921, long after its submission. In the same year Frank Knight, a farmer's son from the American Midwest (who would come to loathe Keynes and all he represented), published a book, *Risk, Uncertainty and Profit*, in a different style but with a related argument. Keynes and Knight emphasised the uncertainty that arose from the necessarily imperfect nature of human knowledge. The future was not just unknown, but unknowable.

Donald Rumsfeld expressed the difference between risk and uncertainty with uncharacteristic clarity. Rumsfeld famously distinguished 'known unknowns – the things we know we do not know' from 'unknown unknowns – the things we do not know we do not know'. This chapter will mainly be about risk – the things we know we do not know. The next chapter will deal with uncertainty – the things we do not know we do not know.

The claim made by the SEU school is that analytic tools can enable us to cut through much of this uncertainty with probabilistic reasoning and formal modelling. These approaches would provide the necessary underpinning for the growth in derivative markets after 1970 and the explosion of credit after 2000. They originated in the work of Ramsey and Savage, and received major extension in the modern portfolio theory of Markowitz and the capital asset-pricing model of Bill Sharpe. In the remainder of this chapter I'll make the case for this approach, ahead of a critique in Chapter 8. Let's understand the claims of SEU by returning to Robb Caledon.

Think probabilities

The year was 1976, and a bill to nationalise British shipbuilding was going through Parliament. If the bill became law, the assets and liabilities of the yard would be assumed by the government and the shareholders would receive around 100p per share. If the bill failed, the shares would be worthless, because the company was insolvent. It was sustained only by its creditors, who hoped the state would bail them out. The shares were selling in the market at around 40p.

I had to be persistent to buy these shares. The brokers I called told me that the Labour government was incompetent, and nationalising shipyards was a silly idea. They were right. They told me that the shipyard was on the point of financial collapse and yet the share price was twice what it had been two months before. They were right about that too. They told me that I risked losing everything I invested. Again, they were right.

All these observations were justified, but none seemed relevant. With youthful enthusiasm, I was applying the lessons I had been taught. Think probabilities – plan for different scenarios, think about the consequences of each and assess their likelihood. Be detached – don't be caught up in events and confuse what you want to happen with what you expect to happen. Mind your portfolio. The risk that is relevant to you is the overall risk of your whole investment portfolio, not the risk associated with the individual securities it contains.

Probabilities were central to my approach. Probabilities are essential to gamblers, though frequently ignored by them. The probability that a fair coin will show heads is one-half. This is a statement about frequency: if you toss a fair coin many times, approximately half the calls will be heads. If you can be bothered to toss the coin many times, you will confirm this statement.

The ancient Greeks laid the foundations of modern mathematics. Although they gambled, they never discovered the – elementary – mathematics of probability, which was not developed until the seventeenth and eighteenth centuries. Two elements of that framework are particularly important in understanding the principles of investment – statistical distributions, and expected values. Statistical distributions describe the probabilities of different outcomes of repeated random events. If you toss a fair coin twice, the probability that you get one head and one tail is a half, and the probability of each of two heads or two tails is a quarter. After many throws, approximately half the calls will be heads, and the distribution of outcomes is described by the most famous of all statistical distributions – the normal distribution – with its familiar 'bell-shaped' curve. The normal distribution is ubiquitous – it describes a wide variety of social and natural phenomena, from the distribution of voting intentions to the heights of the voters. The assumption that the normal distribution can be applied to the distribution of daily movements in securities prices is commonly made in financial economics. It is an assumption that is illuminating, but not true.

The second concept derived from probability theory is expected value. The expected value of a gamble is measured by multiplying the values of the outcomes of a gamble by their probabilities. If a coin-tossing game will pay you £1 if you win, and nothing if you lose, then its expected value is 50p. Despite the name, the expected value is not what you should expect. You will definitely not get 50p from a single toss of that coin.

But the more repeated events there are, the more likely it is that the outcome will approach its expected value. If instead of gambling to win £1 on a single toss, you were to gamble to win 50p on each of two consecutive tosses, the distribution of outcomes is less extreme. There is now a one-in-four chance of winning £1, from two heads, and a one-in-four chance of winning nothing, from two tails. Half the time, one coin will come up heads and the other tails, and you will indeed receive the expected value of 50p. If you gamble for a penny on each of 100 throws of the coin, the expected value is still 50p, and again you will probably receive something close to this figure.

Comparing distributions

In investment matters you will be concerned not just with the expected value but with the overall distribution of gains and losses. In particular, you will want to know what could go wrong. You might ask 'What is the worst that could happen?' The worst that can happen is that you will be convicted of a grave crime of which you are entirely innocent, or that you will be murdered by a passing psychopath. But these events are extremely rare. What you really want to know about is outcomes that are bad but not completely unlikely. Contemplate, for example, the worst 1 per cent of outcomes, and then imagine the best of these conceivable outcomes. This is to take a gloomy view, but not so gloomy that you spend your life in bed. (Though note the observation above that more people die from falling down the stairs than in aircraft accidents. Still, you would increase your probability of death substantially by descending the stairs.) There is no escape from risk and uncertainty.

An outcome that will be exceeded 99 per cent of the time is called the first percentile of the frequency distribution of outcomes. It is not the worst that could happen, but the best of the worst 1 per cent of possibilities. Similarly, an outcome that will be exceeded 90 per cent of the time is the tenth percentile, and you might look at this percentile if you don't want to be quite so pessimistic. Table 5 shows the first percentile of the cumulative frequency distribution of outcomes for the coin-tossing game. On a single toss of a coin, zero is a very likely outcome. The first percentile of the distribution is zero – and indeed zero is the value of all percentiles up to the 50th. If you spread your bets across 100 tosses, however, the first percentile is 38p – on only one per cent of such trials will you win less than 38p, and on 99 per cent of occasions you will win more.

The value-at-risk models used by most financial institutions today seek to measure and control risks by setting values for these low percentiles of the frequency distribution of outcomes. The bank asks 'How much could we lose on a bad (say, one in a hundred) day?' The first percentile of the distribution of daily outcomes gives the answer to that question.

Table 5: **The cumulative frequency distribution from tossing a coin**

Percentile	Winnings			
	1 toss	2 tosses	20 tosses	100 tosses
1st	0	0	26p	38p
10th	0	25p	36p	44p
49th	0	50p	49.7p	49.9p
51st	£1	50p	50.3p	50.1p
90th	£1	75p	66p	56p
Gain on each head obtained	£1	50p	5p	1p
Expected value of winnings	50p	50p	50p	50p

The same method can be used to describe the upper tail of the distribution. You will obtain the 90th percentile of a distribution at least 10 per cent of the time. So the 90th percentile on a single toss is £1. Just as every percentile below the 50th is zero, every percentile above the 50th is £1. For a gamble spread over 100 tosses, however, the 90th percentile is only 56p. You can expect to make more than 56p only 10 per cent of the time. To decide whether one distribution is preferable to another, it isn't really sufficient to make comparisons of a single percentile. The first percentile is a rather unlikely outcome. The prudent person, rather than the committed pessimist, might focus on the 10th percentile. You would have to be very gloomy to ignore altogether the good outcomes at higher percentiles, and you will want to look at the 50th percentile, the median outcome. In banks, the traders tend to look only at the high percentiles, the risk managers only at the low ones. This creates tension between them, which is sometimes constructive, often fatal.

The examples with a relatively small number of trials (one and two tosses) have lower pay-offs at low percentiles, and higher pay-offs at high percentiles. The worse outcomes are worse, and the better outcomes are better, in games of one or two tosses than those of games with twenty or a hundred tosses. That is what we mean by saying a strategy is riskier: low percentiles have worse outcomes, high percentiles have better ones.

In the coin-tossing game, the 50th percentile of all games – whether two tosses, twenty tosses or a thousand tosses – is the same, at 50p, and therefore the median and expected value are the same. (The single toss is different, because an outcome of 50p – the expected value – is impossible; the 50th percentile is either zero or £1, depending on whether you are a glass-half-empty or glass-half-full type of person.)

But this equivalence of median and expected value holds only if the probability distributions are symmetrical. In coin-tossing, good and bad outcomes are equally likely. On 100 tosses, you suffer a 10 per cent chance of falling more than 6p short of the expected value of 50p, and also a 10 per cent chance of getting more than 6p above the expected value. Many risk distributions, however, are asymmetric. The tailgating driver mostly gets to his destination a few seconds quicker, but occasionally dies in a car crash. The 10th and higher percentiles of these distributions are all good; the first percentile is terrible. The median outcome – the 50th percentile – is much better than the expected value, since the expected value must factor in the catastrophic losses that occasionally occur.

The outcomes of a lottery are also asymmetric, but in the opposite way. The lottery ticket buyer usually loses, but might, with low probability, win the jackpot. The 50th percentile, even the 80th percentile, of the outcomes of purchasing a single lottery ticket are lousy – you lose your stake – but the 99.9999th percentile makes you a millionaire. Tailgating and lottery tickets have highly asymmetric distributions.

The coin-tossing game has another important property: the most likely outcome is that you win 50p. Even on a game of two tosses, there is a 0.5 probability that you will win 50p as against a one in four probability of either nothing or £1. The most likely outcome is called the mode of a distribution, and many – though not all – symmetrical distributions have this property.

Thus there are three different ways of measuring what statisticians call the central tendency of a distribution. The expected value is the mean of the distribution. The median is the 50th percentile: you are equally likely to do better or worse than the median. And the most likely outcome is the mode. The coin-tossing game has the property that mean, median and mode are all, at 50p, the same.

But this is true only because the coin-tossing game has a particular – though common – structure. The outcomes follow what is called a binomial distribution, which becomes the normal distribution when the number of trials is large. These distributions describe what is likely to be observed if the result of a process is the product of adding up the consequences of a large number of repeated but independent events: there is an obvious affinity between the normal distribution and the outcome of a random walk. Many real-world phenomena are like this, which is why the normal distribution is so widely encountered.

But many are not. And theorems that apply to the outcomes of repeated trials do not help us much in thinking about one-off events to which SEU asks us to apply subjective probabilities. If I had thought the subjective probability of Robb Caledon being nationalised was 0.7, then the (subjective) mode and median of the distribution of outcomes was £1 and the expected value 70p. If my subjective probability had been 0.3, the (subjective) mode and median would be zero and the expected value 30p. If your commute to work is scheduled for forty minutes, forty minutes is probably the mode. The most likely – though perhaps not very likely – outcome is that the train arrives on time. The median will be a bit more – the train more often arrives late than it arrives early. And the expected value will be greater still – the train will sometimes be very late but never very early.

Few people without some training in statistics distinguish carefully between the three measures of 'central tendency': expected value – the average of outcomes; median – the representative outcome; and mode – the most likely outcome. And one of the reasons for the popularity of assuming a normal distribution is that you don't have to make this distinction, because the normal distribution has the property– unusual even among statistical distributions – that all three measures of central tendency are the same. But failure to understand these distinctions is potentially highly misleading in financial markets, where many distributions are asymmetric and discontinuous. There is not much exaggeration in saying that such failure was a major contributor to the global financial crisis.

The method of comparing distributions by comparing different percentiles of outcomes is quite general. One distribution is riskier than another if it yields worse returns at lower percentiles and better returns at higher percentiles. There will be a crossing point. The lower the crossing point, the more attractive is the riskier distribution. If one distribution has worse outcomes in its lowest five percentiles and better returns at all other percentiles, it is more likely to be acceptable than one for which the crossing point is at the 50th percentile.

A common technique simplifies the comparison of distributions with the aid of a mathematical trick. Many statistical distributions, including the normal distribution, are completely described by two parameters. One parameter is the mean or average, of the distribution – what is the average height of a population? The other is a measure of variability – how many people are over six feet or below five feet? If you know the average and the variability, then you know everything about the normal distribution. If two distributions have the same expected value, then a comparison of a single percentile – any percentile – will be enough to tell you which is riskier.

The usual statistical measure of variability is the variance or standard deviation. The Greek letter sigma is commonly used for the standard deviation. This term has entered popular usage, so that 'a six-sigma event' is an event that is, or should be, very improbable. The Sharpe ratio, which is the ratio of expected return (relative to a benchmark) to standard deviation, is widely used by quantitative investors. If the analysts' distribution of returns were normal, or followed sufficiently closely another of the family of common statistical distributions – and if the parameters of these distributions were known – then techniques such as value at risk and Sharpe ratios would be extremely valuable. The mathematics of probability, which opens the way to the application of powerful statistical tools, could be applied to the analysis of unique political and economic events, such as the failure of legislation and the future of a shipyard. To see some of the possibilities, let's go back to Robb Caledon.

My ship came in

The fate of Robb Caledon was a risk – a known unknown. People sometimes make probability statements about known unknowns, as when they say, 'The probability that Parliament will approve the shipbuilding nationalisation bill is a half.' Such a statement is called an expression of personal, or subjective, probability.

When I talked about tossing a coin, I used the terms 'probability' and 'frequency' interchangeably. But I can't do that for one-off political events. Someone who makes that statement about the shipbuilding bill is not saying 'If Parliament considers the bill one hundred times, the bill will be passed on fifty occasions'. They are making a statement of personal opinion, which sounds like a statement about probabilities. But can such a statement be interpreted in this way?

The idea that risk and uncertainty can be handled with the aid of personal probabilities is often called Bayesian, after the Revd Thomas Bayes, an eighteenth-century clergyman who made important contributions to probability theory. Bayesians believe that each of us has a mental probability distribution of likely and unlikely outcomes, which we constantly revise as new information becomes available. Bayesians further believe that the mathematical rules for calculating compound probabilities (and hence statistical distributions) are universal. These rules can be applied to personal probabilities in the same way as they can be applied to frequentist probabilities. There are some obvious difficulties in the use of rules that are based on the observation of repeated events – such as tossing a coin – in the interpretation of one-off events – such as shipbuilding nationalisation.

Coin-tossing appears to be truly random. Whether the shipbuilding nationalisation bill will be passed is certainly not random. The fate of the bill will be the result of specific political developments, which – if only we had enough information and insight – we might hope to explain and predict, and can certainly describe after they have happened.

However, both Bachelier's notion of the random walk and Samuelson's explanation of that notion through analysis of the ways markets handle information seem to provide a justification for the use of probability theory to describe the – unique – evolution of securities markets. Bachelier and Samuelson realised that the ways in which financial markets process information – the ways expectations of tomorrow's events are incorporated into today's prices – will create patterns that have the appearance of randomness. This apparent randomness may allow us to 'think probabilities' even in situations where events are determined by deliberate human action rather than by chance.

Such apparent randomness of outcome doesn't mean or require that securities prices move for no reason, or that when the Monetary Policy Committee is in a locked room it makes a decision by tossing a coin. God does not play dice, Einstein said, and the remark is illuminating even though there is argument over whether its substance is true. There are underlying explanations of most physical and natural phenomena even if our understanding of these explanations remains imperfect. Randomness of outcome means that, when you have analysed all that is known about the economic and monetary situation, and have understood the attitudes of the different members of the Monetary Policy Committee, it makes sense – or is at least conceivable – that the range of decisions available to the Committee can be described with a probability distribution.

But such a probability distribution is subjective. Different people may assess it differently. Many people do not find it easy to think probabilistically about what interest rates will be, whether Robb Caledon will be nationalised or what they will be doing in retirement. They ask instead 'What is going to happen?' A committed Bayesian believes that, however we *express* our attitudes to risk and uncertainty, personal probabilities govern our decisions. We can discover these buried probabilities by asking questions such as 'How much would you be willing to bet on interest rates being above 5 per cent in twenty years' time?'

Securities markets elicit information by constantly offering such gambles. 'How much would you be willing to pay for a share in Robb Caledon which will pay 100p if the nationalisation bill goes through?' The market asks that question every day by giving you the chance to buy, or sell, Robb Caledon shares. It asks you to bet on future interest rates every time it quotes a price on a bond.

To make this link from probabilities to market prices, we have to assume that personal probabilities can be used to calculate expected values. If my personal probability that the shipbuilding nationalisation bill would pass was 0.5 (it was higher) and the potential pay-out was 100p per share, my subjective expected value of a purchase was 50p. The implicit rule is to compare the expected value of 50p with the market price of 40p. Since the expected value – given my subjective probability – was above the market price, the stock was a good buy.

While the assertion that 'a fair coin falls heads with probability a half' seems to be an objective statement about the world, and can be verified by experiment, personal probabilities are unavoidably subjective. One day the dust will have settled, and Parliament will either have approved the nationalisation bill or not. The finale was nail-biting – so much so that in 2012 the decisive vote was the dramatic highlight of a play, *This House*, by James Graham at London's National Theatre. The House of Commons approved shipbuilding nationalisation by a majority of one, and I duly received the payment of £1 per share. I was pleased with myself, but that doesn't mean my personal probability was right. Nor, if the bill had failed, would that necessarily mean my prior judgement of subjective probability had been wrong. A Bayesian would say that the stockbrokers I consulted had personal probabilities different from mine and that was why they had not recommended the shares.

Did the price of 40p, against a possible pay-off of 100p, mean that 0.4 was the average of everyone's personal probability? No, it doesn't. Many people, like those stockbrokers, attached low personal probabilities to nationalisation – if they had ever thought in this Bayesian way, which is doubtful – and many more people had not considered the matter at all. The price of 40p indicates that the number of people who found the investment attractive was sufficient to hold all the available Robb Caledon shares. Since the shipyard was small, this number did not have to be large (the company never had more than a few hundred shareholders). Only a few people would have to have personal probabilities in excess of 0.4 to establish the price of 40p.*

The metaphor of the market as voting machine is often used in this way to infer probabilities from market prices. On a Bloomberg screen you can find implied probabilities that the Monetary Policy Committee will change interest rates. Commentators sometimes say '"The market" is assuming a 30 per cent per cent chance of an interest rate cut'. But such anthropomorphism should be viewed here, as everywhere, with caution.

Still, there seems to be a profit opportunity if your subjective probability differs from that of Mr Market. In buying Robb Caledon I was attempting to take advantage of just such an opportunity. With an expected value of 50p and a share price of 40p there was an expected profit of 10p. But, just as you will never receive the expected value of 50p when you toss a coin once, so the expected value was not what I would receive from my Robb Caledon purchase. I would either have lost 40p or gained 60p. If I had lost, I would not even have had the consolation that if I had bought the share 100 times, I would almost certainly have made a profit. Coin-tossing is a repeatable event. The proposal to nationalise Robb Caledon was unique.

Still, if you always approach one-off risks in this probabilistic manner, while you will lose some and win others, over the long run you will probably come out ahead. That's a good argument, though not a conclusive argument, for the SEU approach. You will need to be sufficiently detached to ride both the swings and the roundabouts with equanimity. But it does not make the Bayesian approach to risk assessment objective or value-free. Frequentist probabilities and subjective probabilities are different. Frequentist probabilities are facts; personal probabilities

---

* Strictly speaking, this would not be true if it were easy to sell Robb Caledon shares short. At the time it was not possible at all. And even now, holding an asset 'long' is much easier than holding it 'short'.

are opinions. Subjective probabilities are not objectively right or wrong, even with hindsight. The passage of the nationalisation bill did not vindicate my decision to buy. A decision that has a good outcome is not necessarily a good decision, and vice versa. When you can comfortably say to yourself, 'Buying Robb Caledon shares was the right decision even though I lost my entire investment,' you have learned to think probabilistically.

You have also learned why most people – and especially most large organisations – find probabilistic thinking difficult. But you have also learned why individuals who have learned to think probabilistically and can make their own decisions – such as Buffett and Soros – have an advantage over others whose ability to take risks is constrained because they will be judged by superiors who will certainly exploit the benefit of hindsight.

Diminishing marginal utility

The principle that risky outcomes should be judged by their expected value was one of the earliest notions in probability. Daniel Bernoulli, an eighteenth-century mathematician, who played a major role in developing this theory, quickly identified a difficulty. Many people did not, in real life, make decisions by reference to expected value. Many people would prefer a 50 per cent chance of winning £1 million to a 10 per cent chance of winning £5 million, and the certainty of £500,000 in cash to either. But the expected value of all of the outcomes is £500,000. An example Bernoulli used to illustrate this problem became known as the 'St Petersburg paradox'.

In the St Petersburg game, a coin is tossed repeatedly. If the first toss of the coin is a head, the player receives £1. If the first toss is a tail, the prize is doubled to £2 and the coin is tossed again. If the prize is not won, it is doubled again, and so on until a head appears and the game ends. There is therefore a 50 per cent probability that the game ends after a single throw and the player gains £1. There is a much lower probability of winning £4 on the third toss. Simple mathematics shows that the expected value of this strategy is infinitely large.

If you think this is not a very realistic game, you should know that two and a half centuries after Bernoulli investment bankers would invent 'payment-in-kind securities', loans on which payment would increase if the quality of the underlying credit deteriorated. In essence, these were St Petersburg games and, like St Petersburg games, not a good idea for either banker or player.

No one will pay more than a few pounds to play Bernoulli's St Petersburg game. Its infinite expected value depends on multiplying large pay-offs by their small probabilities. The game might run for forty throws, by which time you would be richer than Warren Buffett. But few people seem willing to pay much for that opportunity, given the near-certainty of loss and the possibility of ruinous loss. The resolution of the St Petersburg paradox that is most widely accepted today was known in Bernoulli's time. Jimmie Savage would articulate the reasoning most clearly, and in a manner that would have great influence on financial economics. The St Petersburg paradox, he suggested, is the result of what economists call 'diminishing marginal utility'. The first million is a lot better than the second million, or at least that is what people think before they've got their first million. By the time you have $50 billion, as Warren does, the prospect of another million is of little consequence. So $50 billion is valued at much less than 50 million times $1,000, and the expected *utility* of the St Petersburg game is correspondingly low even if its expected *value* is high.

People who prefer a sure thing to a gamble with the same expected monetary value – people who prefer £500,000 in cash to a 50 per cent per cent chance of £1 million and who are not impressed by the St Petersburg game – are described as risk-averse. The standard hypothesis is that most people are risk-averse when they invest. They are also risk-averse when they insure: they accept a certain loss in return for giving up the gamble that their house will burn down or that they will have to pay unexpected medical bills. The insurance premium will generally be greater than the expected value of the claims; otherwise the insurance company would be unprofitable. Expected value is relevant to the insurance company because it can use its portfolio of policies to think frequencies rather than subjective probabilities.

Diminishing marginal utility can account for risk aversion. Such risk aversion can be significant only when the amounts you gain or lose are large relative to your wealth. Think of a gamble in which you can win, or lose, £1, and suppose you already have £14,265. If you refuse the bet, you will still have £14,265, while if you accept it you will have either £14,264 or £14,266. Few people would think there was much difference between these outcomes. Fewer still would think 'I'd much rather see my wealth increase from £14,264 to £14,265 than see it increase from £14,265 to £14,266'. If the amount you are gambling is relatively small relative to your wealth, then you should simply assess small bets by reference to their expected value.

This conclusion has many lessons for intelligent investors who follow SEU. Since most individual investments will be small relative to your overall portfolio, far less your overall wealth, expected values are usually the right way to deal with risk. That leads to another implication of thinking SEU, and perhaps the most significant one: always look at risk in the context of your portfolio as a whole, rather than its individual elements. Focus on the outcome, not the process. The 'mind your portfolio' principle is fundamental to intelligent investment. To see its consequences I'll go back once more to Robb Caledon.

Mind your portfolio

In 1976 the Labour government promoting the shipbuilding nationalisation bill was struggling and unpopular. Margaret Thatcher had recently become Conservative leader, and her party was gaining support. The government might lose a vote of confidence in the House of Commons and be forced to call an election, which the Conservatives would probably win. This sequence of events happened in 1979, and Thatcher became Prime Minister.

Such a political development was the main risk faced by holders of Robb Caledon shares, because a Conservative government would abandon plans to nationalise shipbuilding. While Labour's fall would have been bad news for Robb Caledon, it would have caused delight around the City, and the wider stock market would have risen immediately. Let's suppose that stocks would have been 5 per cent higher as a result of Labour's defeat. And suppose that you had £5,000 to invest.

Consider three possible portfolios:

- put all the money into Robb Caledon;
- put all your money into blue chip shares; or
- buy 250 Robb Caledon shares for £100 and put the rest of your money into blue chips.

Here is the value of your portfolio if the bill is passed, and if the bill fails.

Table 6: **Value of alternative portfolios depending on the fate of the shipbuilding nationalisation bill of 1976**

	Robb Caledon only	Blue chips only	Mixed portfolio
Government survives	12,500	5,000	5,150
Government falls	0	5,250	5,145

Which portfolio would have been best? With hindsight, of course, you should have gone for the first, and dived into Robb Caledon's docks. But it is easy to be a successful investor with hindsight. If you felt sure the Labour government would fall, you should have gone for the portfolio of blue chips. The first portfolio is extremely risky, suitable only for the most hardened speculator. The paradox is that the least risky portfolio is not the second, which focuses on safe assets, but the third, which includes a small holding of Robb Caledon shares.

In this example, adding a small investment in a very risky asset reduces the overall risk of the portfolio. You are sure to end up with around £5,150. The risk associated with a portfolio is not measured by adding up the risks of each individual element. A combination of risks may be less risky in whole than in part.

I thought Robb Caledon was an interesting speculation for two reasons. All three portfolios would have had the same expected value if the probability that the bill would be passed were slightly more than 0.4. My personal probability that the bill would pass was a good deal higher than Mr Market's. If I viewed the Robb Caledon purchase in isolation, the question of how much higher it would have had to be to have made the purchase worthwhile would seem to depend on how risk-averse I was.

But the 'mind your portfolio' principle transforms the way you approach this problem. If I had bought some blue chips, then, however risk-averse I was, Robb Caledon would have been worth buying because its shares would go down when other shares would go up and vice versa. An asset with this property is called a hedge, and adding a hedge to a portfolio reduces overall portfolio risk, even if the hedge is, in itself, a speculative investment – such as Robb Caledon. So the shipyard was doubly attractive.

Assets don't have to be hedges to reduce the risk in a portfolio. It is sufficient that individual risks are not perfectly correlated with each other. If you bet £1 on a single toss of a coin, you win

£1 or zero: if you bet 50p on each of two different throws, you win 50p half the time: if you bet 1p on each of a hundred throws, what you will win, as Table 5 shows, will be very close to 50p. This is the power of diversification. A small share in a large number of independent risks is much more certain than the outcome of any of the risks taken separately.

Hedging is the purchase of assets whose returns are negatively related to the returns on assets you already own. Diversification spreads risks across many securities whose individual risks – like the outcome of the toss of a coin – are unrelated to each other. The risk and reward of a portfolio, and the relationship between them, are determined not just by expected values and the variability of return. The portfolio risk also depends on the extent to which returns from different assets are related to each other. A risk-averse individual can build a low-risk portfolio from a collection of risky assets through hedging and diversification if the risky assets are appropriately selected. It is impossible to overstate the importance of this idea for intelligent investment.

The variability of a statistical distribution can be measured by its variance or standard deviation. A related measure – called 'covariance' or 'correlation' – looks at how the variability of two different distributions is related. Similar assets have a high covariance, hedges a negative one. In a coin-tossing game the covariance between the outcomes of successive trials is zero because successive trials are independent. The probability that the next toss is a head is not affected by whether the last one was a head or a tail.

What does it mean to say that the returns from investments are independent of each other? Suppose one company is drilling for oil in Kazakhstan and another has entered a new drug in clinical trials in the United States. These outcomes are independent – the dry hole in Kazakhstan does not influence the drug trial. The risks that a shareholder loses because an exploration does not find oil or that a drug trial fails are called specific risks, because their outcome is determined by factors that are specific to the company itself. However, the returns to shareholders in Shell and in Glaxo are probably correlated. There is no direct connection between oil companies and pharmaceutical companies. But the two businesses depend on economic prospects in the same countries, and the share prices of both companies are influenced by the same vagaries of market sentiment. These common risks, which affect all businesses, are described as 'market risk'.

The relationship between the risk on an individual share and the market risk of a portfolio that follows the market as a whole is described by the parameter *beta*. Mathematically, *beta* is computed from a regression equation that estimates the effect of market movements on the security in question. A security will have a *beta* of one if a 1 per cent market movement will change its price by 1 per cent.

A share may have a low *beta* for one or both of two distinct reasons. Shares will have low *betas* if their risks are unrelated to the overall risk of the market. The prices of shares whose returns are derived from oil wells in Kazakhstan, or whose fortunes depend on the results of clinical trials, will have little correlation with the share prices of BP and Glaxo, the type of stock that dominates market indices. A share will also have a low *beta* if, although its returns are related to overall market risk, the company's activities are not very volatile.

Companies such as food retailers or utilities, whose sales will be little affected by economic recession, have low *betas*. Conversely, shares whose performance is very sensitive to the general economic cycle – producers of steel or basic chemicals – might have *betas* that are greater than one. An index, which by definition yields the average return on the market, will have a *beta* of one. For this reason, it is common to call the average return on an asset class 'the *beta*' of that asset class. '*Alpha*' is then a measure of the extent to which a fund manager beats that average return – the outperformance after adjusting for the risk of the manager's portfolio. Lovers of the Greek alphabet will find that derivatives markets extend the lexicon to *gamma*, *delta* and beyond.

But *beta* is key to the capital asset pricing model (CAPM). This is the most influential economic theory in modern investment analysis. It is important to understand its structure, its effect on investment thinking and practice – and its limitations.

The capital asset pricing model

Risk-averse investors will need to earn a premium over the yield on a safe benchmark such as 4.25 per cent Treasury 2055 or indexed 1.25 per cent Treasury 2055 if they are to buy less secure assets. The greater the risk, the greater the premium. But what is the relevant meaning of risk?

At the beginning of this chapter I described the gulf of incomprehension that emerged when economists explained to business people their approach to risk. The latter group did not recognise any operational value in the distinction between specific and market risk that the economists believed was so important. Most people, including those business people, would describe an investment like Robb Caledon as extremely risky. They would say the same of drilling for oil in Kazakhstan, or a clinical trial for a new drug or accepting a fixed-price contract to develop new defence technology. They would think of a big holding in HSBC or BP, by contrast, as safe but boring.

The 'mind your portfolio' principle says that this view gets matters the wrong way round. Robb Caledon and the clinical trial are not really speculative, because the risk can be spread and diversified. So long as the risk of any of these individual stocks is only a small part of your portfolio, you can employ diversification to sleep soundly at night. Conversely, stakes in HSBC or BP are risky because investors cannot hedge or diversify them much – the returns from these investments are likely to be broadly in line with those of the market. Suppose everyone thought this way. Suppose everyone was a 'rational' investor, motivated by the principles of SEU. Then the general opinion would be that shares with specific risks were not very risky, but shares with market risk were. That general opinion, like all general opinions, would be 'in the price'. The implication is that what appear to be risky securities – shares in Robb Caledon or oil exploration in Kazakhstan – would offer lower yields than boring blue chips because the speculative shares have specific risks while the blue chips suffer market risks. This idea is the basis of the CAPM, which won the Nobel Prize for its inventor, Bill Sharpe (of the Sharpe ratio). In the CAPM, risk and reward are determined by the *beta* of a security. Robb Caledon had a *beta* around zero, because the risk was entirely specific (the company may even have had a negative *beta*, because its share price might have gone up when the market went down, and vice versa). As an addition to an existing portfolio, though not as a single investment, an investment with a low *beta* is almost as good as a risk-free asset, and will therefore yield very little more than a risk-free asset. An asset with a *beta* of one will have the same expected return as the market as a whole, and investors will demand a higher return still for an asset with a *beta* above one. In principle, this approach can be applied to all assets, not just shares. You can calculate *betas* for different kinds of property and for other asset classes. Commercial risk measurement services offer quantitatively minded investors estimates of *beta* for the whole range of securities they might buy.

There is another customer base for these risk measurement services. The cost of equity capital to a firm is derived from the long-run expected rate of return on its shares. The expected return on equity is the combination of the *beta* of the individual firm and the equity risk premium for the market. For adherents of the CAPM this expected return is the return required by the market and, therefore, the basis of the cost of capital estimates needed for the DCF appraisal of business investment.

Companies such as Robb Caledon, or a small oil exploration company, or the pharmaceutical business whose fortunes ride on a single clinical trial, should have a low cost of capital because the risk of investment in them, although large, is perfectly diversifiable. Companies such as HSBC and BP, with returns likely to be more in line with the overall market, should have a higher cost of capital. This is the argument that the government economists were presenting to the defence contractors, who did not believe it.

And empirical evidence is not very favourable to the economists. The CAPM follows directly from the notion that people both should, and do, follow SEU. It predicts that the returns on different securities will be determined by two factors: the overall return on the market and the *beta* appropriate to that security. There are problems with both parts of this claim. SEU explains the risk premium in terms of diminishing marginal utility. Investors do not judge risky ventures at their expected value because they value the second million of their wealth less highly than the first. But this factor doesn't seem to be nearly large enough to account for the size of the historical equity premium – the difference between the yield on shares and the yield on safe assets. Models based on risk aversion from diminishing marginal utility struggle to explain why the risks of equity investment would, in an SEU framework, justify a risk premium even as high as 1 per cent.

The data in Chapter 2 suggested that over the last twenty years the difference in return between safe assets and shares has been around 5 per cent. The longer-term analyses of Elroy Dimson and his colleagues support figures of similar magnitude with analysis from many markets over periods as long as a century. The inexplicably large difference between the predictions of SEU-based models and the observed equity premium is the 'equity premium paradox'.

The second component of the CAPM is the use of *beta* to explain relative returns on different assets. The most exhaustive empirical study of the issue, by Eugene Fama and Kenneth French, concluded that estimates of *beta* contributed nothing to an explanation of the historical pattern of returns. These results have been disputed, but have not really been refuted.

Perhaps my business people, shaking their heads around the table, gave the answer. The CAPM describes what the world would be like if everyone behaved according to the principles of SEU. But the failure of its counterintuitive predictions suggests a world in which people don't behave that way. If the cost of capital were significantly lower for firms such as defence contractors, speculative oil drillers or small drugs companies than for businesses with mainstream activities that followed closely the business cycle of major economies, then you might expect that people who had developed successful corporate careers would have noticed. I am sure those at that table were not dissimulating when they said that they had not. And nor had their bankers.

As SEU took hold in the 1950s, a French economist, Maurice Allais, developed a critique. Allais gave examples of common decisions that seemed to violate the principles of SEU (the Allais paradoxes). He wrote in French (no major economics journal would accept such an article today), and hinted that the whole exercise was an American plot. Although the power of his analysis created continuing nagging doubt, he failed to shake the consensus. Two decades later, two psychologists, Danny Kahneman and Amos Tversky, would undertake experiments in which they offered their subjects choices among risks. They found frequent examples of behaviour inconsistent with SEU. All these men would eventually receive the Nobel Prize for founding the subject now known as behavioural finance or behavioural economics. The motivation for behavioural finance is recognition that many people don't behave as SEU would seem to require.

Many real-life investors don't think probabilities, don't mind their portfolio and, above all, don't remain detached. They engage with the process, instead of focusing cold-bloodedly on the outcome. They are fixated by screens and, if out of the office, are obsessively attached to their smartphones. They feel upset when shares they own go down (even if you are Warren Buffett your shares will fall in value on almost half of all the days you own them). Some people need a premium to contemplate the risk of loss at all, even before they take specific account of what those losses might be.

SEU and CAPM suggest you need a premium much less than 5 per cent to compensate you for the risks of equity investment. The evidence suggests you will nevertheless earn that 5 per cent, because other investors, who don't think the SEU way, are wary of investments that seem risky to them but need not be risky for you. The CAPM says you have to pay a price for diversifying your portfolio. The empirical evidence says you probably don't.

SEU and CAPM are theories that are illuminating but which, as explanations of actual behaviour in financial markets, are not true. They are illuminating, in part, because the investment strategies they suggest are more profitable if others don't adopt them. The equity premium paradox works in your favour, if you think SEU and others don't. As with EMH, the intelligent investor can gain by understanding these theories, but will lose by believing them. That is why this chapter is the longest and most complicated, but also the most potentially rewarding, in this book.

8

A World of Unknowns

Unknown unknowns

There were no derivatives markets in the savannahs, where our ancestors developed modern brains. Casinos (in which the blue chips were the highest-value counters) came into being only at a late stage of evolution, although gambling developed at an early stage of history. Hunters gambled in the evenings around the campfire and used animal bones as primitive dice. Human lives were always full of uncertainties, but pure risks – the well-defined problems found in games of chance which can be described using a frequentist approach to probabilities – were invented for popular amusement.

The claim made for SEU is that this calculus of probabilities derived from the gaming room can be applied to one-off events, such as the progress of shipbuilding nationalisation, as well as to repeated events, such as tossing a coin. Here is Milton Friedman, doyen of the Chicago economists who were founding the theory of finance, in 1976 (not entirely coincidentally, the year in which I bought those Robb Caledon shares):

> In his seminal work, Frank Knight drew a sharp distinc-
> tion between risk, as referring to events subject to a known
> or knowable probability distribution, and uncertainty, as

referring to events for which it was not possible to specify numerical probabilities. I have not referred to this distinction because I do not believe it is valid. I follow L. J. Savage in his view of personal probability, which denies any valid distinction along these lines. We may treat people as if they assigned numerical probabilities to every conceivable event.

The fate of Robb Caledon was a risk – a known unknown. Either Robb Caledon would be nationalised or it would not. Its shares would be either worth 100p or nothing. Some issues in financial markets are of this kind. Interest rate risk and credit risk seem to be known unknowns. But there are also many uncertainties, unknown unknowns – events that cannot be sensibly described with probabilities, because we simply do not know what these events might be.

SEU works well for 'known unknowns'. If all potential states of the world are known (even if the one that will materialise is not), if the outcome will be clearly and definitively recorded, if the processes that determine that outcome can be treated as random, then SEU is a sure guide to action. The gamble on Robb Caledon had all these characteristics. There seemed only two possible outcomes; the time-scale was short and defined; the consequences of each outcome appeared clear. But this case was exceptional. I have difficulty in thinking of another occasion in my investment lifetime in which the issues were posed so sharply.

And even then, there was an important difference between the fate of Robb Caledon and the toss of a coin or throw of a dice: the result of the vote on shipbuilding nationalisation was no random event. The outcome would be the result of a political process – the complexity of that process well illustrated in Graham's play – and any assessment of the likely result was properly a matter of expert judgement.

When President Obama held the crucial meeting to determine whether to go ahead with the raid on Osama bin Laden's

Abbottabad compound and 'asked for confidence that bin Laden was in the Abbottabad compound, the estimates ranged from 10 per cent to 95 per cent certainty'. Obama responded to these estimates: 'I'm accustomed to people offering me probabilities. In this situation, what you started getting was probabilities that disguised uncertainty as opposed to actually providing you with more useful information.' As discussion continued, the President interrupted. 'This is fifty-fifty. Look, guys, this is a flip of the coin. I can't base this decision on the notion that we have any greater certainty than that.'*

Obama did not mean that he thought the probability that bin Laden was in the compound was 0.5; still less was his decision a flip of the coin. He was using these phrases, as people often do, to describe radical uncertainty. The mission was subject to unknown unknowns. He, and his advisers, simply did not know, and, as he recognised, the probabilistic statements 'disguised uncertainty as opposed to actually providing you with more useful information'.

Obama recognised the limited value of probabilistic statements even in relation to 'known unknowns'. Keynes went further. Between the completion of his work on probability and its publication the great economist had become famous for his polemical denunciation of the Versailles Treaty which ended the First World War. In a celebrated passage he described the confidence of the pre-war mood. The English upper-middle class viewed its comfortable, stable environment as a permanent condition. Consols reached their all-time high in 1897, as Queen Victoria celebrated her diamond jubilee and the British Empire extended round the world. Even in July 1914, with the end of dreams only weeks away, the bond market held steady.

If the world of the English middle class was transformed by

---

* John A. Gans, *The Atlantic*, 10 October 2012; Mark Bowden, *Vanity Fair*, November 2012.

the war that followed, the world of the central European middle class was shattered. Wealthy families, whose lifestyle had seemed secure, lost everything in the default of Russian bonds, as a result of hyperinflation in Germany and central Europe, and the expropriation of Jewish property.

The future has not become any more certain. The collapse of the Twin Towers was a major event for financial markets, as for international politics. No one, on 10 September, could sensibly have framed or answered the question 'What is the probability that the World Trade Center will be destroyed tomorrow by a terrorist attack?' Keynes claimed that there could be no scientific basis for an assessment of probabilities in the face of uncertainty. The right response to the question 'What will interest rates be in twenty years' time?' was, he suggested, 'We simply do not know'. A question about the level of interest rates is one that might be answered probabilistically. But Keynes's confession of radical uncertainty even in that connection was oddly prescient A holder of British government bonds in 1941 could not have been certain whether he would be repaid in sterling, in Reichsmarks or at all.

Investors are vulnerable to defined, identifiable risks – interest rate risk, momentum and mean reversion in share prices. But investors are also vulnerable to radical uncertainty. Questions like 'What is the future of the Middle East?' 'What will be the economic consequences of China's rise?' or 'How will economic and political systems deal with climate change?' are open-ended. We cannot fully describe the range of outcomes, and decades from now there will still be disagreement over what the outcomes proved to be.

We may attempt to transform these open-ended questions into more narrowly defined ones such as 'Will Bashar al-Assad still be in power in 2018?' or 'What will be China's GDP, or the average world temperature, in 2025?' Even if it were possible to make such predictions with any confidence – and it is not – most answers would not tell people what they really want to know. Imagine a time traveller from the nineteenth century inquiring about the nature of our world. Such a traveller would not know enough about today's world to be able to frame sensible questions, or to appreciate the answers. 'How do you find the way to the airport?' 'I listen to the directions from my smartphone' is not a possible conversation. We suffer not just from ignorance of the future but also from a limited capacity to imagine what the future might be. People who are today concerned about conflict in the Middle East, China's rise, or climate change, would not have been worrying about these issues thirty years ago. They would have been worrying about the Cold War, Japan's economic pre-eminence and the effects of AIDS.

These uncertainties of the 1980s have largely been resolved, and in ways that few people expected. But the key point is not that we mostly fail to anticipate the answers but, rather, that we mostly fail to anticipate the relevant questions. Those English middle class families Keynes described did not conceive the possibility of the catastrophes of the twentieth century – the stalemate of the First World War, the influenza pandemic, the murder of millions of people by deranged dictators. The same was true of transformative political and economic developments – the rise and fall of Communism in Russia, decolonisation, the development of information technology, the changed role of women in society.

Such failure of imagination is inevitable. If you could anticipate the functions and uses of the personal computer, you would already have taken the main steps towards inventing it. To describe a future political movement or economic theory or line of philosophical thought is to bring it into existence. If you can estimate the probability of the invention of the wheel, you have already invented it.

Many great geopolitical events were unknown unknowns:

the First World War, the rise of Hitler, the attack on the Twin Towers. But unknown unknowns are also part of everyday life. Your journey home from work lends itself to description in frequentist terms. You have a rough mental probability distribution of outcomes in your mind, reflecting the schedule and reliability of trains, the variability of traffic conditions. But the outcome is also determined by events. You meet a long-lost acquaintance, you see an item in a shop window that attracts your attention, you slip on the pavement. You did not anticipate such events because you had not thought about them, and could not sensibly have attached a probability to them if you had.

More of these events will disrupt your journey than will accelerate it, which is why your estimate of journey length will be below its expected value. Most people think of risk as an adverse event rather than a distribution about a mean (this was another source of the gap of comprehension at my meeting between the business people and the economists). For good reasons, our thinking about an uncertain world is partly probabilistic, partly not.

In this light, consider again the risk appraisal tools described in Chapter 7, which looked at the outcomes associated with various percentiles of the frequency distribution of outcomes. Your routine experience of how long it takes you to get home from work is likely to be described well by a standard statistical distribution. But the same is not true of experiences that are non-routine: the occasional emergencies, the accidents, the days on which events at work make it impossible to go home at all.

These events are rare, but most extremes of the frequency distribution of outcomes are the product of these out-of-the-ordinary events. When the credit crunch began, in August 2007, David Viniar, chief financial officer of Goldman Sachs, told news reporters that his firm had experienced a 25-sigma event several days in a row. A 25-sigma event is one with a probability so low that the noughts required to express the probability would occupy an entire line on this page. Goldman Sachs could not expect to encounter a 25-sigma event on even one day if it had existed for the entire history of the universe. Of course, what had happened was not a sequence of 25-sigma events. Markets had developed in ways that were not properly considered in Goldman Sachs's risk models.

If a coin comes up heads twenty times in a row, you should consider the possibility that the coin or the person tossing it is biased, before you conclude that the one in a million probability that the outcome is the result of twenty tosses of a fair coin has materialised. The limits of probabilistic reasoning are set by the limitations of the models on which they are based, and any model is an abstraction from a more complex context. The actual distribution of outcomes is the product of a combination of the risks that the model describes and the uncertainties associated with the applicability of the model. That is the fundamental reason why a model can often be illuminating but will almost never be true. We use different tools in the face of uncertainty. Most often, we tell stories.

Narratives and patterns

If I ask people what they think is going to happen, they will usually respond with a story rather than a probability distribution. Thinking probabilities does not come easily to the human mind. Telling stories and constructing narratives do. The stockbrokers I called in 1976 could not separate in their minds the question of whether shipbuilding *would* be nationalised from the question of whether shipbuilding *ought to* be nationalised. They told a story about what they thought would happen, heavily influenced by what they thought should happen. They pontificated about the market and complained about the government, as old-fashioned stockbrokers were prone to do.

We weave stories and fit events and expectations into them. There is evidence of halo effects – if we like something or someone, we interpret everything we know about them favourably – and of confirmation bias – people interpret new evidence in a manner consistent with the view they have already formed. The people who extended credit to subprime borrowers in the belief that house prices always went up, like the people who planned the Iraq war and thought it unnecessary to plan for the aftermath because troops would be greeted with garlands of flowers, were victims of halo effect and confirmation bias. Expectations had been confused with hopes and dreams.

Narratives and probabilistic thinking fit uncomfortably together because thinking probabilistically means thinking, at the same time, of incompatible events – that Robb Caledon will go bankrupt, that Robb Caledon will be nationalised. It might have made sense to buy Robb Caledon shares even if you thought the bill was likely to fail. The issue for the probabilistic thinker was whether the expected value was above the market price, so that the shares might have been a good buy at 10p even if you thought the bill would fail. It may be appropriate to hold indexed bonds even if you do not think that inflation will rise, if you believe – and you should – that inflation *might* rise.

Many people find it hard to reason in these ways. Scott Fitzgerald wrote, 'The test of a first-rate intelligence is the ability to hold two opposing ideas in mind at the same time and still retain the ability to function'. And thinking probabilistically requires that capacity: Robb Caledon will be nationalised, Robb Caledon will not be nationalised.

The most systematic way of trying to handle incompatible futures is scenario planning, a technique pioneered by Shell and widely used in business. Scenario planning demands multiple narratives. Work out two, three or four internally consistent projections of the future, and plan for what you might do in each. But my experience is that if you try to talk about the future in scenarios, you will always be approached by someone who asks 'So what do you really think is going to happen?'

Our ability to tell stories is a valuable asset, the means by which we make sense of disconnected information. But in financial markets this skill often misleads. Bachelier and Samuelson discovered that purposive and directed behaviour in securities markets can produce outcomes with the appearance, and mathematical properties, of randomness. But we resist randomness. The search for patterns in randomly generated data warms the heart, as it hurts the wallet.

Mirages, systems and hot hands

Our abilities in pattern detection often lead us to observe systematic relationships that do not exist, or to confuse underlying causes with statistical noise. Such confusions help chartists stay in business. Popular discussion, based on a poor understanding of probability, tells of a 'law of averages' – if there has been a run of heads, the next toss must be a tail. But the probability of head or tail remains at 50 per cent. There is no law of averages, but there are many random walks. Chaos and randomness are rare in nature, but common in financial markets.

Hopeful investors and tipsters trail through historic series to find systems that would, in the past, have yielded substantial profits. There will always be some such systems, but that doesn't mean these systems will be profitable in any, far less all, future periods. Many 'anomalies' in efficient markets disappear once they have been identified. This would be the case even if it were not also true that the very process of trading on the anomaly reduces or removes its profitability. The 'hot hand' – an outstanding series of scores one after the other – is a well-known phenomenon. Careful statistical analysis of sporting records suggests that there is not much evidence for 'the hot hand'.

Sequences of extraordinary performance are no more frequent than would be expected from chance alone. But long sequences of brilliant scores (or mistakes) stick in the mind.

Are there investment managers with the 'hot hand'? Even if investment returns were the result of pure chance, some managers would seem to have a record of success. But if returns are the result of chance, you cannot expect that these managers will perform any better in future than anyone else. And mostly they don't. The persistence of performance of OEICS (mutual funds, unit trusts) has been the subject of extensive analysis.

Table 7 is a representative illustration of recent results, based on data compiled by Vanguard UK (who market passive funds). If you are looking for a manager who will perform well over the next five years, any manager who has been in the top three quartiles is equally likely to do well. Really badly performing funds, however, tend to remain really badly performing funds. Perhaps this consistently poor performance is the continuing effect of high charges and turnover; perhaps, too, even if there is little evidence of manager skill, there are some fund managers who really have no clue.

Table 7: **Percentage of funds in each performance quintile, 2004–9, with above-median performance in 2009–14**

Quintile	1st	2nd	3rd	4th	5th
	52	55	54	47	36

Source: Vanguard UK

Be warned, however, that funds that perform in the top quintile in one five-year period are more than averagely likely to be in the bottom quintile in the succeeding three-year period. Probably this is because closet indexed funds, which differ little in composition from their benchmarks, are not likely to be either top or bottom performers. The funds that shoot the lights out are specialist funds in what prove to be fashionable sectors, or idiosyncratic managers who hit it lucky. Even if there were no long-run mean reversion, such funds would stand a fair chance of being laggards (as well as leaders) in any three-year period.

There are a very few fund managers, like Buffett, whose record of outperformance is so persistent and continues long after it has been widely identified, so that the evidence of competence over chance seems irrefutable. But you will be fortunate indeed if you identify one. The accumulation of evidence of the kind revealed in the Vanguard research has led the FCA to require fund management groups to state that past performance is no guide to future performance. The intelligent investor should take heed.

The hot hand is frequently – and mistakenly – detected when what we see is the result of an asymmetric statistical distribution that combines frequent small gains with occasional very large losses – an activity sometimes described as picking dimes in front of a steamroller. I call these Taleb distributions, after a book in which Nassim Taleb offers many illustrations (Taleb, 2001). I like to use the analogy of tailgating – the practice, which I often see in France, of people driving at high speed on the motorway just a few metres behind the car ahead, flashing lights to demand that the vehicle ahead give way. Tailgating drivers save a few seconds on most trips. But occasionally you see their smashed cars on the side of the road. Participants dissociate the infrequent failures from the frequent successes. The early arrival is the result of their skilful driving; the crash is caused by bad luck, or the mistakes of others. The judgement of the drivers is vindicated by their success so far.

Tailgating is practised by those who fail Fitzgerald's test; the ability to hold two opposing ideas in mind at the same time and still function. If you ask the tailgating driver what he thinks will happen, his answer will be that he will get home quickly and without incident; and on the vast majority of occasions he will be right. The cautious driver, however, also has in his or her mind an image of smashed cars at the side of the motorway and the sound of ambulance sirens. And both groups think in terms of stories, neither in probabilities.

The 'carry trade' is a Taleb process in financial markets. Interest rates vary across classes of borrower and across currencies. Riskier borrowers pay higher interest rates. If markets price credit risk correctly, then the premium from the higher interest rate will equal the expected value of the losses from default. For example, if a certain type of borrower will fail to repay with a frequency of 2 per cent per year, then a bank with a portfolio of such loans will break even if it charges interest rates 2 per cent higher than prime.

But the distribution of gains and losses on these loans is not symmetrical. Most borrowers meet the principal and interest as they fall due, and the lender collects, year in, year out, the 2 per cent premium. But when the loan fails, the loss is often the full amount outstanding. As with the tailgating driver, lenders win most of the time on risky loans, but when they lose, they lose big-time. And when the credit bubble burst, they did exactly that. The northern European banks which lent to Greece at spreads only 0.2 per cent higher than those available on German bonds were, in an SEU view of the world, assessing the annual probability of a Greek default at 0.2 per cent, or 0.2 per cent higher than the probability of a German default. But actually they were not thinking probabilities at all. They had found reasons for dismissing the possibility of a Greek default from their minds.

Still, like the tailgating driver, people who collect these regular profits congratulate themselves on their prowess, win the admiration of their bosses and justify both their own bonuses and those of their superiors. Beneficiaries of Taleb distributions leave their more cautious competitors behind, so a process of rivalry forces others to follow, and to suppress any private doubts. From time to time accidents happen. There is a car crash, a Greek default. The losses are large, described as unpredictable, unanticipated, exceptional. One-time heroes are fired. The process begins again. The same financial follies are repeated.

You may wonder why many positions in large corporations are filled by people of apparently modest talent, find it inexplicable that dealers with so little knowledge or skill are applauded for their trading success, be surprised at the stupidity of drivers who take large risks for seemingly inconsequential gains. The answer to all of these paradoxes is the same: the people you see are on the upside of their Taleb distribution (and may remain there until they retire).

All political careers end in failure, goes an old saying, because politicians tend to continue until their luck runs out. The same phenomenon is common in the financial world. In any activity in which there is a random element in performance, the outperformers of one period, on average, will show subsequent deterioration, and the underperformers will, on average, improve. Road accidents fall when speed cameras are installed, because speed cameras are installed where there have recently been accidents. This statistical result would be observed even if the camera had no effect on the behaviour of drivers. Statistics seem to show a pattern that may not be there. This is known as the regression fallacy.

And so it is with fund managers. The data in Table 7 are compiled by examining only those funds which completed two five-year periods. Unsuccessful investment funds are much more likely to close, or to be merged into other funds, than successful funds, as Table 8 demonstrates. Without adjusting for these 'lost' funds it is easy to conclude that fund manager performance is better than it is. The Vanguard research is distinctive because the company has tried to eliminate this source of error. Survivor bias means that the funds, gurus and pundits from whom we continue to hear have better historical records than their peers, but this does not mean they are any more likely to be right in future.

Table 8: **Percentage of funds in each performance quintile, 2004–9, surviving to 2014**

Quintile	1st	2nd	3rd	4th	5th
	84	74	72	61	49

Source: Vanguard UK

Perhaps survivor bias is part of the resolution of the equity premium paradox. I'm writing this book about investing in shares in Britain, not about how to invest in Chinese bonds or South American utilities, both of which were popular choices a century ago. The markets we look at, and invest in today, are markets that have performed well in the past. There were no books written in the 1920s on investment in Russia, but if there had been, they would have had to acknowledge that recent performance did not justify an investment.

As with managers, so with asset classes. Markets show short-term positive serial price correlation, but long-term negative serial price correlation. So don't be tempted by advertisements displaying how much money has been made recently in housing or commodities – that is more likely to be a signal to sell than a signal to buy. Assets that have recently done badly deserve attention – but not indiscriminate attention. The objective is always to exploit negative market sentiment to buy cheaply. Detect regression towards the mean; correct for survivor bias; beware data mining.

Models and their limits

Models are an indispensable part of modern finance, and all banks and fund managers use them. The professionalism and sophistication of models and modellers have increased steadily. Anyone equipped with school mathematics can do a discounted

cash flow (DCF) calculation. The Markowitz model of portfolio selection, the basis of the CAPM, is more complex. But
even if Milton Friedman worried that Markowitz's work was
outside the scope of the economics of the time, the techniques
are quite simple (and today well within that scope). The Black–
Scholes model of option pricing, introduced in the 1970s, is both
dynamic and stochastic (it involves differential equations and
probability distributions).

These models are not rocket science (though they are often
called such), but they do require some university-level training
in maths or a maths-based subject. Today an understanding of
the frontiers of finance theory demands an advanced degree in
maths or physics. Because the financial services sector is very
profitable, financial institutions offer large salaries to able mathematicians, but the executives to whom they ultimately report
have little understanding of what these employees do.

You don't have to understand what is under the bonnet of a
car to drive it, and similarly you can be a competent manager of
a pharmaceutical company or an electronics business without
deep familiarity with the underlying chemical or physical characteristics of the product. But you cannot drive a car if you don't
understand what a car does, and you cannot organise the marketing, manufacture or distribution of a product if you don't
understand what the product can do – and what it can't.

Senior people in the financial sector – bank executives or
fund managers – are not themselves able to build the models on
which financial sector activities depend. That is not a problem.
The problem is that the techniques are so far outside their comprehension that they do not understand the limitations of the
models. While professing scepticism, they take too seriously
the conclusions that the models generate. Their attitude might
be described as one of cynical naïveté. Executives seek 99 per
cent certainties from their risk management systems without
appreciating that in an uncertain world there are never 99 per

cent certainties. This was Mr Viniar's error. Ninety-nine per cent probabilities are derived within models whose applicability to the problem being analysed is never 100 per cent certain (and rarely measurable). The first percentile in the distribution of outcomes is typically generated by events that were not incorporated into the structure of the model. As will almost have certainly been the case when the coin comes up heads twenty times in a row, the model, which represents the process as twenty independent tosses of a fair coin, is almost certainly inadequate to describe the real problem.

The attempt in Chapter 6 to apply DCF calculations to asset valuation illustrated a recurrent problem for all models in business and finance. Not only did we not know the numbers that the model required, but the outcome was very sensitive to the assumptions made in entering these numbers. This leads all too often to bogus quantification. People invent numbers to derive supposedly scientific answers to questions whose answers are fundamentally unknowable.

If you have a well-trained financial adviser – one with a financial planning qualification or, better still, a CFA certification – then he or she will very likely build a model of your portfolio in the Markowitz tradition, emphasising the variance and covariances of different assets. That is what financial advisers are taught to do. Risk assessment models in large financial institutions have a similar structure.

In line with the principles of SEU and CAPM, these models have three critical inputs:

- What is the expected return on each asset you hold?
- What will be the volatility of that expected return?
- What will be the correlation between the volatility of the return on a particular asset and the volatility of your portfolio as a whole?

But neither you nor your adviser knows, or can know, the answer to these questions.

The difficulties fall into two main groups:

- The assumptions made about the statistical distributions that link the data to the model.
- The reliance on history for that data.

I'll take each of these issues in turn. A common assumption is that short-term movements in securities prices can be described through a normal distribution. If we look at day-to-day movements in share prices, it appears that the normal distribution fits them quite well. But there is a problem of 'fat tails': there are many more extreme events than these statistical distributions would permit. If share price movements fitted the normal distribution, it is improbable that a market fall such as that of the US market on 19 October 1987 – a twenty-sigma event – would occur even once in the entire history of the universe. But when several such 'once in a blue moon' incidents happen in the course of a few years – as in the last decade, or in Mr Viniar's experience in 2007 – it is time to rethink one's model.

Fat tails are a particularly troubling problem for people who are modelling risk in financial markets, because they suggest that these models fail in precisely the extreme situations in which they are most needed. Although the most common reaction to the problem of fat tails is to note the problem and ignore it, there are two main strategies that attempt to deal with the issue. One approach involves *ad hoc* modification to make the results of classical statistical distributions correspond better to reality. Examples are generalised autoregressive conditional heteroscedasticity (don't ask) and a technique more attractively labelled 'robust statistics'. These approaches continue to assume that there is some correct description of the world enabling the properties of its prospective behaviour to be deduced from historical information – that we can find models that are not just illuminating but true. They presuppose that we confront risks rather than radical uncertainties.

An alternative, perhaps more interesting, critique developed by the mathematician Benoit Mandelbrot, rejects the assumptions of classical statistics altogether. Mandelbrot looked at charts of security prices and saw not a random walk but a beautiful process known as 'fractals'. You encounter fractal geometry when you look at a snowflake through a microscope and discover that, whatever magnification you set, the picture you see is the same.

Distributions that follow fractal processes show altogether different properties from those of classical statistics. These 'power law' distributions have fatter tails, and extreme events play a much larger role in outcomes. The physical analogies are not the diffuse movements of solids in solution described by Brownian motion but earthquakes and avalanches – constant small slips, often imperceptible, punctuated by large shifts. Those analogies correspond to many people's experience of financial markets.

Whether you use the distributions of classical statistics or the different mathematical structures of Mandelbrot's approach, the information you must use to build a model comes from data on what these returns have been, and how they varied, in the past. For good reasons – this historical record is the only objective information available. But, as we have seen, such figures may not be a good guide to the future. Investment allocation models based on recent experience will probably suggest that a high proportion should be devoted to equities. You may also be encouraged to invest more in alternative assets. That is because the returns from equities have in the immediate past been more than sufficient to compensate for their volatility. Alternative assets have also yielded high returns that were not strongly correlated, on a year-by-year basis, with other investment classes. But the model tells you these things only because someone has already told these things to the model.

No model can tell you what expected future returns on different asset classes will be, or the future correlation between these returns. Robb Caledon was a hedge, whose price would move in the opposite direction to the main UK indices. But you would not have learned that by studying past covariances. Indeed, you would have found the opposite. Stocks subject to political risk tended to have high *betas*, moving with the general market by often violent amounts.

Only the peculiar circumstances of 1976, in which the government proposed to nationalise the company for more than it was worth, gave that share its particular risk profile. If broad economic conditions had improved, lifting the price of most stocks, there would probably have been little impact, in either direction, on the share price of the shipyard. Neither in the past nor in the present was there any stable correlation, positive or negative, between Robb Caledon and the general market.

Such observations illustrate why historical measures of *beta* have limited value. Students of statistics are introduced to the alleged correlation between the stork population and the birth rate. The example illustrates that correlation does not imply causation. Storks do not bring babies, nor do babies attract storks. The correlation is the result of a common underlying factor that influences both variables – births are a function of population, and dense populations attract storks – rather than the product of a direct causal relationship between them.

But almost all correlations between security prices are of this kind: they result from common economic influences rather than direct causality. Since correlation and causation are not the same, only an understanding of the underlying causal mechanism can make it possible to know whether a correlation will or will not persist in any particular time period. The correlation of stork population and birth rate would continue to hold if new households moved into the neighbourhood, but would not hold if a predator struck the storks or more efficient contraception became available. One relationship between Robb Caledon's share price and general market movements applied under a Conservative government, and a different one held under a Labour government. Only information outside statistical analysis can tell us that.

The antidote to errors of data interpretation is general knowledge, what many people call common sense: the disparate facts about the world that we apprehend but do not articulate systematically, and which inform every decision we make. Keynes was a successful investor, as well as a man who achieved success in many other fields, in part because he brought to all his activities a range of experience and knowledge of both ideas and affairs probably unparalleled in the twentieth century.

The requirement for general knowledge drawn from outside the model does not make the model useless. A model that makes assumptions about correlations between variables – even arbitrary ones – can illustrate ways in which careful diversification can improve the relationship between risk and return. But the quantitative precision claimed for the results of these exercises is generally spurious. I am a better investor for having learned, and built, models of portfolio selection. I am a better investor partly because these models are illuminating. I understand better the relationship between risk and return as a result. But I am also a better investor because I understand the mistakes made by people who think these models are true.

Forecasts and their limits

If financial experts have limited ability to analyse the past, what of their ability to foresee the future? The commentators you hear on CNBC and other news channels make projections of general trends – the rise and fall of companies, industries and countries – and forecasts of specific economic variables – inflation, economic growth rate, exchange rates.

The record of the market pundits in anticipating events is poor. But this does not diminish the demand for their services. The power of conventional thinking strikes again. What is valued is not genuine knowledge of the future – to the very limited extent that such knowledge exists – but insight into the mind of the market. Keynes's analogy of the beauty contest is again relevant. The objective is not to predict what will happen, but to predict what others will themselves shortly predict.

The world in the 1990s experienced an unprecedented era of political and economic stability under American hegemony, following the end of the Cold War. The unthinking but contagious optimism of the era fuelled the conventional thinking of the New Economy bubble. Books and blogs proclaimed that the Dow Jones index, less around 6,000, would go to 36,000, or even 100,000, on the back of ever-soaring earnings and the disappearance of the risk premium. (It is currrently around 18,000.) These complacent beliefs were strikingly similar to those Keynes described for Britain exactly 100 years earlier. And in the 'noughties' politicians announced the 'great moderation' until they were hit by the most serious financial crisis in eighty years.

Since we are ill equipped to handle inevitable uncertainty, the future is seen through the terms of the near present. The opening in the last twenty-five years of Russia and Eastern Europe, China and India to the market economy is the most important economic development of our lifetimes. But the main beneficiaries of this opening will be the populations of the countries concerned. While it is certain that much money will be made in China, that does not necessarily imply that there is much money to be made there by you and me. And the rise of China and India has not exactly passed unnoticed.

People who pronounce on future geopolitical developments are mostly talking not about tomorrow but about today. They tend to project current trends to an exaggerated extent and with exaggerated speed. As a result, they overestimate change in the short term while underestimating change in the long term. They treat current events as more momentous than they really are – hence 'It's different this time' or portentous talk of 'new paradigms'. Simultaneously, such commentators fail to anticipate the transformational effect of events that have not yet happened and of which they can know nothing – the unknown unknowns that shape our lives. The safe course is to talk about current preoccupations, and that is what successful pundits mostly do. We can all then agree in being astonished by the pace of change.

Economic forecasts of recession or recovery, of interest rates and exchange rates, are part of every investment conversation. Fund managers routinely deliver an assessment of general economic prospects to clients. The EMH should make you suspicious when people who profess special insight into the future reveal that insight to large audiences – the value of such insight would surely depend on knowledge of it not being widely available. Professional forecasters have little, or nothing, to add to public information – information that is printed every day in the newspapers, which can be ascertained every hour of the day on the internet and which is available for free.

Such economists are valued, and rewarded by their employers, for their television manner rather than the accuracy of their predictions. It is a common perception that economists always disagree – two economists, three opinions. The facts are quite otherwise, at least as far as economic forecasters are concerned. There is typically far less divergence between forecasts than between forecasts and outcomes.

For economic forecasters, as for other financial pundits, it is better to be conventionally wrong than unconventionally right. To see correctly what others have failed to see, or chosen to ignore, damages careers more often than it advances them. Such prescience undermines the claim – so important to those who disclaim responsibility for what went wrong on their watch – that what happened could not have been foreseen. Ask the people who tried to warn their superiors of the dangers of a terrorist attack on the United States, or of the fragility of the financial system ahead of 2008.

The weaknesses of forecasting are compounded by the difficulty of specifying how exactly changes in GDP, or interest rate changes, will translate into market prices. Politicians, people in business and finance and the public at large display cynical naïveté in their attitudes to economic forecasts, as in their attitudes to models – a mixture of scepticism and credulity. They express disdain for economic forecasts as they lap them up. Most professional economists regard this forecasting activity as embarrassing and ridiculous, but it continues because the demand is insatiable. People want answers to questions that cannot be answered and refuse to accept the limits of knowledge in the face of uncertainty. They justifiably deride those who profess knowledge of the future which they do not have. 'Economic forecasters are always wrong.' Less justifiably, they also deride those who disclaim such knowledge, and who emphasise that the future can only be described through many divergent, yet plausible, scenarios.

'Give me a one-handed economist', Harry S. Truman is reported to have said. But if he did, it was a foolish remark. Many issues are best assessed through 'one the one hand, or the other' debate. Robb Caledon might have been nationalised, or it might not. Prudence acknowledges both possibilities.

The economic environment is like the weather. We cannot forecast it accurately, but we know quite a lot about its broad properties – it won't snow in England in July, and it might rain on any day of the year. General knowledge of this latter kind is already 'in the price', and people who claim more specific knowledge of the future are mostly charlatans.

The common mistake is to believe that the uncertainty described by Keynes and Knight can, through diligent research or analytic sophistication, be transformed into the well-defined, quantifiable risk that responds to the techniques developed by the successors of Ramsey and Savage. Keynes correctly observed that the only justified answer to many questions about the future is 'We simply do not know', but no one is rewarded for saying that. Many people in the financial services sector profess knowledge of the future they do not have, and cannot have. In contrast, legendary investors such as Buffett and Soros stand out for their readiness to acknowledge the limitations of their – and all – knowledge.

Here is Soros:

My financial success stands in stark contrast with my ability to forecast events … With regard to events in the real world, my record is downright dismal. The outstanding feature of my predictions is that I keep on expecting developments that do not materialise.

(Soros, 2003)

And here Buffett:

In many industries, of course, Charlie [Munger] and I can't determine whether we are dealing with a 'pet rock' or a 'Barbie'. We wouldn't solve this problem, moreover, even if we were to spend years intensely studying these industries … Did we foresee thirty years ago what would transpire in the television manufacturing or computer industries? Of course not. (Nor did most of the investors and corporate managers who enthusiastically entered these industries.)

(Buffett and Cunningham, 2002, p.85)

Recall Keynes's 'There is no scientific basis on which to form any calculable probability whatever. We simply do not know.' The intelligent investor knows that he or she does not know and (like Buffett, Keynes and Soros) can enjoy the luxury of acknowledging that ignorance. Professional investment experts mostly cannot acknowledge such ignorance – they are hired to provide answers to unanswerable questions. Never mind, they are well paid for it. But not, if you are an intelligent investor, by you.

Approaches to risk

In this and the previous chapters I've described both the dominant SEU theory and the more eclectic and pragmatic approaches to risk and uncertainty favoured by Keynes and Knight. It is time to pull together the strands and spell out their implications for intelligent investors. In SEU theory, the term 'subjective' has a double significance. The probabilities are subjective, and so are the valuations of outcomes.

Probabilities and values differ between people but, once established for any individual, are held consistently. If the risks are the same, you use the same probabilities whatever the pay-offs; if the pay-offs are the same, you attach the same valuations whatever the probabilities. There is a powerful underlying logic to this approach. The reasons the SEU school is today dominant in risk analysis in financial markets can be traced, directly and indirectly, to a clever argument constructed by Ramsey. If you don't adopt the SEU approach, people can devise schemes that will make money at your expense. The process is called a 'Dutch book'. (Offended residents of the Netherlands have attempted, without success, to track down the origins of the phrase.) In a Dutch book, you make a series of choices, each of which you believe is to your advantage, whose net effect leaves you worse off. The only sure means of preventing inconsistency in your choices is to follow the precepts of subjective expected utility. The Allais paradoxes described compellingly attractive Dutch books.

While SEU may appear a good way of thinking about risk, it is certainly not the only way of thinking about risk. Ramsey's argument was never as decisive as it appeared. In the uncertain, constantly changing world that Keynes and Knight correctly perceived, it is impossible to be sure whether behaviour is consistent or simply stubborn. You are steadfast. I am pragmatic. There is no objective basis for the claim that two similar situations are indeed identical.

The findings of behavioural economists are often interpreted as evidence of irrational behaviour. This interpretation is simplistic. The demonstration of supposedly irrational behaviour in the principal Allais paradox rests on the human tendency to value certainties much more highly than extremely probable events. There are good reasons for this trait. There is no such thing in everyday life as an event with a calculable 99 per cent probability. The first percentile of a distribution is generally encountered as a result of uncertainties outside the model. A common feature of these behavioural experiments is that the subject applies a rule that makes sense in everyday life – which is full of uncertainty – in an abstract experimental situation in which problems can be reduced to risks that are precisely defined and described.

There are choices in which rigorous application of the principles of SEU seems to make sense – Robb Caledon – but mostly calculations have to be tempered with the more qualitative judgement that enables us to handle uncertainty. It is not easy to draw a clear line between situations for which SEU is relevant and situations for which it is not. There is tension between people who have learned to 'think SEU' and those who have not. That was the situation President Obama faced in deciding whether to go ahead with the raid in Pakistan.

These conflicts between different perspectives on risk are as old as history. Throwing dice is one of the oldest forms of gambling – bones shaped like cubes were used for this purpose thousands of years ago. Games of dice and other forms of gambling were invented precisely because they create conditions in which a probability-based SEU approach is valuable. The modern casino similarly allows people who 'think SEU' – the operators – to make money at the expense of people who do not think SEU – the punters. The casino, like the insurance company, is concerned with expected values. The motivations of the gamblers in the casino and the customers of the insurance company are more complex.

The ability to 'think probabilities', to apply the premises of SEU, is one that will save you from costly mistakes at the casino. But in an uncertain world in which risks cannot be clearly identified, we don't approach all questions probabilistically because the probabilistic approach often isn't useful. If people turn out not to have consistent personal probabilities, the reason may be that a scheme of personal probabilities is incapable of fully describing the way they think about the First World War, the Twin Towers or even their daily journey home from work.

Detachment means that you focus single-mindedly on the outcome of a risky activity and ignore those aspects of the process that you cannot control. This is also difficult. There is evidence that we worry more about risks we cannot control than about those we can. This may be why so many people are nervous about flying, but far fewer are nervous about driving, even though it is far more dangerous.

Sometimes involvement gives pleasure, as when we cheer the horses we have backed at the races. Some people experience a rush of adrenalin as lights flash on the fruit machine or as the roulette wheel spins. Sometimes involvement in events we cannot influence causes anxiety, as when I turned to the news to hear the progress of the shipbuilding nationalisation bill through Parliament.

In a world of unknowns, engagement is part of the process of managing uncertainty. To be detached about mountain climbing or buying a lottery ticket is to miss the point of these activities.

Regret for our mistakes is part of the process by which we learn from them. Compartmentalising our decisions and the information relevant to them – a process known as mental accounting – is the only way we can cope with a complex world.

But whether pleasurable or painful, the experience of engagement is costly. The thrill of the race and the excitement of the casino are paid for by the majority of punters who lose. Sleepless nights worrying about which way Members of Parliament will vote on shipbuilding nationalisation bring no benefit – my attention is not going to affect the outcome. But the prospect of experiencing those sleepless nights dissuades most people from undertaking investments, like buying shares in Robb Caledon, even if the odds are attractive. If you are detached you will pay no special attention to the prices of shares you have sold or decided not to buy. But you will!

People often tell me that they do not want to manage their own investments because they do not have the time – or inclination – to monitor their portfolio daily, as professionals do. But this can be a positive advantage. You can be free of the depression and euphoria generated by short-term price fluctuations that convey no meaningful information about fundamental value. Professional investors must come to the office and check their screens every day.

But training yourself to think in line with the principles of SEU will give you a technique that will serve you well in investment decisions. We don't naturally or easily think probabilistically, achieve detachment or always make decisions in the light of the totality of our circumstances. But if you want to make money in financial markets, there are substantial rewards to training yourself to think in that way. That is why this chapter and the preceding one, which are the most difficult in the book, may also be the most profitable.

If you don't practise SEU, you will be Dutch-booked – sold products that will be financially rewarding for the promoter but not for you. For years I taught that people would behave in line with SEU precepts since others would make money at their expense if they didn't. The logic was correct, but the conclusion was wrong. People often don't behave in line with SEU precepts, and others do make money at their expense, and that is a large part of what financial markets are about. Conversely, if you can learn to 'think SEU', then you will often make money at the expense of people who don't.

It isn't always a mistake to be Dutch-booked. The enjoyment of the daydream some people feel as the national lottery draw approaches, the excitement of watching the roulette wheel spin, the worry that is removed by buying an insurance policy – these feelings are real. But they are also expensive, and the other side of the Dutch book is the profits of the lottery and of insurance companies. If you can successfully suppress emotions of excitement and regret, you will be financially better off. You may prefer to enjoy these experiences, and I'm certainly not going to label you irrational in consequence. But this is a book about how to be a successful financial adviser to yourself. And one of the best pieces of financial advice you can give yourself is to familiarise yourself with the principles of SEU.

But people who think SEU are not necessarily more successful in life than people who do not think SEU, only more successful in not losing money at the casino. In casinos, the house wins and the punters lose. But perhaps the punters have the money to stake, and the attractive women on their arms, because they are over-confident. They tend to view life in terms of lively stories and vivid narratives rather than the abstract world of Bayes's theorem inhabited by nerdy economists.

So the evolutionary argument that SEU will drive out other methods of thinking, popular with these economists, is wrong. Around the campfires of those savannahs, *bon viveurs* and entertainers brought together groups that contained many different personality types – the enthusiastic, energetic hunters who killed the game and the more analytic tribesmen who focused on dividing it out. All these groups cooperated and prospered, as they do in modern financial markets. The world accommodates different approaches to risk and uncertainty, and so must you.

9

Modern Developments
in Financial Markets

Derivatives

In September 2000 Jim Chanos read the notes to the accounts of
Enron. Enron's filings with the Securities and Exchange Commission ran to thousands of pages, including many notes printed
in small type. The notes were ignored by the many Wall Street
analysts who promoted Enron shares and didn't know, or didn't
care, about the detail of the accounts. (The only Wall Street
analyst to have been consistently critical of Enron, John Olson,
left Merrill Lynch in 1998. His departure followed a complaint by
the firm's investment bankers, who feared being excluded from
Enron transactions.) The notes described the complex relationships between Enron and associated companies. Chanos was not
impressed by what he read.

If you own a security, you are 'long' of that security. If you
own a security, and you don't like it, you can sell it; if you don't
own it, and you don't like it, you can refrain from buying it. But
Chanos and the fund he managed, Kynikos, took such a negative view of Enron that they wanted to sell it even though they
didn't own it. (The hedge funds that speculated unsuccessfully
in Volkswagen a decade later similarly believed that the Porsche

bid would fail and they could buy the shares they did not own at a lower price. They were right on the first point and wrong on the second.) Selling a share you don't own is called 'establishing a short position', and the market for derivatives allows such trades. Derivatives are securities whose value is derived from the value of other securities. However complex the contract, almost all derivatives are based on shares, bonds, property, commodities or currencies.

Someone who is long in a security profits when its value rises. A short seller profits when the shares fall. When Enron shares plummeted, Chanos and other short sellers made substantial profits. The usual method of short selling today is to take out a 'contract for difference' (CFD). Suppose the share price today is 100p. A contract for difference is an agreement that can be terminated at any time either to pay or to receive the difference between 100p and the market price. The value of the contract for difference varies from day to day in line with the market price. Such contracts are a means of speculating on price movements. Not much up-front cash is required. When Enron's market price fell to zero, the holder of a suitable contract for difference could close the transaction and receive what the market price of Enron shares had been on the day he made the agreement.

A contract for difference, like all derivative contracts, is made with a counterparty – typically an investment bank. The bank may, but need not, hedge its side of the contract by itself buying, selling or 'borrowing' the shares. That decision will be part of the bank's management of its own portfolio of risks. A retail investor can engage in spread betting as an alternative to a contract for difference. The substantive transaction is the same, but, under UK law, gains on CFDs are subject to tax (and losses are deductible), although gambling winnings (including the proceeds of spread bets) are not. Another derivative contract is a 'swap'.

Interest rate swaps are the most common. You exchange an interest rate that varies from day to day for an interest rate that is fixed for a period of years. Mortgage lenders use swaps to offer retail investors a choice of fixed and variable rate products. People who take out mortgages often trade in derivative markets even though they don't know it; their lender is buying a swap contract on their behalf. When retail investors buy structured products, such as the enhanced bonds and protected equities I describe below, they are often buying derivatives.

A futures contract is an agreement to buy or sell something in the future at a price that is fixed today. Futures have a long history. A merchant might have to wait three months till a ship reached port, and would be vulnerable to price changes while his cargo was at sea. A farmer might wish to establish, now, how much he will get for his crop at harvest time. The earliest futures contracts brought such producers together with users who, on their side, were concerned about how much they might have to pay for the raw materials they would need. Such contracts enabled both parties to meet their requirements with greater certainty – to hedge. But you can buy a futures contract without any need, or intention, to hedge. You can buy it to speculate, and that is what most purchasers of futures contracts do.

The price of buying a future is governed by the present price of the asset. If a commodity does not deteriorate physically, its price three months from now can't be more than the price today, plus the cost of storing it for three months. But if there is a physical shortage of the commodity today, the current price could be higher than the future price. This 'backwardation' is occasionally seen in commodity markets, but at the time of writing there are surpluses of most commodities.

Storage costs influence the relationship between futures prices and current prices. There is also a financing cost. Money that has been borrowed, or which could otherwise be invested, is tied up in the purchase. A physical commodity needs to be warehoused and insured. For securities there is only the financing cost, and the cost of holding the security will be reduced if there is a dividend on the share, or interest on a bond, during the holding period. Interest rates differ in different currencies – generally there will be one interest rate at which banks borrow and lend dollars, and different interest rates at which they borrow and lend euros or pounds. The cost of owning a currency is the difference between the interest rate on that currency and the interest rate in your home country.

An option confers the right, but not the obligation, to buy or sell at a specified price, known as the 'strike price'. Some options have a fixed exercise date, while others can be exercised at any time until they expire, but since you usually won't want to exercise an option before expiry the difference isn't great. Since the option confers right but not obligation, an option seems preferable to a futures contract, which entails both right and obligation. If the option were free, it *would* be preferable. But while you can usually buy a futures contract in a commodity or a security for something close to the current price, you have to pay a premium for an option. The right to buy is known as a 'call option', while the right to sell is called a 'put'. What are these options worth?

Two influences on value are obvious. The longer the life of an option, the greater its value. The value of a call option diminishes, and the value of a put option increases, the higher the strike price relative to the current price.

There is another, less obvious, principle of option pricing. The value of an option increases with the volatility of the underlying asset. The riskier a security, the more valuable are options in it. This may seem paradoxical, but note that the riskier the asset, the more likely it is that you will be glad you own an option rather than the security itself. An option to buy £1 for £1 is not worth anything. An option to buy a £1 lottery ticket for £1 is valuable because you need exercise the option only if the ticket turns out to be a winner. Until the 1970s assessments of option value were guesses. That was before publication of the Black–Scholes model of derivative pricing, which analysed the relationship between the option price and the security price.

The apparently scientific basis for assessing the value of derivatives this model provided was essential to the subsequent explosion of derivatives markets. The value of the option therefore depends on its exercise price, its expiry date and the volatility of the price of the underlying security. Given these parameters, the standard model calculates an option value on the basis that successive price changes are independent of each other (follow a random walk) and follow a normal distribution. That procedure is fine if these assumptions of independence and normality hold. But there are strong reasons to query both. Deviations from a random walk arise from momentum or positive short-term serial correlation. The 'fat tail problem' – extreme events happen more often than the normal distribution allows – is especially troubling. Option valuation models seem to work well in relatively placid times, but it's not so clear that they work well when markets are unsettled. That's a major problem, because it is in unsettled markets that options are most useful, most profitable and most dangerous and the need for measures of what they are worth is most urgent.

'Mind your portfolio' – look at your investment portfolio as a whole. Most derivatives are, in themselves, risky investments – the return on an individual transaction is very uncertain. But adding derivatives to an existing portfolio can reduce the risk or improve the expected return on the portfolio without additional risk. A futures contract can hedge a portfolio against a market fall; a put option will limit the maximum loss. Derivatives can lock in profits or anticipate future needs, or allow you to benefit from a market rise while limiting risks. But hedging and insurance aren't the main reasons why people buy derivatives and related products based on them. They buy them because they think they are a good bet.

The normal experience of gamblers is that only the house

makes money in the long run. This is as true of speculation in derivative markets as it is elsewhere. Valuing derivatives is complex, and there are no correct answers. But the financial institutions that sell derivative products have access to sophisticated computer programs, extensive databases, Black–Scholes and other models, and roomfuls of maths and physics PhDs. These institutions are better at valuing derivatives than are the fund managers, treasurers of big companies and public authorities who characteristically buy them. Buying derivatives because you think they are cheap, rather than as hedges in a programme of portfolio diversification, is almost certainly a mug's game. The risks are in the price, and if you think the risks are not in the price, the most likely reason is that you are wrong. Why do I want to buy what they want to sell?

Trade in derivative markets has grown steadily, and the products have become more opaque. Some people – notoriously Alan Greenspan, former chairman of the Federal Reserve Board and author of what some called 'the Greenspan doctrine' – explained this growth in trade in terms of an ever more sophisticated risk allocation. Perhaps the German regional banks which invested in asset-backed securities related to the value of subprime mortgages in American inner cities did so because they were particularly knowledgeable about these loans, or believed they hedged or diversified other assets in their portfolios. More likely, victims of information asymmetry, they did not understand what they were doing.

When assets are difficult to value, they will be owned by people who overestimate that value. Most derivatives are bought by people who are making a mistake, and the proliferation of ever more complex financial instruments, hard to assess even with sophisticated models, encourages such mistakes.

There is a history of spectacular failures in derivatives markets. Sometimes credulous individuals in public agencies or large corporations fall for a sales pitch. In the 1990s many embarked on programmes of trading in derivatives or structured products whose nature they at best dimly understood. The municipality of Orange County went bust after trades made by the appropriately named Robert Citron came unstuck. The London borough of Hammersmith and Fulham was spared similar embarrassment when the courts ruled that the council had no authority to gamble with local residents' money and the banks could get lost.

Naïve incompetence is not confined to local authorities. Major US companies – even the mighty consumer group Procter & Gamble – suffered large losses from speculative derivative trading programmes. A second-line investment bank, Bankers Trust, was particularly aggressive in marketing these programmes to its clients. Ultimately the angry reaction of clients and threats of litigation destroyed the reputation of the bank. Financial institutions themselves are frequently victims as well as perpetrators. Managers of profitable trading divisions within banks receive large bonuses and may not be inclined to question closely how the profits are made. Traders who begin with honest losses may turn to fraud to conceal these losses. Nick Leeson achieved notoriety as the rogue trader whose speculations at Barings destroyed one of Britain's oldest investment banks, but in 2008 Jérôme Kerviel surpassed Leeson's record by helping his employer, the French bank Société Générale, lose €5 billion.

The most famous of all derivative related failures was the demise of Long-Term Capital Management in 1998. This collapse received particular attention – and caused particular joy in some quarters – because of the personalities involved. Founded by John Meriwether, a legendary Salomon trader, the management team included two Nobel Prize-winners, Bob Merton and Myron Scholes (of the Black–Scholes model). LTCM relied on arbitrage trades based on fundamental value – reversion to the mean in relationships between similar but different securities. But momentum may drive prices sufficiently far away from fundamental value for sufficiently long to exhaust the patience, and the resources, of investors – 'markets can be wrong for longer than you can be solvent'. Apparently unrelated bets proved to be correlated in the widespread panic that followed the Asian financial crisis and Russian debt repudiation of 1997–8. The scale of LTCM's borrowings – the magic of leverage meant that this relatively small fund had liabilities of trillions of dollars – was such that the Federal Reserve orchestrated a rescue operation.

Many derivatives in modern securities markets are complex. However elaborate, they are mostly based on combinations of the four basic mechanisms I have described above: shorts, swaps, futures and options. Most retail investors will not trade in derivatives directly. But they may do so through hedge funds and structured products, or through funds that invest in hedge funds or structured products.

When bonds were no longer boring

Bonds are intrinsically boring investments. The market in shares is associated with, and contributes to, the growth of companies and their investment and expansion. Over time businesses grow and investors share these profits. But Treasury 4.25 per cent 2055 is, well, just Treasury 4.25 per cent 2055. However often you trade, however many derivative securities you construct on the back of it, the government will not pay a penny more or a penny less.

And, once upon a time, bonds were boring. The Government Broker, recognisable by his top hat, would assess the bond market on behalf of the Bank of England. He (a female Government Broker was even more improbable than a female Prime Minister) was a partner in Mullens & Co., and frequently bore the surname Mullens. Nick Carraway, the colourless narrator of Scott Fitzgerald's 1925 American novel *The Great Gatsby*, was a bond trader.

Mullens & Co. disappeared in Big Bang, and within a very few years the former backwater had become the roughest of seas. The causes of the change in the nature of bond markets were not so much Big Bang itself as financial innovations that originated in the United States and were imitated in London. An early idea was the strip, which separated the income from the principal of a bond, so that one person might receive the £4.25 interest per year for forty years and another the £100 principal at the end of forty years. Some people might have needed income, while others wanted to secure a future liability. But in the 1970s and 1980s several distinct innovations turned the bond market into an exciting place. The introduction of an interest rate futures contract on the Chicago Mercantile Exchange, almost simultaneous with the work of Black and Scholes at the neighbouring university, was the beginning of the development of derivative contracts related to bond markets.

The 'junk bond' was invented by Michael Milken, whose graduate school thesis demonstrated that the premium interest rate attached to risky bonds was more than sufficient to offset the probability of default. Most of the bonds Milken studied were once sound securities whose issuers had fallen on hard times. Milken's innovation was to issue bonds that were obviously highly risky from inception. Milken pioneered the issue of junk bonds, and for a few years the investment bank he worked for, Drexel Burnham Lambert, almost monopolised that market. The idea was to issue very large quantities of low-quality bonds to enable people without much money to take over very large companies. Using the results of his graduate school research, Milken argued that junk bonds would produce returns in excess of those available from conventional investments. Few students find, as Milken did, a thesis subject that will make them unimaginably rich.

Junk bonds allowed the takeover of RJR Nabisco, the food and tobacco conglomerate, by KKR, a private equity business. For a decade, before Gent's Vodafone acquired the German opera-tor Mannesmann and AOL merged even more disastrously with Time-Warner, this transaction would stand as the largest acquisition in history. The junk bond movement reached its apotheosis when an unstable Canadian of large ambition but smaller talent, Robert Campeau, used junk bond finance to acquire many of America's largest department stores, including the iconic Bloomingdale's (and damaged those businesses, in some cases irreversibly, as he failed to stave off the bankruptcy of his fragile empire).

Banks created asset-backed securities, bundling together packages of loans and dividing them into safer and riskier tranches. 'Mortgages are math', declared Lew Ranieri, who ran the fixed interest department at Salomon Brothers and promoted the mortgage-backed security. Ranieri would be a central figure in Michael Lewis's coruscating 1989 account of the trading floor at Salomon. Two years earlier, Tom Wolfe had described the New York of that era in his novel *The Bonfire of the Vanities*. Wolfe's central figure, Sherman McCoy, Master of the Universe, was, like Nick Carraway, a bond salesman. But in a very different environment.

Alternative assets

The first hedge fund was established by Alfred Jones, a journalist who, having undertaken research for an article on fund man-agement, concluded that he could do much better himself. Jones traded aggressively, and profitably, through the 1950s. Hedge funds attracted wide popular attention with the bet against ster-ling by the Quantum Fund of George Soros in 1992 and came into the spotlight again with the failure of Long-Term Capital Management in 1998.

Until 2000 hedge funds were used only by rich individuals and a few sophisticated institutions. Academic endowments, notably those of Harvard and Yale, were early and successful supporters. After the end of the New Economy bubble, investors searched for new ways of generating the high returns that had seemed to come so easily in the 1990s. They turned to hedge funds. Exceptional individuals such as Soros had been able to command high fees for their services, and newer funds set their charges at the same level. The prospect of such fees proved irresistible to many people in investment banks. As newcomers rushed through the door, Soros made for the exit. So did another legend, Julian Robertson, who seriously misjudged the New Economy bubble. While the long-term performance of his Tiger Fund rivalled that of Soros, Robertson may have lost more money in his last year than he had made throughout his career.

Different hedge funds pursue different strategies. A long/short fund will deploy the stock-picking skills of its managers to select losers as well as winners. Jim Chanos, who helped expose Enron, specialised in taking short positions. A market-neutral fund will hedge its exposure to general market movements. It will focus on alpha and eliminate *beta*. A macroeconomic event fund in the style of Soros aspires to predict major financial and political developments in the world economy – such as Britain's EMS failure – and trades on the basis of these forecasts.

Arbitrage strategies, such as those deployed at LTCM, rely on stable relationships between the prices of related, but different, securities. Such pairs might be currencies within a region, or the debt and equity of the same company, or the shares of an acquiring company and its potential target. As at LTCM, arbitrage strategies are often based on complex modelling. Relying on history in this way is dangerous, as it proved to be for the LTCM partners.

Distressed debt funds buy bonds of businesses or countries in financial difficulty. These funds may hope to profit from buying below fundamental value, or to increase that fundamental value through litigation or the threat to block proposals for financial reconstruction.

In the 1980s investment banks established proprietary trading operations – their own internal hedge funds. LTCM emerged from what was for years the most successful of these, at Salomon. But Salomon's proprietary trading activities were curtailed after Warren Buffett took charge, and finally closed when Citigroup acquired the business. Proprietary trading nevertheless became a major activity for most large banks (including Citigroup). These 'prop desks' benefited from the information that flows continuously through the bank; despite Chinese walls, the conflicts of interest between these trading activities and the interests of clients are obvious. The 'Volcker rule', introduced as part of the Dodd–Frank legislation in response to the 2008 financial crisis, limited the extent of prop trading activities by banks, but the detail proved complex and the subject of endless negotiation, in which paid lobbyists for banks played the dominant role. Senator Dodd and Congressman Frank might write the principles, but the industry would write the detail.

Although most hedge funds are based in London or the United States, for legal and regulatory purposes they are normally registered offshore. While the City of London (and its increasingly important annexe at Canary Wharf) remains the centre of London's financial services business, hedge fund managers emphasise differentiation and exclusivity by clustering in St James's (and, in the US, in Connecticut). Charging typical fees of 2 per cent of funds under management and 20 per cent of profits, the managers can afford West End rents.

The fee structure, in effect, shares profits but not losses. Investors look for reliable month-by-month appreciation in the value of their funds, and hedge fund managers are closely monitored by reference to this metric. Both the incentives and the supervision encourage the adoption of strategies with Taleb characteristics – frequent small profits, even at the risk of occasional large losses.

Managers take performance fees for their skilful driving, but are able to walk away from car crashes with only their reputation damaged. Hedge funds make extensive use of the 'carry trade', which relies on interest rate differentials between good and bad credits, or strong and weak currencies.

Retail investors cannot easily access major hedge funds, as a result of regulatory restrictions and high minimum investments, and many of the most highly regarded funds are closed to new investors. Retail investors have the opportunity to invest in more conventional open- or closed-ended funds which themselves invest in hedge funds. Since many hedge fund managers reveal only limited information about what they do, intermediaries may be helpful, but expensive. These funds of funds can diversify across funds with different strategies. The returns on, say, a long/short fund should not be correlated with the returns on, say, a distressed debt fund. Historical analysis supports this claim. But do not count on the stability of historic correlations in times of extreme financial strain. Funds learned this lesson in 2007–8.

The shift from mainstream to alternative investments also favoured private equity. Private equity is a means by which investment institutions, either directly or through managed funds, invest in unquoted businesses. Before the late 1990s, private equity used to be more or less synonymous with venture capital – the provision of funds for start-up and early stage businesses.

Not all private equity deals were of this kind. Some very large transactions were financed through junk bonds, as described above, but that boom ended with the collapse of Drexel Burnham Lambert, the imprisonment of Michael Milken and the relatively unsuccessful outcome of the massive acquisition of RJR Nabisco by KKR. As large corporations restructured in the two decades that followed, unwanted 'non-core' divisions were often sold to consortia led by their managers and funded by private equity. The newly established business was often refinanced or the subject of a fresh IPO within a few years. Many individual managers became very rich through these transactions, a development that helped to raise the pay aspirations of all executives.

The search for new investment avenues after 2000 led to rapid growth in the funds available for private equity, and the scale of the typical transaction again grew rapidly. Private equity funds would buy an established business from the existing owners. These owners might be other companies, family and founding shareholders or, increasingly, the shareholders of public companies quoted on the stock exchange. The largest private equity deal in the UK was the takeover of Boots, the high street chemists and a listed public company, for £11 billion, including more than £8 billion of debt.

In this type of a transaction private equity has come a long way from its roots in the provision of funds to small, growing businesses. Private equity investment became an indirect, expensive and exclusive method of buying shares in medium and large companies similar to those in the main index. The returns from such investment will therefore be correlated with the returns from other equity investments, but, given the leverage involved, the *beta* associated with the equity is well above one.

The concentrated share ownership of private equity deals allows more effective monitoring of company management. Such concentrated ownership has been common for many years in continental Europe. Public companies find their ability to focus on fundamental value inhibited by the earnings management process of analyst guidance and quarterly reports. Some patient private equity investors are willing to hold their financial investments for many years, thus facilitating longer-term strategic thinking and productive investment. But the major private equity firms, and the investors who back them, are generally in search of a rapid exit. The objective is normally to sell the company or to float it on the stock market within three to five years, returning the money obtained to the investors in that particular fund.

I described in Chapter 6 the numerous ways in which businesses can enhance earnings in the short term. Private equity, and the threat of takeover by private equity, has increased pressure to use these strategies. During a recent stay in a hotel, looking at the frayed carpet and overpriced extras, I thought 'This hotel has been bought out in a private equity transaction'. It had been. It is easy to enhance the earnings of most businesses if your time horizon is three years.

Both the citizen and the investor should be concerned about the difficulty modern management faces in taking a long-term view of the growth and development of the business. The public company encounters the blight of quarterly earnings reporting; the private-equity-owned business must accommodate the time-scale of investors seeking a rapid exit for quick profit. This short-termism is reinforced by the incentive schemes offered to managers – even, or perhaps especially, the so-called long-term incentive schemes that now constitute a large part of executive remuneration. (Long-term is typically three years.) Even if you are concerned with the fundamental value of the business in which you own shares, the managers may not be.

It is difficult for the investor to judge the historic success of private equity, far less its prospective future returns. Some private equity houses may have been able to supervise management teams more effectively than can public markets. Some may possess skills that add value through financial engineering. Private equity houses recently had (but no longer have) access to debt financing whose pricing did not reflect the risk involved. The reporting of historical performance is confounded by survivor bias – it is the more successful investors who are raising new funds – and by the capacity of leverage to produce very high returns to equity investors in a period of rising share prices (with the opposite effect when share prices are falling).

Against these potential advantages must be set the certainty of charges. 'Two and twenty' is a common charging basis for both hedge funds and private equity investments. The private equity house takes a management fee of 2 per cent of the fund per year, and 20 per cent of the profits, known in private equity as the 'carried interest'. Like other investment managers, they may also arrange for many of their own costs to be directly or indirectly charged to their funds. When these percentages are applied to large transactions – such as those of Boots – the numbers become eye-watering. Many hedge funds and private equity managers have become very rich very quickly. But what of the customers' yachts? 'Two and twenty' reduces an 8 per cent underlying return to 5 per cent. A retail investor will normally make an investment in a hedge fund or private equity fund through a fund of funds or a feeder fund, for which a further charge will be made. Tax and inflation take a further bite of the return. In this way an 8 per cent yield on the underlying investment might only be 2 per cent in the hands of the saver.

Such figures make no sense. Returns on financial investment are ultimately governed by returns on productive investment. While some investors in hedge funds and private equity will make excellent returns from a mixture of skill and luck on the part of their managers, most stand no chance of earning profits commensurate with the risks. Hedge funds and private equity are not the only alternative assets. Other options include commodities such as: oil, gold and other metals; undeveloped land such as farms, forests and building plots; and collectables such as wine, art, jewels and furniture.

Commodity exchanges, large and active, meet the needs of people who produce or use the physical commodities. Commodities have always been a fertile field for speculation by those who believe they can anticipate 'the mind of the market'. If this is you, then good luck and good fortune; you will need good luck to preserve your good fortune. If you simply want to invest, there are funds whose value is linked to commodity prices, which I will describe in the next chapter.

The years since the financial crisis have seen extraordinary gyrations in commodity prices. The price of oil, the most widely traded and used commodity, reached almost $150 per barrel in June 2008, then fell to below $50, again rose over $100 and subsequently dropped to $30. Plainly these fluctuations have little connection to fundamental value. But fundamental value is what matters in the long run, and over the long run commodity investment has not been very profitable. Despite continuing worries about forthcoming resource scarcity, new technology and new discoveries have more than offset the exploitation of existing reserves. It is cheaper to own commodities in the ground than in a warehouse, and mining companies are generally better investments than the commodities themselves, and are good portfolio diversifiers. The aphorism that a small minerals company is a hole in the ground with a crook at the top is, however, often true. London's Alternative Investment Market has become a magnet for small resource companies, many of dubious provenance, from around the world.

Other alternative assets are marketed to private investors either as hot tips or as additions to a diversified portfolio. The general rule is to avoid these areas unless you have specialist knowledge. Timber offers attractive tax concessions – and is therefore not very attractive to those who do not benefit from these concessions – and is in over-supply in Britain as a result of excessive tax advantages and subsidies in the past. Land with remote prospects of future planning permission for building has recently been widely marketed by 'advisers' – i.e., salespeople.

Buy wine, art, jewels or furniture if you like wine, art, jewels or furniture. While it is certainly possible to make money in these investments, the differences between buying and selling prices are wide, and there is none of the regulatory apparatus that protects small investors in securities markets. If you are expert, and even more if you are not, buy only collectable items you like.

Structured products

A structured product is a security whose risk and return characteristics have been created by financial engineering. Such engineering can take the form of packaging one security with others, splitting the risk and return from an asset into several components, combining a security with a derivative based on the same or another security or, frequently, a combination of all these methods. A synthetic investment resembles a fund, but the issuer does not hold the underlying assets to which its value is related; the risks may be hedged through derivatives (but need not be).

Financial engineering sounds complicated, and the legal and economic structure of these instruments is indeed complicated. But good financial engineering is like watchmaking. Its objective is to create products whose properties appear simple, even if the underlying mechanisms are not. Much financial engineering, however, is more like the skills of the illusionist: what the audience sees is not the reality.

The aim of financial engineering is either to increase the yield on bonds with little addition to risk or to reduce the risk in equity investment with little loss of return. I'll call these two basic types of security 'enhanced bonds' and 'protected equities'.

Protected equities came into vogue in the 1980s. The use of a derivative would reduce the risk of a share portfolio. A variant called 'portfolio insurance' involved a rolling programme of computerised trade known as 'dynamic hedging'. This mechanism came unstuck on 19 October 1987, when the US market fell sharply. Dynamic hedging triggered many sell orders. These led to further price falls, and many of the transactions that the trading strategies required simply could not be executed. Portfolio insurance aggravated market volatility and often failed to provide the 'insurance' its customers sought.

For several decades the main protected equity products

available to the retail investor were the with-profits funds of insurance companies. These policies sought not only to provide retail investors with a diversified portfolio – including equities, bonds and property – in a single purchase, but also to insulate the returns from short-term fluctuations in the value of investments. The company's actuaries would hold back profits in good times in order to support returns when markets fell.* But in the market setback of 2000 the smoothing process failed. The traditional with-profits model, no longer attractive to either savers or providers, has no long-term future.

Innovative new protected equity products are now widely marketed. This type of product might promise that your portfolio will never fall by, say, more than 5 per cent in a quarter. Another might give you a proportion of the upside (but not the downside) in the FTSE index over the life of the product. All of these instruments are constructed from packages of derivatives and can be divided into their underlying components. The first is an index fund combined with a put option; the second is a deposit combined with a call option.

Few retail products now offer, as life policies once did, a portfolio diversified across all asset categories. A new development is the lifecycle fund, which varies the asset composition of a portfolio according to the age of the holder. The mechanism assumes that most people want to reduce volatility (and will accept a lower return in consequence) as they get older. I'll discuss that proposition further in Chapter 11. Both protected equity and lifecycle products are worth considering by lazy and timid investors. But

---

* This scheme can work only if the companies involved maintain large reserves. As this type of investment is wound down, ownership of the reserves that companies built up from their with-profits funds – 'orphan assets' – is controversial. But competition forced companies hungry for new business to pay an increasing proportion of their investment returns. (In 1999–2000 Equitable Life, perhaps the best-regarded provider of these products, came close to collapse.)

you will always find it cheaper to achieve the same balance of risk and reward from your own diversified portfolio.

The enhanced bonds most frequently offered to retail investors are usually, and misleadingly, called 'guaranteed bonds', which are aggressively marketed by financial advisers. The guarantee applies to the income from the bond but not to the capital. The small print explains that you will usually get your capital back, but that you might not. Such securities are sometimes known as 'precipice bonds'. Another structured product designed to give the promise of high return is a 'kick-out bond'.

Decline offers of these products. The issuer of these bonds writes a complex derivative contract with an investment bank. The bank makes a payment but is entitled to receive a much larger sum if the complex combination of events described in the small print materialises (the 'punt'). The premium pays for the higher interest rate you are 'guaranteed' (and for the marketing expenses of the bond, which will be substantial).

The investment bank has done its own modelling and considers that the punt is a good deal. But if the punt is a good deal for the bank, it is a bad deal for you. It is very unlikely that you would buy this kind of complex gamble with negative expected value as a stand-alone product. Once again, you can apply the 'mind your portfolio' principle to the structured product by analysing its components. You will get to the same answer quickly and simply through two other principles: 'Why do I want to buy what they want to sell?' and 'Keep it simple'. Both these maxims are good guides in the world of structured products; both tell you not to go there.

If you adhere to the 'mind your portfolio' principle you will not want to buy structured products. The structured product alters the risk/return characteristics of individual investments. What matters to you is the risk/return characteristics of your overall portfolio. You can and should achieve the overall objectives – the balance of risk and return – by balancing your overall mix of investments and addressing the risk relevant to your own investment objectives. Mind your portfolio! You do not need funds or companies to gear or diversify on your behalf because you can do these things yourself. The best and cheapest way of limiting the risk in shares is to hold a lower proportion of your assets in shares.

But rigorous application of the 'mind your portfolio' principle is hard. Many intelligent investors will feel better if they limit the risk on the individual components of their portfolio as well as the risk on the whole portfolio. Others like the risk and return combination offered by particular structured products. One of the very first structured products, and still the one with most appeal to retail investors, is an enhanced bond from the British government. The premium bond was introduced in 1956 in showman style by the future Prime Minister, Harold Macmillan. The bond offers no income, only the chance to participate in a monthly prize draw. The premium bond is a combination of a deposit account and a lottery, and since the deposit rate is competitive and the lottery is fair, the combination is an attractive proposition for people who are interested in both holding bonds and entering lotteries.

This method of analysing a structured product unravels the financial engineering of the product's designers. The technique can also be applied to any structured product, and should be applied by anyone who adheres to the 'mind your portfolio' principle. Split the package into its component parts, and ask whether each component is something you would want to add to your portfolio.

A bond issued by a company will offer a higher return than a British government stock, but at a higher risk. Corporate bonds used to be the province only of institutional investors, but more recently some companies – either small ones trying to avoid the costs of traditional securities issuance or large ones well known to the public – have issued 'retail bonds' designed to appeal to small savers. For example, Tesco has issued a 5 per cent bond maturing in 2020, and an index-linked 2019 bond with an interest coupon of 1 per cent. These both trade at prices above their par value of £100 and have respective GRYs of around 3.6 per cent nominal and real zero respectively.

There is a greater possibility (though still not a very large one) that the company will default than that the British government will refuse to pay interest and principal as they fall due. The bonds are issued by Tesco Bank rather than the principal company, so if Tesco Bank fails to repay, you cannot raid Tesco stores and take your money in groceries, though you might think that a default would be so damaging to the reputation of the retail business that Tesco cannot allow it to happen.

But apply the component test. The 2020 Tesco bond has a GRY of about 2 per cent (often called 200 basis points) higher than the Treasury 2021 stock described in Chapter 3. Purchasing the Tesco security is equivalent to buying a completely safe bond and offering to insure the credit risk associated with Tesco. You promise to pay out £100 if Tesco defaults in return for a premium of 200p per annum. The margin has increased since the bond was issued in 2011 because the perceived credit risk attached to Tesco has increased.

Seen as a hybrid of bond and insurance, the deal sounds less attractive. You do not have the information needed to assess credit risk. Credit insurance is an activity whose returns are strongly correlated with your overall portfolio (a situation in which Tesco defaults on its bonds is likely to be one in which there is mayhem in other financial markets). The additional risk and return that the corporate bond implies relative to the government bond is probably not a risk you would add to your portfolio if it were offered on a stand-alone basis.

Many markets offer bundled products. Buy one, get the second half-price. Television programmes are sold as packages of channels. Buy coffee and croissant together. Eat the dishes on a *prix fixe* menu. The cost of the menu is typically less than the cost of the separate components. Not so in financial markets, where the cost of the structured product is generally higher than the cost of the components and the premium is the source of the financial engineer's profit. No one would buy a *table d'hôte* menu at a price higher than the sum of the same items on the *à la carte* menu. The premium also indicates that structured products are often bought (in my view, mostly bought) by people who misunderstand them. The analogy of the illusionist is more relevant than the analogy of the watchmaker.

The market for structured products illustrates many issues of information asymmetry. Asking 'Would I choose to buy each of the separate components of this package?' is an important discipline both in the restaurant and in financial markets, but especially in financial markets. Because structured products are often bought by people who are making mistakes, they are usually better bought second-hand.

Michael Milken used data on the past performance of bonds with high credit risk to create the junk bond market in the 1980s. But there was a difference between bonds that became junk – the distressed securities of good companies that had fallen on hard times – and those that were intended to be junk from the beginning. The fallen idols were often cheap because unwilling holders needed to be rid of their unsuccessful investments at almost any price. The sale might stave off embarrassing questions from bosses or trustees. Or it might be necessary because many investors are not allowed to hold low-quality bonds by regulatory constraint or internally imposed rule.

The newly minted junk bonds were in a different category. The potential holder always needs to ask the question 'Why do I want to buy what they want to sell?' These instruments failed the component test. The design of the gamble was unattractive. There was a small probability of large loss, and that loss correlated with a general market slide. The odds offered were poor, for the usual reason – the costs and fees of setting up the arrangements. When complex products fail, as in 2008, the reputation of similar securities becomes toxic.

When the securities have been sold to retail investors (and sometimes when they have been sold to professional investors), financial advisers risk being sued for having recommended the securities to clients for whom they were unsuitable. Often there were few, if any, clients for whom they had ever been suitable. The market value of these instruments may fall even below their fundamental value. But these complex products create more pitfalls than opportunities. If you are going to hold bonds, hold bonds. Complex financial engineering is expensive, and the expense is likely to be yours.

10

The Conventional Investor

Establish your portfolio

Every financial adviser is trained to begin by asking you to define your investment objectives and your attitude to risk. As your own financial adviser, you need to pose these questions to yourself. The professional adviser must tick boxes to complete the 'fact find' so he can move on to sell you products, having fulfilled his regulatory obligations. You really want to know the answers because they will determine your investment strategy.

Are you a net saver or a net spender? Are you building up assets to pay a deposit on a house, or to spend later, or to provide for your children's education or your own retirement? Or have you reached a stage at which your concern is with managing existing assets to support your standard of living? Most people before retirement are, or should be, net savers. Many people, after retirement, will be net spenders. People before retirement need to consider how much they can afford to save. People after retirement need to consider how much they can afford to spend.

If you gathered nuts for twenty-five years, and planned to retire for twenty-five years, you would need to set aside half your nuts for your old age (Table 8). If you can earn a return on your investment, you can save less. But at present long-term government bond rates are below 3 per cent. On this basis, you would need to save more than a third of your income. This is a calculation of great political and economic significance. Current interest rates render effective retirement planning funded by savings invested in long-term bonds more or less impossible.

As an investor planning for retirement, you have to aim for a higher rate of return, from 'risky' assets. If you achieve an 8 per cent target rate of return, 12.7 per cent of income will grow to a cache large enough to meet your needs. You can now eat more than 85 per cent of the nuts you collect.

Table 9: **Save now, spend later**

Percentage of income needed to maintain the same spending power in retirement with a saving/spending period each of twenty-five years						
Realised rate of return (p.a.)	10%	8%	6%	4%	2%	0
Percentage of income required to save	8.5	12.7	19.0	27.3	37.9	50.0
Percentage of income available to spend	91.5	87.3	81.0	72.7	62.1	50.0

Every 2 per cent that you gain or lose in investment return will make a big difference. You can sacrifice more than 2 per cent through poor investment performance, bad timing of sales and purchases or unsuitable allocation across investment categories. You might (but need not) lose 2 per cent in tax, and you might (but need not) lose another 2 per cent by paying more than you need in fees and charges. And you might (but need not) lose 2 per cent, or more, by making large allocations to assets that advisers describe as low-risk investments which offer lower but more predictable returns.

In this and the following chapters I will describe how you can minimise the leakage of return under each of these headings. I'll suggest how to turn the timing of investments to your advantage, and how to approach asset allocation and stock selection. I'll direct you to the most tax-efficient forms of investment. I'll stress the importance of keeping down costs and charges, and explain how to do it. And I will offer practical guidance on how to think about risk and uncertainty based on the principles outlined in Chapters 7 and 8. The lesson of that discussion is that you don't necessarily have to accept low returns to achieve low risk. If risk is defined as failure to meet realistic objectives, then reconciling yourself to low returns is a high-risk strategy, not a low-risk one. Defining your investment objectives leads to your – subjective – definition of risk.

Chapter 2 described the essential preliminaries to intelligent investment – listing assets and liabilities, reviewing your banking arrangements and your mortgage. Now you need a stockbroker. Most people still have an image of the stockbroker derived from the days before players replaced gentlemen: grand but seedy; with good social skills and connections; streetwise but not clever; well off but not hard-working. These people still exist, mostly outside London, but are a dying breed. They have been superseded by wealth management, or 'private banking', services that banks and brokers offer to well-heeled clients. Many readers of this book will not even qualify. These services will levy annual management charges or substantial commissions on purchases and sales, or both. They are expensive. You will find it much better value to buy yourself a nice lunch than to let wealth managers entertain you to one.

There is now a digital alternative to the wealth manager: the robot-adviser. The robot-adviser is an online service that does not need expensive premises, employ salespeople dressed in expensive suits, invite you to Ascot or make excessive charges. A robot-adviser (such as Nutmeg, to whom I am an adviser) will build you a diversified portfolio cheaply. If you are seriously nervous about taking any of your own investment decisions, this approach will allow you to forget about your savings. But if you have got this far through this book, you should be willing, and equipped, to manage a portfolio yourself.

Your stockbroker should be an online share-dealing service. The Retail Distribution Review has – as regulation so often does – made life more complex in the short term, but has helped bring fund charges down and in the long run may lead to a simpler and more transparent environment for the retail investor. You need an execution-only service, in which you make decisions and give instructions yourself. These services are cheap, because computers do most of the work. Unless your savings are very small, you should aim for a service that offers trades at around £10 and charges a flat fee rather than a percentage of the value of your portfolio. This flat fee should not be more than £100 or so a year, and it should be reduced if you trade. You should also look for a provider who offers access to good indexed funds – such as Vanguard – without charging you a percentage of your investment for doing so. At the time of writing, Alliance Trust Savings ticks these boxes, but you should make some up-to-the-minute comparisons.

The securities that you buy will be held electronically in the nominee account of a bank or other financial institution. If the regulations are complied with, your savings will be safe, but I am less convinced than I would like to be of the guaranteed effectiveness of these arrangements. The Financial Services Compensation Scheme protects the first £75,000 of investment through any individual firm. In practice, as proved to be the case with Northern Rock and other failed banks, official intervention will probably ensure you do not lose out. But if your portfolio is large, you might consider splitting it between different providers (you could have your SIPP, ISA and general portfolio with different institutions) or using the option allowed by a few firms (such as Charles Stanley) of holding shares in your own name through the Stock Exchange's electronic Crest system. You can obtain paper certificates, but there are much higher costs and other practical disadvantages.

When you set up your brokerage account, you will want to take advantage of the substantial tax exemptions available to retail investors. These have been substantially increased since the first edition of this book. An ISA (Individual Savings Account) is free of tax on income or capital gains. A SIPP (Self-Invested Personal Pension) allows you to roll forward the money you invest in it free of income or capital gains tax, and additionally gives you tax relief on your annual contribution. The maximum investment in an ISA is £15,240 a year, rising to £20,000 in 2017. Platforms offer self-select ISAs at low or no cost. The new 'lifetime ISA' will extend this favourable treatment still further and add a government bonus; this scheme is designed for younger people saving towards a house purchase or retirement.

The limits for investment in a SIPP are higher, but the rules on contributions, once fairly simple, seem to be made more complex every year. The corollary is that the rules for taking money out have been relaxed, with the overriding constraint that normally you cannot make any withdrawal until you are fifty-five (SIPPs are designed for retirement savings).

If you are a member of an occupational pension scheme provided by your employer, the limits on your SIPP contributions are reduced on account of the benefits of the occupational scheme. As a result of the new auto-enrolment state provisions currently being introduced, everyone in employment in the UK will have some pension associated with their work by 2017. But the prescribed contribution levels for this new compulsory state scheme are very low. You should plan to have your own SIPP. You are entitled to opt out of your employer's scheme and transfer its value to your SIPP; you will not normally want to do this while your employer is contributing to your occupational pension, but you may well want to exercise this option at retirement. Nevertheless, the tax advantages and simplified administration of a SIPP make it attractive to navigate the constraints and contribute as much to a SIPP as you are allowed.

Although irksome and in some respects complex, these restrictions on contributions are not very constraining for someone planning to build up savings for retirement. ISAs and SIPPs both enhance returns and simplify administration, and the two schemes complement each other. If you are planning to build up your savings slowly, you should focus on an ISA and benefit from its flexibility. Anyone building a larger portfolio should begin with an ISA but expect to place a significant fraction into a SIPP.

You may have to pay tax on savings outside the scope of ISAs and SIPPs. But you are now able to receive £5,000 of dividends and £500 of interest tax-free. On any excess over these limits, a higher-rate taxpayer pays tax on dividends at 32.5 per cent and on interest at 40 per cent. The practical consequence is that in future a couple should be able over fifteen years to accumulate well over £1 million in tax-free vehicles if their income is sufficient to allow them to save this amount.

While securities will be the main component of your investment portfolio, the 'mind your portfolio' principle implies that you should consider insurance at the same time as you contemplate investment. You should think probabilities when you take out insurance. But your insurance company will also think probabilities, and it knows probabilities well. That is its business.

You should be detached. While it is vexing to have your television stolen, or to lose your bag on holiday, insurance will not bring back either your television or your bag. The financial loss from a stolen television or a lost bag is probably less than the loss you will incur on a bad day on the stock market. Much of the premium on policies that insure against these minor contingencies goes not to pay policyholders but in the administrative costs of small claims.

So anyone who is truly minding their portfolio, and recognises that the insurance company has calculated the expected value of their policy, will insure only things they cannot afford to lose. You need insurance against your house burning down, but not to replace the bedroom carpet; you need insurance against being hospitalised in the United States, but not for the cost of an extra night's hotel accommodation because your plane is delayed.

Many people find this advice difficult to accept. Insurers observe that their customers have little appetite for policies that rarely pay out, even though low-probability risks are precisely those for which insurance is appropriate. Policyholders like the reassurance of occasional small cheques even if such cheques add up to much less than their premiums.

You will be financially better off if you can 'think SEU' and learn to control these emotions, but it is difficult, even for people educated in intelligent investment, to exercise such control. Regret is a powerful human emotion, even if often an unproductive one. If you can't refrain from kicking yourself, or if your spouse can't refrain from kicking you, when an uninsured television set is stolen, then you should take out the policy. This strategy is, however, likely to cost you money – even after taking account of the insurance companies' cheques.

Pay less

Over the fifty years that Warren Buffett has been in charge of Berkshire Hathaway, the company has earned an average compound rate of return of over 20 per cent per year. For Buffett himself. But also for his investors. The lucky people who have been his fellow shareholders through all that time have enjoyed just the same rate of return as he has. The fortune he has accumulated is the result of the rise in the value of his share of the collective fund.

Suppose that Buffett had deducted from the returns on his own investment – his own, not that of his fellow shareholders

– a notional investment management fee, based on the standard '2 per cent annual charge and 20 per cent of gains' formula of the hedge fund and private equity businesses. There would then be two pots: one created by reinvestment of the fees Buffett was charging himself and one created by the growth in the value of Buffett's own original investment. Call the first pot the wealth of Buffett Investment Management, the second pot the wealth of the Buffett Foundation.

How much of Buffett's $70 billion would be the property of Buffett Investment Management and how much the property of the Buffett Foundation? The – completely astonishing – answer is that Buffett Investment Management would have $64 billion and the Buffett Foundation $6 billion. The cumulative effect of 'two and twenty' over fifty years is so large that the earnings of the investment manager completely overshadow the earnings of the investor. That calculation tells you why it was the giants of the financial services industry, not the customers, who owned the yachts.

The least risky way to increase the returns from your financial investments is to minimise agency costs – to ensure that the return on the underlying investments goes into your own pocket rather than someone else's. The effect of charges on investments is so large that it is as important to understand the structure of charges as the principles of investment analysis. The first charge that hits you when you invest is the spread between the buying price and the selling price. For government bonds and for blue chip shares, such as Vodafone, this spread will be extremely small, and you can deal at any time in any quantity you like. The only other dealing costs are commission (you should expect to pay less than £15 for an internet deal) and government stamp duty on shares, which is 0.5 per cent. The total cost of making and realising an investment of £10,000 in a FTSE 100 company should be less than £100 (1 per cent).

Small companies are different. The spread between buying and selling prices may be 3 per cent or 4 per cent. Even a purchase of £10,000 may require a telephone call rather than a mouse click, and telephone orders will usually entail higher commission. The difference between what it will cost you to buy and what you will get if you sell could be as much as 5 per cent.

The effect of these costs on returns depends on the frequency with which you deal. Online trading is so inexpensive and easy that you may be tempted to trade often. Only one thing eats up investment returns faster than fees and commissions, and that is frequent trading. Do not succumb. Do not accept the invitation to subscribe to direct market access. The total costs of running your own portfolio should be less than 1 per cent per year.

Investing in actively managed funds will cost you more. The choice of funds available, both open- and closed-end, is unbelievably wide. There are more funds investing in shares than there are shares to invest in. This situation doesn't make sense, and is both cause and effect of the high charges. Costs need to be high to recover the expenses of running so many different, mainly small, funds that all do much the same thing. At the same time, the high level of charges encourages financial services companies to set up even more funds.

Table 10: **Available UK retail investment funds, at end-2015**

Asset class (%)	Number of funds	Average size (£m)	Median total expense ratio
Sterling bonds	82	570	0.8
Global bonds	82	501	1.1
UK equities	267	181	1.5
Global equities	201	400	1.6
Japanese equities	54	384	1.7
North American equities	97	474	1.7

Source: ThomsonReutersLipper

The proliferation of funds means that choosing a fund may be no easier than choosing individual investments. You can hire an adviser to recommend funds. There are also many advisers. The problem seems to multiply itself, as do the fees. The size of the fees attracts more advisers, and so on.

If you own a mainstream British unit trust for five years, it is possible that the direct and indirect costs and charges you incur in buying, holding and selling that investment will total 3 per cent a year. Other investment funds may cost you more. The total charges on a fund of hedge funds are such that it might yield less than a government bond even if the underlying investments returned more than 10 per cent per year.

Costs and charges for funds fall into three broad categories:

- Annual costs of managing and administering the investment. Regulated investment funds must quote this figure, formerly called the total expense ratio (TER), but now described as the ongoing charges ratio.
- Costs and charges incurred in buying and selling your investment, which include initial fees, commission charges, and any difference between the quoted buying and selling price. The effect of these charges on your annual return depends on the length of time for which you hold the investment.

The expected reduction in yield (ERY) is the sum of the first and second of these costs, under a specified assumption about the length of the period for which you hold the fund. The ERY may also include some part of the third cost heading:

- Costs incurred by the fund manager and charged against the value of the fund (e.g., commission on the manager's transactions and the difference between the buying and selling prices of the underlying securities).

Annual management charges range from 0.1 per cent or 0.2 per cent for some indexed funds to 2 per cent or more for an insurance policy-linked fund or a hedge fund. Other administrative costs will usually be between 0.2 per cent and 0.4 per cent. If you buy a fund of funds that invests in other funds, you may have to pay more than one level of these charges. Some funds also charge a performance fee, which gives the managers a share of any profit, or of outperformance relative to a benchmark. If you buy one of the funds commonly recommended to neophyte investors, you will probably end up in an open-ended fund, or life assurance bond, linked to a selection of mainstream UK shares.

Probably to your detriment. Table 11 describes the median performance of UK investment funds. The median UK equity fund underperformed its benchmark by around 1 per cent per year over five and ten years. Bond funds were worse, and only property funds offered any glint of outperformance.

Table 11: **Relative performance of UK retail investment funds, 2005–15**

Median cumulative outperformance (percentage figures) relative to relevant sector benchmark to 31 December 2015	5 years	10 years
£ Corporate bond	−4.30	−15.18
UK gilt	−5.42	−11.00
UK All companies	−5.79	−8.67
UK property	0.87	−3.04

Source: ThomsonReutersLipper

You may be tempted to think that, even if you can manage your UK investments yourself, you need to find a manager to invest overseas. The thought is wise, the conclusion not. If UK investors struggle in other markets, so do UK fund managers, particularly in the largest overseas market, the United States (Table 12). You will normally do better to diversify overseas through a passive vehicle.

Table 12: **Relative performance of UK retail investment funds in non-UK asset categories, 2005–15**

Median cumulative outperformance (percentage figures) relative to relevant sector benchmark to 31 December 2015	5 years	10 years
Global equities	1.7	–0.4
Global bond	0.3	–11.9
North American equities	–15.3	–32.2
Japanese equities	–1.0	–7.0

Source: ThomsonReutersLipper

Of course, half of all funds do better than the median. But the data in Tables 7 and 8 in Chapter 8 suggests that persistent outperformance is rare. As Table 13 demonstrates, your chance of finding a fund that persistently outperforms its benchmark is low. The clear lesson is that the representative UK retail open-ended fund does not provide performance to justify its charges and that most fund managers have little or no investment skill.

Table 13: **Percentage of sterling-denominated open-ended funds outperforming relevant index (at December 2015)**

	Over 5 years	Over 10 years
UK equity	47	28
European equity	42	27
Global equity	10	11
Emerging markets equity	26	15
US equity	5	5

Source: S&P Dow Jones SPIVA survey.

Many supposedly actively managed funds are closet-indexed – although they claim to be actively managed, their composition is very close to the make-up of the UK index. That minimises the risk – to the manager – that the fund will significantly under-perform the market. If the largest holdings are BP, Shell, HSBC, Vodafone and Glaxo, the fund is closet-indexed. You can achieve a similar result much more cheaply yourself, and you should.

How can so much be charged for so little? The underlying problem is one of information asymmetry. The marketing of financial services emphasises quality, not price, and for good reasons. You don't want to be operated on by a surgeon who says that he is not the best, but that he is cheap. It would be worth paying more – a lot more – to get a good fund manager. But since it is hard to identify a good fund manager, good and bad managers all charge high fees, with the consequences described above. It is hard to escape the dilemma posed by this market inefficiency.

The basis of charging for funds for retail investors is currently changing as a result of the retail distribution review (RDR), which puts further pressure on financial services firms to make their charges explicit. The market is changing rapidly as a result of these regulatory innovations. But whatever the outcome, you should ensure that for UK investments you do not pay an initial charge, or only a nominal one, that you do not pay a management charge of more than 0.5 per cent p.a. and that the total of charges does not exceed 1 per cent p.a.

In the United States the Vanguard group, a not-for-profit company with a messianic founder, John Bogle, has become market leader in retail fund management with charges substantially lower than the US, or UK, norm. Vanguard principally offers passive funds. Today the largest providers of retail funds in the US are specialist asset managers such as BlackRock, Vanguard and Fidelity. These specialised businesses do not suffer the conflicts of interest inherent in the cross-selling of retail products or the simultaneous provision of investment banking services to companies in which the funds invest. In the UK (and even more in continental Europe) banks have a large share of the funds market, typically with high management fees. However, the worst US fund managers are greedier, and probably more corrupt, than their British counterparts.

In 2009 Vanguard established an operation in the UK. This is still small, partly because Vanguard has imposed a £100,000 minimum investment. However, it is possible to access their funds with much smaller amounts through the platforms of Alliance Trust Savings and Bestinvest (up-to-date details should be available from Vanguard's web site). The most attractive equity-based funds for small investors are generally indexed funds and investment trusts (closed-end funds) with low charges and significant discounts to underlying asset value. I'll discuss these options in more detail later, and also the – necessarily more expensive – options available for property investment. These funds provide sufficient choice for normal purposes. All of them can be accessed through your online execution-only share-dealing account.

The conventional investor's portfolio

Where to begin? Many people will sensibly start the job of being their own investment manager as conventional investors. The conventional investor is hesitant to trust his or her own judgement, and prefers to rely on the consensus of professional opinion. The conventional investor is probably hesitant to 'think SEU' and is still not quite convinced that a share such as Robb Caledon is part of a low-risk investment portfolio. I shall describe a strategy for the conventional investor and then suggest how that strategy might be developed by those who are more ready to use their own judgement.

Even twenty or thirty years ago the commonest form of long-term saving was through the investment funds of life assurance companies, which managed a complete range of investments – shares, bonds and property. In this way the conventional investor could hand over investment allocation decisions to a fund manager. But recent returns on with-profits policies have been poor, the basis on which returns are determined opaque, and these policies are no longer attractive investments (except to those who sell them). Even conventional investors must now make some asset allocation decisions of their own.

Large institutions that are conventional investors get advice on asset allocation from consultants, such as Mercer or Willis Towers Watson. Most of these firms originated as actuarial practices (actuaries measure the liabilities of insurance companies or pension funds) and have broadened their business activities. Consultants will usually base their advice on portfolio models of the Markowitz variety and on their knowledge of what other similarly placed investors are doing. The activities of consultants are a means of disseminating conventional thinking.

The public reports described in Chapter 2 show what these conventional investors do. In 2012 the average local authority pension fund held between 60 and 65 per cent of its portfolio in shares as a result of the decisions of its managers and trustees, with their consultants. Slightly less than half of these shares were in UK companies, the balance in foreign equities. The typical pension fund held 15 to 20 per cent in bonds, 5 to 10 per cent in property and around 10 per cent in cash and other assets.

The conventional investor can simply and cheaply replicate the portfolio of these institutions with a sum as small as £10,000. The share components can be purchased through either an index tracking unit trust or exchange traded fund. If you want to retain the home country bias characteristic of conventional investors you will want to hold a significant proportion of the equity element of your portfolio in UK shares. That implies a UK index tracker. The balance should go into a fund which invests in developed world equities excluding the UK. Vanguard offer both types of funds with an ongoing charges ratio of 0.15%. You might choose to divide £6500 equally between these two funds.

Two thousand pounds is earmarked for bonds. You may be able to hold bonds in your internet stockbroker's account, but some basic dealing services do not offer this option. You can buy British government stock online through the Debt Management Office. But – absurdly – you may actually find it cheaper to buy a fund, and Vanguard give you access to a global bond fund which gives you diversification across a range of currencies and maturities.

Finally, there is £1,000 for property. You are not going to buy a property of your own for £1,000, so your choice is between funds. The simplest way is to buy shares in a closed-end fund. When I started writing this book, these funds were at a premium, but as the book was completed they were at substantial discounts to the reported value of the underlying property. The two largest British property companies, Land Securities and British Land, each own a diversified range of prime properties, mostly in the UK. The shares of these companies are mostly held by institutional investors.

And that is it. You have £500 left for cash, rounding, or more adventurous choices. With four clicks of a mouse you have a diversified portfolio similar to that adopted by a well-advised large investment fund with long-term aspirations to total return. And you have constructed it at low initial and ongoing cost. You can safely forget about this portfolio for a long time – years if you like. Your investments may or may not do well, but their performance will most likely be similar to, but better than, the balanced portfolio a consultant or adviser would construct on your behalf. Similar to, because it reproduces the balanced portfolio of the conventional institutional investor; better than, because you have greatly reduced the costs of establishment and management.

You should have aspirations to do better still. The conventional investor should consider separating a part of his or her portfolio in order to test his or her own judgement. You might begin with that £500. As experience and confidence grow, the plan is to devote more and more funds to intelligent investment.

11

The Intelligent
Investor's Strategy

Developing a strategy

Conventional investors – often tacitly, sometimes knowingly – employ a conventional approach to risk, based on SEU. In that approach, risk has the same meaning for everyone: i.e. short-term volatility. The well-advised conventional investor finds a balance between risk and return by selecting a point on the 'efficient frontier' described by Harry Markowitz. The appropriate choice of the point on the frontier depends on your 'risk appetite' or 'risk tolerance'. Risk has a market price, determined by the average risk appetite of all investors. A financial adviser will quiz you to establish your 'risk tolerance'; this interrogation is an essential part of the 'know your client' exercise which all financial advisers and investment consultants must undertake.

Actually, most conventional investors do not really think this way: they mostly follow conventional wisdom and do what other people in loosely similar situations do. When Markowitz was asked how he had invested his own retirement savings, he replied:

I should have compared the historical advantages of the asset classes and drawn an efficient frontier. Instead, I visualised my grief if the stock market went way up and I wasn't in it, or if it went down and I was completely in it. My intention was to minimise my future regret. So I split my contributions 50/50 between bonds and equities.*

For the intelligent investor, risk is *not* short-term volatility of asset prices. Risk is failure to meet realistic aspirations. So the intelligent investor needs to begin by defining his or her investment goals. Every individual has different objectives, but the purposes of investment generally fall into a few broad categories. Most people need to save for retirement. You may want to save for some other specific purpose: to make a deposit on a house, or to buy a secondary property, or to fund your children through college or help them buy their own apartment. You may have a lump sum to invest, perhaps from inheritance or from the sale of a property or business. A cautious person will not want to splurge it right away but hopes to earn returns in order to enjoy a more comfortable standard of living in future. Or you may have no very clear objective in mind – you are saving for a rainy day, or perhaps for a sunny one.

Whatever his or her objectives, the intelligent investor thinks total return. In Chapter 2 I suggested that 8 per cent was an appropriate target for that total return – a figure which includes both income and capital gains, but is measured before allowing for tax and inflation. But the intelligent investor should plan around another, lower, rate of return figure – the prudent spending rate. How much can you draw from your investments without impairing their long-term capacity to allow you to maintain or increase the level of expenditure to which you have become accustomed?

The prudent spending rate is a key concept for the trustees

---

* Interview reported by Jason Zweig 2008.

of endowments: the managers of the Norwegian oil fund, the overseers of the Harvard endowment, the trustees of the Gates Foundation. Because sophisticated investors like these think total return, they are no longer bound, either legally or in their own planning, by the traditional convention that you should match your spending to the income you receive – the total of the dividends, interest, rents, etc., arising year by year. But faced with considerable volatility of total return as a result of gyrations in market prices, they have to make decisions as to how much it is provident to spend. And so will you. If you have built up a fund for retirement, or benefited from a windfall, you will need to construct a portfolio of assets and decide how much you can safely withdraw each year.

The definition of income given by the economist John Hicks provides the starting point. Hicks defined 'a man's income as the maximum value which he can consume during a week, and still expect to be as well off at the end of the period as he was at the beginning' (Hicks, 1946, p. 172). (The sexism is remarkable since Hicks's formidable wife was a much better practical manager than her husband.) So if you plan for an 8 per cent total return, and achieve it, you could spend 8 per cent of the value of your portfolio each year and still meet Hicks's test.

Well, not quite. First, 8 per cent is a target, not money in the bank. Prudence suggests you should plan on the basis of a lower return, and therefore spend less. Second, taxes will eat into your total return. I've suggested you might allow 2 per cent for that, giving a realistic target return of 6 per cent. Third, inflation will erode the value of your assets. Even if prices rise at only 2 per cent per annum, you will need to earn a 2 per cent total return simply to stand still. Taking these factors of prudence, tax and inflation together, you might conclude that spending 3–4 per cent of assets each year would be consistent with Hicks's test. This is the sort of prudent spending rate widely used by sophisticated charitable funds such as university endowments. US foundations are required to spend 5 per cent of the value of their assets each year. This is to prevent the establishment of trusts such as the Netherlands foundation of Ingvar Kamprad, the fabulously wealthy Swedish founder of IKEA, which spends very little and grows indefinitely in value. The prudent spending rate should be a little less than your target rate, converted into a real post-tax rate of return, and should be revised from time to time in line with experience.

As an individual, you might choose a prudent spending rate a little higher than 3–4 per cent. Trustees must be more conservative than individuals. Universities hope to exist for ever. When a US agent asked us for how long St John's College had been investing in real estate, we were able to respond, 'More than 450 years'. You, however, are mortal. Ben Franklin famously remarked that only two things were inevitable: death and taxes. For individuals, both are inevitable; for charitable institutions, neither applies. In setting a target rate of return, you might plausibly conclude that one roughly offsets the other. You can spend more than a fund with an indefinite time horizon, because you are mortal and there is no point in being the richest person in the graveyard; but you are probably subject to heavier taxation than the endowment. Older people, therefore, might be a little less conservative than younger ones – conventional wisdom tends to have it the other way round. Enjoy those round-the-world cruises!

Buying an annuity was a traditional method of providing for security in old age by converting a lump sum into a fixed lifetime income. In the modern world these investments are not attractive. Annuity rates are poor, because of high charges and investment strategies that focus on individually low-risk assets. There is also the problem of moral hazard created by information asymmetry. Annuities are bought by people in good health, not people with low life expectancies. Purchasers of annuities are more long-lived than the population as a whole. So a man aged sixty-five can expect to live another seventeen years, but an annuity for him will today yield, before tax, less than 6 per cent and, if linked to inflation, less than 4 per cent. These are rates available in dollars or sterling; an annuity in euros may offer 1 per cent less. These figures are below a realistic target rate of return even without any drawdown of capital.

Reviewing your goals

Let's turn now to these various categories of investment purpose: relevant planning, saving for a specific goal, prudent management of a lump sum, and 'rainy day' saving.

Retirement planning is critical for almost every household, and even young ones must give it thought. At the beginning of the last chapter I offered an illustrative calculation of what you might need to save. You might want to make a similar calculation based on your own circumstances. You will want to tweak the figures in many ways. You will probably need less in retirement than in your working lifetime. You are likely to spend less, you will pay less tax and you will have some other sources of pension income.

Readers of this book are, on average, healthier than average, so your plan should cover at least twenty-five years of retirement.* But – if you can – you should also plan to save for more than twenty-five years before retirement, to benefit from the extraordinary power of compounding returns. Your capacity to save may increase over time, along with your income. You may already have some assets which can be invested more effectively. Your calculation needs to be tailored to your particular circumstances.

This is the sort of problem that a model helps to solve. Remember that no such calculation will be true; like any model, it gives

---

*Seriously. Life expectancy increases with education and income level.

you the 'right' answer to the arithmetic problem, but not necessarily to the substantive problem – there are too many unknown unknowns. But the exercise can be illuminating and will help to illustrate whether your hopes and plans are feasible. You may want to use one of many useful programs on the internet. But with simple arithmetic you – or your children or grandchildren – should be able to construct a spreadsheet to calculate what you should aim to save for your retirement.

If your investment goal is a specific purchase, the lowest-risk method of achieving that objective may be to buy it now, even if you have to borrow. If you accept that risk is failure to achieve your realistic investment objectives, then both the financial difficulty that may follow excessive ambition and the inability to achieve your financial goals that may result from overly modest aspirations are risks. You will have to balance the risk that servicing the borrowing will prove difficult against the risk that you will not be able to afford to make the purchase in future. We are taught to regard the former, but not the latter, as a risk – to shun failure, but to accept disappointment. But both are sources of unhappiness and regret. The 'mind your portfolio' principle tells you that leverage is not always risky.

If you cannot, or do not want, to achieve your goal immediately, then you may be able to hedge it in whole or part. Buying a property – a secondary residence for yourself or an apartment for your children – is a common investment objective. The clearer you are about the characteristics of such a property, the better placed you are to hedge. Buy-to-let property may be relevant. If you are determined to buy a house in France, then you can bias your portfolio towards property and assets denominated in euros. Another common specific investment objective is to fund the education of your family. There are many schemes to help you do this. Take advantage of any tax breaks offered, but do not pay initial commissions or high ongoing charges to access these schemes. DIY will often be the best route.

The cautious investor of a lump sum will build a diversified portfolio of the kind I will describe below, but should not aim to do so immediately. Gradual investment, drip-feeding your funds into your portfolio, will allow you to benefit from 'dollar cost averaging', a potent 'get rich slow' scheme which I will also describe below.

For the lump sum investor looking to supplement earnings from investment income, determination of the prudent spending rate is critical. Of course, you may not want to spread the benefit over the whole of your life, but the calculation of a prudent spending rate provides a key benchmark. You may well find that annual interest and dividends are less than your prudent spending rate. If so, you will need to sell assets from time to time if your expenditure is in line with your prudent spending rate.

You may find this hard. The notion that a cautious person spends no more than his or her income is firmly ingrained in our culture, and for good reasons. A wise farmer would divide the crop into the amount that should feed his family and provide for their clothes and education – the income – and the amount – the capital – that should be planted for next year's crop. But principles that worked well on the land do not necessarily serve us well in a world of swaps and derivatives. Habits honed by evolution can be costly. It requires discipline to resist mental accounting. One mechanism for challenging this mental accounting is to set up an automatic transfer from your broker's account to your bank.

And then there is the 'rainy day' saver. The most attractive financial goal for most people is to know that no likely contingency will cause financial embarrassment. While your own circumstances will be particular to you, the meaning of financial security for most readers of this book is confidence about their future standard of living. There are several threats to the achievement of such security through an investment portfolio. The portfolio may decline in monetary value through market risk or credit risk. The monetary value of the portfolio may lose its purchasing power through inflation risk. I will discuss below how to control these risks through diversification, emphasis on long-time horizons and a focus on real assets.

But beyond these known unknowns, the world is also uncertain. There are many historical instances of people who thought they had secured their financial future but who were proved wrong. Wealthy central Europeans, who had never expected to work for a living, discovered in the economic turbulence of the 1920s that they had lost all they had, because banks failed or because hyperinflation made their savings worthless. Prosperous Jews thought that owning their own houses gave them security, but discovered that they would have been better off with assets overseas when Nazi persecution made it impossible for them to enjoy their German property.

Many people pay a high price for the appearance of certainty – docile citizens of East Germany, or the people who accepted dull jobs in large corporations in the belief that their jobs were for life. Both groups discovered that the certainty they craved was illusory. To take control of one's own life or financial affairs may seem to create uncertainty, but taking control is a prerequisite of security in a world that is inescapably uncertain.

It is impossible to eliminate financial worries altogether, as those twentieth-century European households discovered. More recently, Mikhail Khodorkovsky and Boris Berezovsky became billionaires in the 1990s as oligarchs prospered from the collapse of the Soviet state. But both these individuals fell out with the Putin regime. Khodorkovsky spent ten years in prison. Berezovsky, who had fled to London, was engaged for years in ruinous litigation with another oligarch, Roman Abramovich, until, bankrupt, Berezovsky was found hanged in unexplained circumstances in 2013. Such vicissitudes of fortune have been the experience of many oligarchs throughout history.

A few investment gurus, harbingers of the apocalypse, recommend gold bars, or the equivalent, which can be cashed in the event of financial collapse. Barton Biggs, Morgan Stanley's long-term naysayer, urged everyone to have 'a farm or a ranch somewhat far off the beaten track but which you can get to quickly and easily'. This is not a realistic recommendation for most people. But there are episodes in history in which coins or jewellery have literally been lifesavers.

Diversification is the key to managing risk

The conventional investor believes that there is a trade-off between risk and return. This is another aphorism that is sometimes illuminating, but often untrue. The assumption of trade-off gives insufficient attention to the 'mind your portfolio' principle. Even if high risk and high expected returns were indissolubly associated at the level of the individual security, it does not follow that the same relationship holds in a portfolio. You cannot measure the risk of a portfolio by simply aggregating the risks of individual investments.

A portfolio that consists of a collection of idiosyncratic but individually risky investments, such as Robb Caledon, can be a low-risk portfolio. Such a portfolio may carry a lower risk, in fact, than a collection of blue chips – stocks which are individually safe, but whose returns are likely to be strongly correlated with each other. For the intelligent investor, risk is a characteristic of a portfolio, rather than of the individual security. This is the illuminating insight of the capital asset pricing model, and that insight remains valid independently of reservations about the truth of the CAPM.

In fact, the insight is profitable for investors precisely because the capital asset pricing model is not true. The pattern of returns on different assets reflects other people's views of risk, uncertainty and security. The risk premium they offer is the product of the average of other people's attitudes to risk. But other people's attitudes to risk are different from yours. They avoid mistakes for which they might be criticised. They are wedded to benchmarks. They focus on the riskiness of individual assets, rather than on the risk of their overall portfolio. Their mistakes, or at least their different approaches to risk, provide your opportunities.

Conventional investors regard risk as short-term volatility of return, but the intelligent investor has a different conception of risk. *Your risk is your failure to meet your realistic aspirations.* Your strategy is the product of your long-term investment goals, and the longer your time horizon, the better the opportunities for you to achieve satisfying combinations of risk and return.

Suppose the premium which volatile assets command over what are conventionally described as risk-free assets is 4 per cent, a common assumption for the size of the equity premium. The magnitude of this figure reflects these conventional investors' fear of short-term fluctuations in the value of their assets. Suppose also the standard deviation of annual equity returns is 15 per cent (approximately the historical average). Then, over the next week, the expected return on an equity investment is less than 0.1 per cent more than the risk-free asset.

And the spread of outcomes is much wider: that follows from the way risk has been defined. Even Warren Buffett and George Soros lose money most days. If the distribution of returns is normal – a reasonable assumption over one week – then there is almost a 50 per cent chance that the 'risk-free' asset will do better. Over a year, however, the expected value of the additional return from volatile assets is 4 per cent and the probability that there will be *some* additional return to compensate for not has risen to around 60 per cent.*

---

*This calculation assumes that the distribution of returns is normal and that successive period returns are independent. As I have explained, there are good reasons for scepticism about both these assumptions. These illustrative figures should be treated as illuminating rather than accurate.

Stretch the time horizon to twenty-five years, and the divergence becomes much greater. The expected value of the 'risky' portfolio is 167 per cent higher. If the distribution of returns is normal, this 167 per cent advantage is also the median and the modal outcome. Only the very lowest percentiles of the distribution of volatile returns will fall short of the returns on the 'safe' asset. In fact, you will do better in the 'risky' asset on almost 99 per cent of occasions. And the longer the time horizon, the more certain it is that volatile assets will outperform (on the assumptions above about risk premium and volatility). The notion that cash and short-dated bonds are less risky than more volatile assets is the product of the confusion between certainty and security identified in Chapter 7.

Moreover, we have seen that there is no such thing as a risk-free asset. Extreme percentiles of the distribution of outcomes are typically generated not by risks but from uncertainties. These extreme events are sometimes the result of very low probability risks incorporated in models – the risk that a fair coin comes up heads twenty times in a row. But disastrous outcomes are most often a consequence of the large-scale breakdown of social, political and economic institutions: the Russian Revolution, the hyperinflation of the Weimar Republic and the lawlessness of the Nazi regime which followed, and, as I am writing this, the breakdown of the Venezuelan state. It is events such as these, rather than runs of bad luck, which are most likely to destroy the value of an investment portfolio.

Even in Britain, such institutional breakdown was within sight on three occasions in the last century: in 1931, when the Great Depression threatened political stability; in 1940, when Britain faced the real prospect of hostile invasion; and in 1974, when securities markets collapsed as a weak government presided over inflation and labour unrest that seemed out of control. The United States weathered the political and economic crisis that had closed the nation's banks as Franklin Roosevelt was inaugurated President in 1933; but the survival of the US market economy was no foregone conclusion. In these latter cases, breakdown was averted. But in none was the margin so wide as to suggest that collapse was inconceivable.

Since distributions of investment outcomes have fat tails, especially at the lower ends of the distribution, even the most conventional portfolio can suffer from events which fall far short of these apocalyptic outcomes. The financial failures with which we are more recently familiar – the 1987 crash, the credit crisis of 2007–8, defaults of Greek debt – represent bad, but not extreme, percentiles of potentially predictable risk distributions (although, as Mr Viniar revealed, even these events were not within the range of possibilities contemplated by Goldman Sachs's risk models*). Big upsets come from even milder crises – the Asian collapse of 1997–8 or the bursting of the New Economy bubble. All these events, however, are sufficiently abnormal to have fallen outside the scope of conventional modelling.

You do not know what investments will pay off in these extreme circumstances, and nor does anyone else. You can build an investment portfolio for a rainy day, but what of a monsoon? The only certainty you can have is that a well-diversified portfolio gives you the best chance that at least some assets will retain their value – as it did for those refugees who fled with their jewellery.

The illusory security of cash and bonds

Over the years since 1980, intelligent investors have been able to make a lot of money in bonds. As worldwide inflation subsided,

---

*Perhaps significantly, Goldman had done more than its competitors to protect itself against the events of 2007–8, suggesting that its qualitative analysis was more reliable than its modelling.

interest rates steadily fell from the peaks they achieved in the 1970s. These declines in short- and long-term interest rates provided capital gains to bondholders. Even Queen Victoria's Consols proved a highly rewarding investment.

But even after inflation had more or less ended in developed economies, bond yields continued to fall and their prices to rise. The policy known as 'quantitative easing' was adopted in response to the 2008 global financial crisis. Central banks – initially those of Japan, the UK and the US, and more recently the European Central Bank – have bought bonds in enormous quantities. The Federal Reserve Board holds US Treasury securities worth trillions of dollars. The resulting distortion of the bond market has made the sector unattractive to intelligent investors.

Safe bonds from stable countries with interest rates that are around zero or even negative do not sound attractive investments, and they are not. If you were thinking of buying the 2046 bund described in Chapter 3, with its 1 per cent redemption yield, you might instead consider an apartment in Berlin or Frankfurt. That investment will yield between 3 per cent and 5 per cent. Even if the rent never rose and the property was worthless by 2046, you would have earned more from the property than from the bund. Instead of a thirty-year gilt, you might consider a closed-end fund such as City of London Trust, with an equity portfolio which currently yields 4.2 per cent. The company has increased its dividend every year for fifty years.

Since safe government bonds today are so unlikely to pay more than other investments over the long run, who holds them, and why? As a result of quantitative easing, governments themselves are, through their central banks, by far the largest owners of their own securities. But even now, most government bonds are in private hands. Some long-dated bonds are held speculatively, by people who hope to sell at a profit next week and have no interest in what happens in 2046. Others are held by institutions which are only interested in what happens in 2046. These are typically pension funds and insurance companies, which have fixed monetary liabilities stretching far into the future, and which are under regulatory or other pressure to find assets that more or less exactly match these liabilities.

But you do not fall into either category. You are not trying to anticipate the changing 'mind of the market', nor attempting to meet a fixed money claim falling due in 2046. With bonds so unattractive that you do not want to hold them directly, you also do not want to hold them indirectly, by participating in insurance or pension funds which hold them in significant quantity.

Cash and short-dated bonds are often described as low-risk investments. But they are not low-risk investments for those who want to protect their future real living standards. Many people find that statement difficult. Part of the problem is confusion between the minimisation of risk and the search for certainty. With cash and short-dated bonds you know – in a sense – what is going to happen; it is highly probable that you will get back the cash you put in. But if security is confidence in your long-term standard of living – the ability to be relaxed about retirement, the confidence that you can provide for your children or one day buy the property you have dreamed about – then cash does not provide that security.

Few if any of your long-term future liabilities are fixed in money terms. Your plans for the future are defined in real terms – the cash needed to fulfil your objectives is dependent on the purchasing power of the money of that future time. The inflation protection provided by index-linked bonds potentially offers greater certainty. Even then it is difficult to match the bonds exactly to your personal objectives. You are exposed to interest rate risk unless the pattern of payments on the bond precisely corresponds to the time path of your planned expenditures. You are also exposed to personal inflation risk – the price of the goods and services you buy is not the same as the representative basket chosen by official statisticians. And the return is extremely low;

currently most maturities of index linked bonds offer a negligible or even negative real yield.

Even in more normal circumstances, cash and bonds have little to offer the intelligent investor. The greater certainty that cash appears to provide is perhaps only the certainty that you will not do well, since nothing can provide certainty that exceptionally unfavourable outcomes are unlikely. Even in a relatively stable political and economic environment, a portfolio of bonds offers little security. Investors in British Consols lost more or less their entire wealth in the course of the twentieth century. A portfolio of indexed bonds would perform better, although this is a modern asset category that has never been tested in extreme conditions. Risks can never be eliminated, and uncertainties are inescapable. The key issue for the intelligent investor is to understand that achieving security does not lie in avoiding all risk – which is impossible – but in diversification. Do not be too vulnerable to any particular contingency, however improbable. Hold as many options as possible against a necessarily unpredictable future.

The relevance of bonds to an investment portfolio is not that they are risk-free, but that they may do well in circumstances in which other investments will not. British government bonds served their holders well in the Great Depression of the early 1930s, and were the only major asset category to do so. In Britain the oil crisis of 1973–4 became a political crisis leading to rapid inflation and a collapse of shares and property values. If indexed bonds had been available, they would have performed strongly, and would almost certainly have been the only asset class to do so.

I don't think cash or conventional fixed interest bonds normally have a role in an intelligent investor's portfolio. You will want to keep enough cash on hand for impulse and emergency purchases. Many, probably most, of the investments in the intelligent investor's portfolio are as good as cash for these purposes.

You can turn an investment in a blue chip share into money in the bank within a week. But we employ mental accounting. We don't think of our liquid securities as cash. Like me, you will probably keep more money in a deposit account than you need. You relinquish return, and gain only superficial security, from these habits.

These conclusions represent a very different approach to risk from that of the conventional investor. Most financial advisers will recommend a mix of safe and risky assets, assuming that the meaning of safety is both obvious and universal, and that investors need to be paid a premium to relinquish that safety. The robo-adviser, constrained by regulation to follow the conventional wisdom, will make similar proposals. But the most rewarding strategy for the intelligent investor is to construct a low-risk portfolio from a collection of assets which the conventional investor perceives as risky.

Contrary thinking

The conventional investor avoids judgements wherever possible. The intelligent investor is willing to make judgements. But most retail investors show bad judgement. The average investor does much worse than the market average mutual fund. The US investment research house Dalbar has for many years measured the average return earned by investors in mutual funds. Over twenty years the annual return to mutual fund savers who invested in stocks has been 5.2 per cent. Not too bad, you may think – until you are told that the total return on the S & P 500 index, the principal US stock market index, has been 9.9 per cent. The average return to holders of bond funds has been a miserable 0.8 per cent against 6.2 per cent for the equivalent bond index. This underperformance – averaging 5 per cent per year – has persisted, year in year out, in the Dalbar analysis.

Why? The average mutual fund investor, with encouragement from the financial services industry, gets timing badly wrong. Momentum effects are picked up most quickly by proprietary traders, next by professional fund managers and finally by the marketing departments of financial services businesses. Their salespeople, naturally, promote the funds that have recently done best. So money floods into fashionable sectors. Retail investors bought technology in 1999–2000, and were encouraged to buy bond funds after equity markets had collapsed. Subsequently, property funds were strongly promoted. In each case, investors bought at the top and quickly incurred losses. Doubtless they will have the same experience in bonds when interest rates return to more normal levels.

Retail investors, towards the back of the crowd, tend to suffer from mean reversion rather than benefiting from momentum. They enter the market when short-term positive serial correlation turns into long-term negative serial correlation. Jaded investors later sell the funds that promised much but delivered little. They get it wrong both when they buy and when they sell. I suspect that more than a few readers of this book recognise their own experience.

Timing peaks and troughs in the market is as hopeless as looking for hot tips. Professional doomsters continually predict market crashes and are, like stopped clocks, occasionally right. Chartists detect patterns or investment indicators that provide buy and sell signals in randomly generated data. There is little evidence of anyone, amateur or professional, generating superior returns from systematic identification of the tops and bottoms of market cycles. George Soros and Warren Buffett understood well that the 1999–2000 New Economy bubble would burst and that markets would crash. But they didn't know the date, and so they didn't profit. Even if you know that long-term mean reversion will eventually lead prices back towards fundamental values, you can't tell when. If Soros and Buffett can't – and no longer try – nor can you.

Once you have accepted that you can't time the market, there is a great deal you can still do. The dismal record of mutual fund investors suggests a place to start. Watch what these people do, and do the opposite. Their underperformance will be your out-performance. Look at the sectors promoted in advertisements. These are the sectors to avoid. When the promotions favour technology and emerging markets, think infrastructure and property. When they show photographs of roads and offices, think technology and emerging markets. Be contrarian. Your aim is to avoid following in the rear of the crowd, and to be travelling in a different – even the opposite – direction.

Modern financial markets are dominated by the power of conventional thinking. People in the financial sector share superficial views with each other and project current trends too far and too fast. Social and commercial pressures, reinforced by ubiquitous benchmarking, encourage professional fund managers to act on these widely shared opinions regardless of private reservations.

There is, almost always, an underlying element of truth in conventional thinking. The internet was an important commercial and social development. The economic progress of China and India does have a major impact on the global economy. This information is 'in the price'. More than that – the herd behaviour of professional investors means that these conventional opinions are more than fully in the price. That is part of the reason why prices display positive serial correlation in the short run and negative serial correlation in the long run. In the short run, momentum drives prices as fashion spreads; in the long run, mean reversion drives prices as fashion fades.

There are two possible ways of exploiting this behaviour. One is to ride momentum. But this is like riding a tiger. The experience will certainly be stressful and exciting, and it may be rewarding for a time, but the difficulty of timing accurately when you get on and when you get off is so great that, sooner or later, it is probable that you will be mauled (as happened to Julian Robertson). There is not much evidence that anyone can do it successfully over a long period. If anyone can do it successfully, it will almost certainly be someone very close to the market, who can detect shifts in sentiment in that brief interval when it is still possible to act but before these shifts are incorporated in prices. It is very unlikely that you will be that person.

In the second strategy – defying the fashion – the retail investor potentially has an advantage over the professional. Not being close to the market means that you are not subject to the pressures the professionals experience. You don't have to talk to trustees or clients who want to act on the news they have read in the newspaper that morning (and which everyone else has also read) – that China is growing rapidly or that the housing market is dull.

The converse of the power of conventional thinking is the power of contrarian investment. There is something paradoxical in the idea that the best way to use the expertise of the financial services industry is to do the opposite of what it recommends. This is not because that expertise is no good. It is because that expertise is 'in the price' and characteristically more 'in the price' than is objectively justified.

Some of the biggest mistakes in my own investment history have been following the crowd when the crowd was going in the right direction – for example, buying European property in 2006, when the mind of the market identified it as an undervalued asset class. Even if the crowd is right about fundamental value (and in that case I think it was), the fashion is 'in the price'. When the fashion fades, so will some of the money you have paid (and within two years it had).

Being contrarian should not be interpreted as perversity, or counter-suggestibility. Begin by limiting your contrarian strategy to broad asset categories and to funds. Be much more hesitant about taking a contrarian view of individual shares.

There is a real likelihood that a share price has fallen because someone knows something you don't. It is a common mistake to believe that if a share once sold for £5 it will reach that value again. A stock which has fallen by 95 per cent from its high has halved in value since the date at which it had fallen from its high by 90 per cent.

A contrarian investor will, however, see cases where a stock has fallen for a specific reason but by an amount far larger than that specific reason would justify, as Buffett did at American Express. The scandal was soon forgotten by both customer and market, and the stock price rose steadily. If, however, the fall had affected all house-builders, or most Japanese stocks, then it is more likely that the explanation of the price fall is to be found in general knowledge exaggerated in conventional thinking than that it is the result of inside knowledge not yet available to the markets.

Contrarianism is equally relevant to your purchase of funds. Buy the funds that aren't promoted rather than the ones that are. Closed-end funds move to large discounts to asset value when the sector in which they specialise falls out of favour, and this is an opportunity to buy.

Market timing

Here is a scheme for beating the market that really works. Imagine a volatile share that sells for 50p in odd years and £1 in even years. If you invest £100 every year in this share, over a ten-year period you will have accumulated 1,500 shares at an average price of 66.7p, well below the average market price, which is 75p.

This system will, on average, outperform the market, and the more volatile the markets, the greater the gains. The method is known as dollar cost averaging. It works through its built-in mechanism for buying more when prices are relatively low and less when prices are relatively high. No judgement is required by the investor that prices are relatively low or relatively high.

Many individuals do, and more should, make regular savings to build up an investment portfolio. Some investment managers use the benefits of pound cost averaging and extol the benefits of a regular savings scheme in their marketing literature. On this occasion, believe them. The benefits are real. But keep an eye, as usual, on their charges. Regular saving is a practice you can organise for yourself through an execution only stockbroker. You do not need to pay someone a commission to take direct debits from your account.

The effectiveness of pound cost averaging illustrates how low share prices are an opportunity rather than a problem for the intelligent investor. Conventional investors are usually excited when they hear that the market is going up, disappointed when they learn that it has fallen. As Buffett has occasionally pointed out, this is odd. We are pleased when we hear that a favourite shop has a sale, or car dealers have reduced their prices. We want high prices when we are sellers, but low prices when we are buyers. We are usually only buyers of clothes or durable goods. However, for shares – as perhaps for cars and houses – we may be both buyers and sellers at different times.

When should the intelligent investor sell? The simple answer is 'not very often'. Frequent trading endangers returns. But sometimes the mind of the market will take a security to a price well in excess of any reasonable estimate of its fundamental value. Money is a means to an end, not an end in itself, and you will sometimes sell investments in order to spend, especially if most of your total return is capital gains. In recent years, the rate at which small companies have been acquired has ensured that portfolios have a regular inflow of cash from acquisitions. This will not be true if you invest mainly in funds rather than individual securities. But if you invest in well-chosen funds, you have even less reason to wish to trade.

Pound cost averaging makes sense for both conventional and intelligent investors. Conventional investors can feel relieved that their approach yields profits without requiring judgement. Intelligent investors know that market timing is unlikely to make money and can feel happy with an approach that is inherently contrarian. The reasoning that makes pound cost averaging attractive applies to decisions about asset classes as well as to decisions about market timing. Let's see how.

Asset allocation

Investment consultants and managed funds follow each other closely. Trustees or managers are required to set benchmarks for asset allocations, and deviations from the norm – the average of what others do – require considered justification. The best way for them to minimise risk is to do much the same as everyone else. This is, of course, not a course of action which minimises risk for their beneficiaries.

When an asset category rises in value, the proportion of that asset class in the benchmark increases. Individual investors may choose to follow the market allocation; institutional investors feel obliged to follow it. Such benchmarking has led to a steady increase in the share of equities, the best performing asset class, in conventional portfolios.

The consequences can be perverse. At the peak of the Japanese stock market bubble of the 1980s, Japanese shares accounted for almost half of the value of all shares – American, European, Brazilian, Australian – in the world. American and European investors, who had thought they were brave if 10 per cent of their assets were in Japan, felt under pressure to acquire more securities in Japan. Fifteen years later, Japanese share prices had fallen, while those in other countries had risen. Today Japan accounts for less than 10 per cent of the market value of world indices.

Common sense suggests that an allocation of half your portfolio to Japan in the late 1980s was far too much, given that Japan never accounted for more than 10 per cent of world output. Most investors did, at least intuitively, understand this. While few people fell comprehensively into this Japanese trap, many investors have been victims of milder versions of the error, buying technology shares, bonds, infrastructure and property at the wrong times. Looking at market weightings when deciding asset allocation leads institutions and fund managers to buy high and sell low. This strategy leads them to purchase overpriced assets in order to achieve desired portfolio weightings.

The search for 'fundamental indices' is an attempt to resist these perverse behaviours. The idea behind a fundamental index is that asset-class weightings should be based not on market value but on some underlying measure of economic contribution. This insight leads intelligent investors to look behind financial assets and judge the value of the productive assets that underpin them. A benchmark for allocation to Japan might, therefore, be Japanese national income as a percentage of world national income, implying a range of 5–10 per cent that would remain unchanged by the vagaries of the Japanese stock markets.

From this perspective the model pension fund portfolio contains a heavy concentration of oil companies, pharmaceutical businesses and banks, relative to the economic importance of these activities. The investor who has thought in terms of fundamental indices is bound to wonder why a conventional institutional portfolio allocates ten times as much to stocks as to property. Very large economic sectors – such as agriculture, education and healthcare, and legal and accounting services – are not represented at all in the model pension fund portfolio, or are represented only in very limited ways.

You can change that. There are few quoted securities in agriculture, education or health, but there are some. There are (as yet) only a few stock market prices for law firms or accountancy practices (the first and largest quoted law firm in the UK was called Quindell, and many people pronounced its name with the stress on the first syllable). There are other businesses, such as recruitment agencies and public relations firms, whose fortunes are closely related. The conventional investor's assets are much less diversified than they might be.

The numbers that emerge from analysis based on fundamental indices may be illuminating but not true – certainly no one should regard them as more than qualitative guides. The illuminating insight is that investors should be wary of allowing fluctuations in market prices to influence their target allocations to different asset classes. If the price of property rises relative to the price of your other assets, consider reducing the proportion of your assets you hold in property, and vice versa. Many people find this paradoxical. Should we really sell securities just because they have done well? In a world characterised by momentum and mean reversion, you should. That way you can realise the benefits of dollar cost averaging in asset allocation as well as market timing.

But what is the right asset allocation? How should an intelligent investor's portfolio be divided between shares, bonds and property? I'm not sure that this is the right way to pose the asset allocation question. To do so supposes that all shares are much more like each other than they are like any of the assets in the other categories, such as property and bonds, and that the same is true in turn of these asset categories.

For the assets that institutional funds typically hold, it may well be true that all the securities within a given asset class are much the same. Their share portfolio will mainly contain large, global companies, whose prices tend to go up and down together; the bonds will mainly be medium- and long-dated government securities; the properties will mainly be well-located, city-centre office blocks with similar prospective growth in both rental levels and capital values. These funds will have followed the conventional investor's strategy of minimising the risks on individual investments rather than the intelligent investor's strategy of looking at the risk of their portfolio as a whole. So when they buy property, they buy whichever category of property their advisers currently tout as the best mixture of return and reward, and they buy several such properties. Following this conventional strategy, they fail to diversify effectively.

The 'mind your portfolio' principle implies that you should look at the expected return from individual assets and their correlation with your overall portfolio. Your objective is that every single investment you buy should significantly diversify your portfolio. You don't need, and probably shouldn't have, an intermediate process of asset allocation. Asset allocation percentages will be the result, not the preliminary, of diversifying investment decisions about individual securities. In the next chapter I'll discuss how these securities should be selected.

12

Intelligent Investment

Diversify

Most financial advisers will tell you that the conventional investor uses a low-risk strategy. I disagree. Between 2007 and 2009 the conventional investor's portfolio would have fallen in value by around 30 per cent. Many pension funds, insurance companies and charities suffered badly during that period. The Harvard and Yale endowments, which had been poster children for effective endowment management, suffered losses of 25 to 30 per cent, and both universities laid off employees. Nor was the fall experienced in the global financial crisis unprecedented. There was a similar setback in 2000–02. The loss in 1973–4 would have been greater, and there would have been additional significant dips in value at other times.

The issue, once again, is the different meanings that different people attach to the term 'risk'. Conventional investors such as local authority pension funds focus on large, widely held stocks. They interpret 'low risk' as meaning avoidance of investments that involve the possibility of loss. Each individual security in their portfolio is low-risk.

From the perspective of pension fund trustees and their investment managers, such a perspective is understandable. As I have emphasised, the major risk a financial adviser runs is not the risk that his clients do badly but the risk that his clients do worse than other people. Every committee and large organisation is crowded with people who will say 'I told you so' when things go wrong. The conventional investor will be reluctant to hold an asset that he or she can be criticised for having bought. I can take more individual stock risks with my personal investment portfolio than I can feel comfortable recommending to those I advise because I don't have to justify decisions to myself, before or after the event. I can adopt this approach even though my personal style is to maintain a low portfolio risk. I am free to 'mind my portfolio', and so are you. The typical institutional investor is not. Robb Caledon would be a risky purchase for anyone managing someone else's funds, because there is a substantial probability of total loss, followed by rebuke from a client or committee possessed of hindsight.

A portfolio indexed to the FTSE 100 or all-share index contains a lot of shares. That is not the same as diversification. Look behind the index and the broad allocations to asset categories and see the disposition of the conventional investor's £10,000. You will have large holdings in the oil majors – Exxon, Shell and BP, and in General Electric, Glaxo, Vodafone, Apple and Microsoft. You will, even after the collapse of the banking sector, have considerable exposure to finance. All these companies sell mainly to the advanced economies of the United States and Western Europe. The fortunes of these global businesses wax and wane with the world economy, and so does market sentiment towards them. Returns from all these stocks are strongly correlated with each other; and stocks like these make up most of the 70 per cent of the portfolio that the conventional investor holds in equities. The conventional investor's portfolio is not well diversified.

An emphasis on diversification implies a different approach to the selection of stocks and funds. Almost everyone thinking about investment opportunities begins by asking the question

'What is likely to go up?' But general knowledge about companies, industries and countries is knowledge that you share with everyone else and which is already 'in the price'. The record of most investment professionals in knowing what will go up is poor. You don't know what is going to go up. That is why you may have been tempted to take advice. But those who offer to advise you have little more, or no more valuable, knowledge than you, and different interests.

The construction of a diversified portfolio requires as much attention to correlation as to expected return. That approach means rejecting seemingly attractive investments because the returns from these investments are correlated with investments you already have. This will happen often, since the rationale of the earlier purchase may also apply to the new one. But using similar arguments to buy more assets of the same kind as those you already own will lead to a high-risk portfolio. Avoid overconfidence in your own judgement.

An indexed portfolio is neither diversified nor contrarian, because the weights in the index are driven by the power of conventional thinking. A more diversified portfolio should offer you expected returns similar to those of an indexed portfolio with lower volatility. (I need to enter again the health warning that if you accept the conclusions of the CAPM, as most finance academics though few practical people do, then the diversified strategy will be so popular that it will force down the average return from adopting it. Perhaps that should be true, but I don't think it is.)

Increasing diversification means holding less in pharmaceuticals and oil companies, and more in sectors whose performance is less strongly correlated with the investments you already hold. General insurance companies and house-builders, for example, may experience cycles of their own that are not necessarily in sync with the general economic cycle.

Think about activities like gold-mining and timber production, whose performance is likely to be very different from that of the general stock market. Diversify internationally. But there is no point in reducing your holding in Glaxo, a UK company, in order to increase your holding in Pfizer, a US company: these companies have very similar businesses. A small pharmaceutical company – whether British or American – whose fortunes will probably rise or fall with the success of individual drugs may offer attractive potential returns (many investors think it is high-risk, as in a sense it is) with lower correlation and hence little risk relative to your overall portfolio. Look to Japan or Russia or Taiwan for less correlated opportunities, but real diversification from these investments will come from companies oriented to their domestic economies, rather than businesses with which you are more familiar. Sony, Gazprom and Lenovo sell to the same people as Microsoft, Shell and Vodafone.

Fund selection

Most investors will, and should, begin with funds rather than individual stocks. Funds may be distinguished by investment style or by sectoral or geographic specialisation. Choose funds whose returns are not strongly correlated with each other – be diversified. Choose funds that are out of favour rather than fashionable – be contrarian.

A web site such as Morningstar or Trustnet will give you a wide – far too wide – selection. In every category there are many similar funds doing similar things. I am not going to recommend specific funds, but the criteria I will describe will narrow the range very considerably.

You might consider exchange-traded funds here, since the range of indexed open-ended funds is limited, and the ETF sector offers a variety of country options. You can invest not just in the US and US indices but also in Brazil, Taiwan and other small and emerging markets. In the larger markets you can choose to focus on smaller or larger companies, or on a particular sector, such as utilities or real estate. Plan to build up a diversified portfolio of such funds, emphasising sectors that are unfashionable.

Then consider an allocation to actively managed funds. Pick two or three idiosyncratic funds with widely different styles and approaches. Such diversification gives a better balance of risk and return. But keep a close eye on charges. A company that charges 1 per cent or more for a closet index fund is ripping you off. Buying a closed-end fund with a low ongoing charges ratio and a large discount to asset value gives you a chance of earning the return generated by the underlying productive investments. Most funds go to a discount of 10 per cent or more from time to time, if you are content to wait. The widening of the discount is a good contrarian signal when it is the result of the unfashionability of the sector rather than the poor performance of the fund. You can easily check whether it is the stock or the sector that is out of fashion by looking at similar funds. If the TER is above 1 per cent, the fund must justify these charges by its distinctive style (low correlation with market indices) and proven success. Few can.

How to distinguish proven success from the 'hot hand'? Favour funds that are strongly identified with an individual. Good fund managers are people rather than corporations, although on occasion good processes are the creation of innovative founders. Idiosyncratic funds with a strong record are typically provided by boutiques, but there are exceptions – legendary fund managers Anthony Bolton and Peter Lynch ran funds for Fidelity.

Buy funds that have a history of good performance, but look for a long history and, above all, ensure that the track record was good both before and after the fund manager became famous. Do not follow names that are famous for reasons other than their investment performance, such as supermum Nicola Horlick or the ubiquitous Richard Branson. Most good track records are the product of lucky streaks and are then aggressively marketed, only to disappear. There is some evidence of investment skill, but it is rare.

Property

While most equity funds are open-ended, most property funds are closed-end. Most such funds are real estate investment trusts (REITs). Companies with REIT status are tax-exempt, so that shareholders are taxed broadly as if they owned a share of the properties of the fund. Land Securities and British Land, the largest UK property funds, are REITs. Some other property funds, such as F&C Commercial Property Fund, achieve a similar effect by registering the company offshore while being listed in London. There are also some closed-end property funds that do not qualify as REITs, typically those with large development programmes or extensive borrowings, or which are invested largely overseas.

Closed-end property funds generally have substantial leverage – much more so than closed-end funds that invest in shares. You need to be careful about this leverage. Your £1,000 investment in a fund might correspond to £3,000 of property and £2,000 of borrowings. If you hold geared assets, you should remember the 'mind your portfolio' principle. An investment of £1,000 in such a leveraged fund, with the balance of £2,000 in bonds, would give you the same property exposure as £1,000 in an unleveraged open-ended fund.

These open-ended property funds mostly do not use leverage. Some, such as Standard Life and Threadneedle, are invested directly in property, and they sell and redeem units at a price that reflects the value of the underlying assets. When the property market fell in 2007, some open-ended funds suspended redemption. Other open-ended property funds, such as Aberdeen, invest only in REITs and other property shares. While some property funds cover a wide spectrum of properties, most have a bias towards particular geographical areas or sectors. REITs, like other closed-end funds, are attractive when you can buy them at significant discounts to their asset value (which, at the moment of writing, you can); again, do not buy closed-end funds at a premium. You should expect to pay higher management charges for a property fund than for an equity fund, because the costs of looking after buildings are greater than the costs of looking after paper.

Foreign property can provide further opportunities for diversification. You can buy foreign property through UK-based funds, but you need not pay additional charges for doing so. You can easily buy REITs or property companies domiciled in American or European markets, such as Vornado (a US REIT which owns prime New York office blocks) or Unibail-Rodamco (a Dutch company, the largest quoted property business in continental Europe).

With such a range of possibilities, it is easy with two or three purchases to construct a portfolio of property assets diversified across different kinds of property – offices, shops, industrial, residential – and across geographical locations – Britain, the rest of Europe, North America.

Stock picking

As your experience of intelligent investment grows, you will wish to consider individual stocks. Even if you have a large, diversified portfolio, you will probably not own more than 1 per cent of the stocks you could buy. That means you can, and should, be extremely selective. It is as though you were speed-dating thousands of potential partners. You are fortunate in being spoilt for choice, and one good reason for rejection is enough.

The basic principles of stock picking follow from Chapters 5 to 8. You are concerned with fundamental value, not momentum in the share price – with the characteristics of the company rather than the stock price history. Conventional investors are unduly averse to specific risk which affects one company alone and which can and should be diversified. You do not mind that an individual stock is risky, so long as it does not add greatly to the risk of your portfolio as a whole. That implies, of course, that you can understand what these risks are.

If conventional investors are sometimes too prone to avoid risk – the known unknowns – they are also too prone to accept uncertainties – the unknown unknowns. Use probabilities to assess risk, be detached and recognise uncertainties by knowing when you don't know.

Everywhere and always in financial markets, you are vulnerable to information asymmetry. The company and its executives know more – or are at least capable of knowing more – than you do. The greater the information asymmetry, the more likely it is that the bargain is in fact a lemon. If you don't understand something, or the affairs of the company or the strategy or construction of the fund appear unnecessarily difficult to understand, do not buy. If the share price is falling for inexplicable reasons, do not buy.

Institutional investors will have access to the research on companies that banks circulate to their clients. You will find it difficult to obtain much of this, although you can see similar material in magazines such as *Investors Chronicle* or in newsletters (tip sheets). These reports are more useful for the information they obtain than for the recommendations (though you will probably have readier access to the latter). You should understand a little of what these analysts do, not in order to reproduce their conclusions, but because their approach and conclusions are 'in the price'.

An analyst will provide 'coverage' of a group of companies

with similar activities. If these businesses are very large, the analyst will be responsible for only a very few stocks, though an analyst of smaller companies may cover twenty or more. The bank that employs the analyst frequently hopes to obtain (or has already obtained) corporate finance business from the companies on which it undertakes research; for small companies, the bank that managed the IPO will often provide the only coverage. This limits objectivity.

An analyst is rewarded for 'good calls'. (The results of ThomsonReutersExtel ratings of analysts, based on opinion polls of institutions, have a major influence on their reputation and remuneration.) A good call is a successful prediction of a sharp upward or downward movement in the share price. But the timescale on which the call is judged will rarely exceed six months. Although many research reports appear to be concerned with fundamental value, a good call will often anticipate a news announcement relevant to the company (generally either merger and acquisition activity or a substantial revision to earnings expectations). Or, in the manner of Keynes's beauty contest, an analyst may make good calls by being quick to assess the changing mood of other analysts.

The favoured analyst will be close to the companies he or she follows, and able to infer from nudges and winks whether announcements will be behind, or ahead of, market expectations. The less favoured analyst – one whose reporting has a critical tone – will be shut out. Analysts who take a negative view of a company frequently receive abuse from chief executives and provoke complaints to the senior management of the banks that employ them.

As I described in Chapter 5, the growth of financial conglomerates transformed sell-side analysts into a sales force for investment banks. Following the New Economy bubble, the damage to the reputations of the firms concerned, and pressure from regulators, forced investment bankers to concede greater independence to analysts. Recommendations still have a strongly positive bias, but the institutions at which they are aimed are able, at least in part, to offset this bias. Analysts' research is focused on short-term earnings announcements and projections.

Most analysts simply project current earnings in a mechanical fashion. Even if they are trying to assess fundamental value, they typically do the calculation by making estimates of earnings and translating them into a DCF model. These analysts' valuations are what is 'in the price'. Estimates of fundamental value play a relatively minor role.

Stock selection

A basic checklist for any company you consider investing in should contain the following points: the company should be clear and transparent in the presentation of its affairs and accounts; and the background and remuneration of its senior executives should suggest that they are experienced in and interested in the business, rather than being primarily concerned with self-aggrandisement or self-enrichment. These are necessary precautions against information asymmetry, and necessary preliminaries to judging risks. If you wouldn't buy a used car from the directors, then you shouldn't buy a share in the company, and for essentially the same reasons.

There should also be a clear, comprehensible business model, based on a distinctive capability that has the potential to create sustainable and appropriable competitive advantage. The only sources of fundamental value are tangible assets and competitive advantage. If you cannot identify tangible assets from the accounts that support the valuation, or don't understand the source of the competitive advantage of the business, then you cannot judge either its fundamental value or the risks associated with it. Avoid unnecessary uncertainty.

You will normally look for companies that are soundly financed. Borrowings should be less than the value of the company's readily realisable assets, and the business should generate cash. Operational risk in a company is inescapable. But when an established business compounds operational risk with financial risk, it adds uncertainty to risk. The company may become dependent on the indulgence of its bank or the vagaries of interest rates, and vulnerable to modest economic or business setbacks. Usually this fragility in profit-and-loss accounts or balance sheets is the product of debt-financed acquisitions or of financial engineering. Both large-scale acquisitions and financial engineering generally give negative signals about the preoccupations of the company's management.

Where the weak balance sheet is the result of recent poor trading, the position may be more interesting. Most players in financial markets tell stories rather than think probabilities. They believe the company is going bust, or that it is not – they rarely express the view that there is a probability of 0.4 that it might, or might not, go bust. Analysts, brokers and fund managers are not often detached. They may still be in love with the purchase they made at a much higher price, or worried by the criticism they might receive from bosses or trustees who possess the benefit of hindsight. As at Robb Caledon, the market price of a risky investment may be a poor guide to the expected value.

Be wary of companies with growing profits and negative cash flow. A new, rapidly expanding business or a firm with a large investment programme may have transparent reasons for continuing external funding. The difficulty of explaining the discrepancy between profits and cash should have steered intelligent investors away from Enron.

You can reduce uncertainties by focusing on stable businesses. There are fewer uncertainties in the market for water – a monopoly whose basic technology was developed millennia ago – than in the market for more competitive and exciting activities, such as computers or biotechnology. Even companies in relatively stable markets can create uncertainty by programmes of acquisitions and disposals. Most of the fundamental value of any company derives from the cash it will generate five and more years into the future. If you don't know what the company will be doing five years from now, how can you assess its value? Such strategic uncertainty is unnecessary and avoidable.

Look for clarity and transparency in the company's account of its affairs: a simple business model based on distinctive capability that offers sustainable competitive advantage; and a strong balance sheet with cash flow generation and a stable business. A stock that meets all of these criteria is unlikely to be a ten or twenty bagger, but you are looking for a reliable 8 per cent annual return, not ten or twenty baggers.

Most companies will fail to meet at least one of these criteria. But there are many more fish in the sea. Your aim is to buy good companies on a contrarian basis, probably when their sector is out of fashion. If investors generally applied these criteria in selecting stocks, their decisions would transform the behaviour of British corporations. And overwhelmingly for the better. There would be less financial engineering, fewer acquisitions, simpler and more modest executive remuneration. And, above all, less emphasis on investor relations activities to influence the mind of the market and more on the creation of fundamental value through the identification and development of competitive advantage in operating businesses.

The preoccupations of most professionals are elsewhere. They are focused on earnings guidance and their quarterly performance figures. They are fixated on 'corporate activity' – a term that is often simply a euphemism for mergers and acquisitions, and more generally means an announcement that may have a material effect on share prices. Such activity is the basis of market gossip, and keeps market turnover high.

The intelligent investor isn't, and doesn't want to be, party to that market gossip. The intelligent investor isn't seeking votes in the ThomsonReutersExtel survey. Your reward comes from good investment returns, not from the bonuses you receive for the business you attract.

13

The Customers' Yachts

'Why do I want to buy what they want to sell?' This question is fundamental to investment. Both buyers and sellers own securities in the hope of income and capital gains. But the returns the buyer will obtain are exactly the returns the seller could have obtained if he or she had held on to the shares. Why should you buy what they want to sell?

In any market in which there is wide and unresolvable uncertainty, and in any market where participants have different information and beliefs, many trades will be the result of mistakes. In financial markets, uncertainty and differential information are endemic. When you trade, you need to be confident that it is not you who is making the mistake. Bear in mind the old gambler's maxim: if you don't know who is the patsy in the room, it is probably you.

Keep it simple. If you don't understand a financial product, don't buy it. We purchase cars and computers and many other things without understanding how they work – it is enough to understand their purpose. We rely on the reputation of Mercedes or Microsoft for our belief that their products will actually deliver what they promise. Many people dislike thinking about money, and would like to hand over their financial affairs to someone they can trust. Unfortunately, such trust isn't enough to deal with product complexity in modern financial markets. The nature of trade in financial services and the ethics and behaviour of financial services businesses are different. Good reputations seem to survive bad behaviour. Many of the suckers who were ripped off in the New Economy bubble came back to be victims of the credit bubble.

Scepticism is appropriate. If it sounds too good to be true, it usually is. In most markets you tend to get what you pay for. But not necessarily in finance. The greater the extent of differential information, the less likely it is that costs and charges represent value. The most certain way of increasing returns on your investments is to pay less in fees and commissions. You are on your own, but in the modern world you are never alone with a computer. The contents of the last chapters are startlingly different from those I would have included two decades ago.

The internet gives cheap and easy access to financial products for everyone, and immediate access to information that once required diligent research. Innovations in financial markets – such as the growth of exchange-traded funds and property vehicles – have transformed the opportunities available to retail investors to build for themselves a portfolio that achieves low risk through wide diversification. The intelligent investor today is in greater danger of trading too much because it is easy than of being deprived of opportunities because access is too difficult.

Securities markets mediate differential information. The activity of trading assimilates uncertainty and disagreement to establish 'the mind of the market'. The market is often described as a voting machine, weighing and evaluating different assessments to arrive at a market view. This line of thought leads to the efficient market hypothesis. All available information about securities, economic developments, the success and failure of business strategies and our political and technological futures is already in the price.

There is something in this argument, although it is a mistake to take it too seriously. The efficient market hypothesis is illuminating, but not true. There are investment lessons and profit opportunities both in what is illuminating, and in what is not true. Across the market as a whole, the profits on financial investment must ultimately depend on the profits on productive investment. For all the intricacies of modern finance, the yield of securities depends on the ability of trading businesses to find profitable ways of serving their customers, on the willingness of tenants to pay rents on shops, offices, houses and factories, and on the ability of companies, consumers and governments to service and repay loans that finance their recent investment or current consumption.

The fundamental value of companies depends on their success in establishing competitive advantages over their rivals, and such sustainable competitive advantages are the only enduring source of superior returns. The value of a property depends on the rents derived from it. The value of a bond depends on the interest it yields and the principal it repays. These determinants of fundamental value necessarily drive securities prices in the long run.

But the short run is very different, characterised by the literal and metaphorical noise of the trading floor. The notion that market prices are the result of a plebiscite on competing estimates of fundamental value is far removed from the reality of frenzied dealing in modern financial markets. Most participants are preoccupied not with long-term economic trends and the competitive advantage of companies but with evolving market opinion and the ephemeral news that passes across the Bloomberg screen.

In an efficient market what is 'in the price' is an average of divergent views. But often what is in the price is the manifestation of a common City view, generally held within the Square Mile but not necessarily well founded. The New Economy bubble was an extreme instance of widely held perceptions that were also widely at variance with reality. Prices that are going up tend to continue going up – markets are characterised in the short term by short-term serial price correlation, or momentum. In the long run prices that have gone up by a lot tend to go down – there is mean reversion to fundamental value. If only we could know when the short run becomes the long!

It is possible, though unusual, to make money out of observing and anticipating market momentum. Some people, though not many, are close to the market and have an intuitive feel for, or perhaps an analytic understanding of, its determinants. Whatever the books on trading will tell you, the chances that the person who makes money out of observing and anticipating these fluctuations will be you, the retail investor, are very small.

The only basis on which the intelligent investor can hope to keep up with, far less beat, the market is by attention to fundamental value. Through attention to fundamental value, the intelligent investor gains a big advantage over investment professionals who are judged on their performance quarterly, or even more frequently. There is no way in which an investor, amateur or professional, who is focused on fundamental value can reliably outperform the market on a monthly or quarterly basis – the noise is far too loud. But, over the long run, mean reversion works in your favour.

Not being party to the conventional wisdom of these professionals gives you an opportunity to be contrarian. Contrarianism requires scepticism but is not perversity. The opportunity for contrarianism arises when the question 'Why do I want to buy what they want to sell?' can attract the answer 'Because they have bad reasons for wanting to sell it'. The investment community cannot afford to ignore the noise, but you can. Patience pays. To a trader, an asset is worth only what he can sell it for; to a long-term investor, the asset is worth the higher of market price and fundamental value.

The principal risk investment professionals run is the risk of underperformance relative to their peers. Most investment institutions benchmark their performance against their competitors and market averages. There are good reasons for this benchmarking, but also malign consequences. But what interests the intelligent investor is how much money he or she makes, not how much money he or she makes relative to other people. Relative performance doesn't pay the bills.

Relative performance has no spending power, but money has equal spending power whether it comes as income or capital gain. Think 'total return'. Treat both income and capital gain as part of the yield on your investment. Set a prudent spending rate by reference to your expected total return over a period of years. If your underlying investment objective is capital growth, then reinvestment of dividends will contribute substantially to capital appreciation in the long run. If your underlying investment objective is to obtain a steady income from investments, an 'income' can be generated, if necessary, through occasional sales from a growing portfolio. A 'think total return' strategy is equally relevant to investors who are accumulating wealth and investors who are using their assets to support their standard of living.

The return on productive investments provides the basis for realistic expectations of what an investment portfolio can yield. If you earn higher returns than the yield on productive investments, these returns can only be obtained at the expense of other people who are obtaining lower returns than the yield on productive investments. This may be because you are willing to take risks that they are not, or because you have a superior investment strategy. But you cannot expect consistently to derive more than a modest premium to market returns from these sources.

Your objectives colour your strategy. One justification for the substantial fees financial advisers charge directly and indirectly to retail investors is that such investors need individually tailored advice. While there are some honest and conscientious independent financial advisers, the majority of people who make contact with small savers do not have the capacity or knowledge to give such advice, even if they had the inclination and the financial motivation. If you still doubt this, test them with some questions about the meanings of terms defined in the Glossary.

I am not convinced anyway that much tailoring of investment strategy to particular needs is required. The most important issue is the stage of your working and investing life. Are you a net saver or a net spender? Most people have broadly similar investment objectives – to support their future standard of living, without more precise definition. For the vast majority of investors, risk is uncertainty about their future standard of living. These objectives define both the meaning of risk and your approach to risk.

I've given a lot of space in this book to different ways of thinking about risk, and described at length in Chapter 7 the theory I have called SEU. Treated both prescriptively and descriptively, this theory completely dominates quantitative approaches to investment today. Intelligent investors should learn to 'think SEU' – to understand its principles but not to follow them blindly. That means learning to think probabilities and expected values. Such an approach recognises that many different outcomes are possible, and assesses, even quantifies, the likelihood of attractive and unattractive outcomes.

SEU implies detachment in investment decisions. If you are a gambler by temperament, you may enjoy the search for a ten bagger, but the expected value of the search is likely to be negative; i.e., it will, on balance, cost you money. If you are concerned principally to minimise the regret that you will feel (or your bosses will make you feel) with hindsight, then the expected value of your strategy is also likely to be negative. These losses of expected value are the costs of emotional involvement with your investments.

The most important implication of SEU is the 'mind your portfolio' principle. Every investment decision should be judged not just by the character of the individual investment but also by the contribution it makes to your overall portfolio. An incidental, but large, benefit of being your own investment manager is that you are the only person who can have complete knowledge of your affairs.

Like the efficient market hypothesis, SEU is an illuminating theory so long as you do not make the mistake of believing that it is true. It is not true either as a prescriptive theory – What should I do? – or as a descriptive theory – How do market participants respond to risks and uncertainties? The conventional view is that you, the typical dumb investor, don't think SEU, but that markets do. This view is mistaken. Markets don't generally think this way, but you often, though by no means always, should. SEU is a powerful tool for thinking about well-defined risks, the things we know we don't know. SEU can describe the risks you encounter when you play roulette, or wonder what the Monetary Policy Committee will decide about interest rates at its next meeting. Risks such as these are things we know we don't know, and for which we can plausibly attach probabilities to a range of defined outcomes. But SEU helps little when we contemplate uncertainties. The things we don't know we don't know. The many situations in which probabilistic reasoning is of little help.

The prevalence of uncertainty explains why SEU thinking doesn't come naturally. We didn't experience the complexities of modern financial markets in the long process of evolution that hardwired our brains, or in the schools and playgrounds where we were taught to cope with life. Many, though by no means all, situations we face in financial markets are ones for which SEU methods are relevant. We make mistakes. Sometimes the mistake is not to use SEU principles when they might help us – as with the stockbrokers who could not take a detached view of Robb Caledon. More sophisticated investors sometimes make the error of using SEU principles where they don't assist – as in the banks whose risk-modelling failed to describe the events that brought them to their knees.

The sophisticated world of modern finance relies on models and forecasts in its assessment of both risks and fundamental values. Most people who are not professionally engaged in building models or producing forecasts respond to models and forecasts with cynical naïveté – a curious mixture of disdain and credulity. At a visceral level such people know that no model can capture the complexity of the world of finance, business and politics, yet they treat the output of models with the utmost seriousness. They believe that economic forecasts convey little useful information, and yet they pay almost obsessive attention to them.

Financial analysis without models is impossible. But investment managers and executives of financial services firms who rely on the output of models they don't understand have relinquished decision-making to a black box. Such individuals profess adherence to science, but their behaviour is indistinguishable from that of earlier generations of decision-makers who consulted the oracle or employed soothsayers to read the entrails. You don't have to be able to build models yourself, but you do have to understand a little of what the models can do in order to understand and make best use of the limited but real insights they can provide. Numbers can illuminate, but can also blind.

You need analysis and models more than you need forecasts. If you were able to see the future, profitable investment would be easy, but you can't. Nor can anyone else. The only useful information that people who predict the level of the stock market a year from now give you when they speak is that you should pay very little attention to anything they say. General knowledge about the future is 'in the price'. Specific knowledge about the future is vouchsafed to very few, and the people who have such information which is not in the public domain are mostly prohibited from trading on it.

Instead of devoting time to speculation about what the future holds, recognise that the future is inescapably uncertain. Equip yourself with options that will be robust to many different contingencies. Options and diversification are the most effective responses to cope with a complex world. Knowing what you don't know gives you a considerable advantage over those, amateurs and professionals alike, who don't know what they don't know. Or, more dangerous still, those who know what isn't so. A broadly diversified portfolio based on real assets will give you considerable protection against risk and uncertainty with little compromise on return. In a 100 per cent efficient market, there might be an unavoidable trade-off between risk and return, but in a partially efficient market there is not. New investment technology using internet dealing means that the retail investor can achieve a diversified portfolio with relatively modest sums.

Modern financial markets are complex, but much of the complexity is for the benefit of providers rather than consumers of financial services. If you don't understand it, don't do it. That simple maxim would have saved both amateurs and professionals billions of pounds over the years. The more recent the years, the larger the savings.

Three simple rules – pay less, diversify more and be contrarian – will serve almost everyone well. If you have an established investment portfolio based on advice, you will almost certainly find that a substantial part of your total assets is in open-ended managed funds that are closet-indexed. This costs you too much and is inadequately diversified. You can transfer this money into a group of exchange-traded funds, closed-end funds and real estate investment trusts on substantial discounts. That strategy will give you exposure to a range of countries, types of security and styles of management. Such a strategy will give you lower charges, and less risk in your overall portfolio. An emphasis on market sectors at a discount will automatically imply a contrarian stance. You will lose what you have already paid in initial charges to set up your investments, but that money has gone anyway. If you are at an earlier stage of your investment career, you can structure your portfolio on these lines from the beginning.

Whether or not you choose to hire a financial adviser, you are on your own. I hope this book can be your companion.

Glossary

Absolute return The total return on a portfolio. Absolute return is measured without benchmarking or reference to market movements. 32

Acquisition The takeover of one company by another. 79

Acquisition accounting Accounting treatment designed to flatter the accounts of the acquiring company. 101

Active management (portfolio) Professional asset selection. Contrast with passive management, which simply follows an index. 53

Agency costs Costs of intermediation, which reduce the returns on financial investment relative to those of the underlying productive investment. 212

Allais paradox A problem in behavioural economics devised by the French economist Maurice Allais which demonstrates a 'Dutch book'. 149, 175

Alpha Outperformance of an investment or investment fund, relative to a benchmark, adjusted for risk. (The *beta* of the portfolio is calculated to measure what part of excess return is accounted for by return to above-average risk.) 145, 191

Alternative investment Asset outside mainstream categories of shares, bonds and property. Traditionally alternative assets were mostly physical objects (such as paintings and commodities), but more recently the term is used to refer to private equity and hedge funds. 193

Alternative investment market (AIM) Market for shares in small companies that do not meet the standards for a full London Stock Exchange listing. 197

American Depository Receipts (ADRs) New York-traded versions of shares from countries other than the US. 34

Amortisation *See* DEPRECIATION.

Anomalies Deviations from the efficient market hypothesis. **61, 79**

Arbitrage A strategy to profit from divergences in the prices of similar or related securities. **43, 187**

Arbitrageurs Traders using arbitrage strategies, especially those that trade between an acquirer's stock and that of the prospective acquisition. **53**

Asset stripping Breaking up a company to realise the value of its underlying assets. **111**

Asset value The value of the assets underlying a security (which may differ from the market price of the security). **52, 111**

Asset-backed securities (ABS) Tradable securities based on a pool of loans. An asset-backed security can have several tranches of security relating to the same asset pool; if the value of the pool deteriorates, the senior tranches will be paid first. **186**

Bagger (as in 'ten or twenty bagger') Speculative stock which increases greatly in value. **26, 258**

Basis point Each percentage point of yield is 100 basis points. **202**

Bayesian The view that degrees of belief can be expressed as probabilities updated with new information. **135**

Behavioural finance, behavioural economics Analysis based on empirical or experimental studies of behaviour (especially towards risk) rather than models of rational choice. **81, 149, 176**

Benchmark The index specified to judge an investment manager's performance. **90**

Best execution The obligation to place a trade at the best price available in the market. **8**

Beta The predicted effect on the price of a security of a 1 per cent movement in the benchmark index. **145, 191**

Big Bang Deregulation of the City of London in 1986. **9, 189**

Black–Scholes model The most widely used model for pricing options. **165, 184**

Blue chips Shares in large companies. **121, 212**

Bonds Securities with fixed interest rates and redemption dates. **41**

BRIC Principal emerging markets – Brazil, Russia, India, China. South Africa has sometimes also been included.

Buy side Investors and their advisers (contrast with 'sell side'). **85**

Call option The right to buy a security at a fixed price at a future date (*see* PUT OPTION). **184, 199**

Capital asset pricing model (CAPM) A model that predicts that expected rates of return will be determined by a combination of the risk-free rate and a risk premium determined by the asset category and the asset *beta*. **147**

Carry trade Arbitrage strategies that yield repeated small profits, usually from interest rate differentials (*see* TALEB DISTRIBUTIONS). **162, 193**

Chartist (*see* TECHNICAL ANALYSIS) Someone who predicts security prices by identifying trends from charts. **59, 159**

Chinese walls Measures (including rules and physical separation) to prevent different divisions (principally buy side and sell side) of a financial institution from exchanging information. **78, 192**

Closed end An investment fund whose shares can be acquired or disposed of only by selling to another investor. Such a fund may therefore sell at a premium or discount to its asset value. **51, 218**

Closet indexation Active management which closely follows the content (and performance) of the benchmark index. **91**

Collateral Provision against a liability. **54**

Competitive advantage The ability of a business to produce at lower cost, or to command higher prices, than other businesses serving the same market. **113**

Complex systems Social or natural systems whose mathematical description demands dynamic, non-linear relationships. **81**

Compound interest Calculation in which returns are increased by interest on reinvested interest. **30, 106**

Confirmation bias A tendency to select evidence that supports views that are already held. **158**

Consensus forecast The median (or perhaps mean or modal) forecast, a product of the tendency of all economic forecasters to cluster together. **65**

Consumer prices index *See* HARMONISED INDEX OF CONSUMER PRICES.

Contract for difference (CFD) An agreement to pay (or receive) the difference between the present and future prices of a security. **182**

Contrarian Someone who buys assets not currently favoured by the mind of the market. **237**

Conventional investor An investor who applies closet indexation. **11, 205**

Correlation Assets are correlated if movements in their prices tend to move in the same direction (*see BETA*). **64**

Cost of capital The cost to a firm of raising capital (typically an average of the cost of corporate debt and the total return required by equity shareholders). **107**

Counterparty The person on the other side of a transaction. Market counterparties are institutions trading securities. **182**

Credit rating An assessment of credit risk, often by a rating agency. **45**

Credit risk The risk that a borrower will fail to meet the interest or principal on a loan. **41, 152**

Day traders Small speculators who buy and sell frequently, perhaps within a single day. **26**

Depreciation An allowance against profits for the fall in value of assets through time or use (*see also AMORTISATION*). **105**

Derivatives Securities whose value is based on the value of other securities. **182**

Diminishing marginal utility A tendency for additions to income or wealth to be valued less by the beneficiary as that income or wealth increases. **139, 148**

Discount rate, discounted cash flow (DCF) The process of discounting future revenues to compute a present value. **106**

Distressed debt Bonds or loans on which the borrower may fail to make payment. **191, 203**

Diversification The process of reducing risk by buying assets whose returns are uncorrelated. **144, 230**

Dividend The dividend on a share is the (usually biannual) payment declared by the company. **35**

Dividend yield The dividend yield is the annual dividend per share as a percentage of the share price. **36**

Dutch book A sequence of apparently attractive gambles which, if accepted, will leave the taker worse off. **175**

Earnings before interest, tax, depreciation, amortisation (EBITDA) A profit figure reported by companies seeking to deliver flattering accounts of their affairs (*see PRO FORMA EARNINGS*). **105**

Earnings guidance The process by which companies influence analysts' forecasts of their earnings. **91**

Earnings per share Profits after tax, divided by the total number of shares in issue. **36**

Earnings yield (*see* PRICE EARNINGS RATIO) Earnings per share, as a percentage of the share price. **98**

Eat what you kill The practice in professional firms of rewarding partners by reference to the revenues the individual partners themselves generate. **104**

Efficient market hypothesis (EMH) The proposition that all relevant information about the value of a security is reflected in its price. **7, 59**

Emerging market Country outside the principal developed economies (e.g., BRIC countries). **52**

Endowment mortgages A scheme to repay the principal of a mortgage from the proceeds of a life assurance policy. **3, 13**

Enhanced bonds A structured product that uses derivatives to provide a higher yield (and risk) than the underlying bond. **183, 200**

Equity An equity interest is the right to receive what is left after prior claims have been met: e.g., ordinary shareholders receive the residual after debts and preferred shareholders have been paid. The owner's equity in a house is its value less the value of any outstanding mortgage. **20**

Equity premium, equity risk premium The expected difference between the return on shares and the return on a safe asset. **32, 108**

Exchange-traded fund (ETF) A fund traded on a stock exchange whose value is linked to an index. **53, 260**

Execution only The service offered by a broker who will deal but not advise. **208**

Exercise price The price on which you can buy or sell a share under option (*see* STRIKE PRICE). **185**

Expected value The average outcome of a gamble, calculated by multiplying potential pay-offs by their probabilities. **128**

Expiry date The last date at which an option can be exercised. **185**

Fat tails A phenomenon in which extreme events happen more frequently than a standard statistical distribution (e.g., binominal or normal distribution) allows. **167**

Financial engineering The attempt to create value by repackaging investment products. **195**

Financial Conduct Authority (FCA) The principal UK regulatory agency. **161**

Financial investment, productive investment Financial investment is investment in securities; productive investment is investment in the activities that give these securities their value. 20

Financial Times **index (FTSE)** The original *Financial Times* index was an average of the prices of thirty leading stocks. Today the most widely used UK indices are the FTSE 100 (one hundred major shares) and the FTSE all-share index (all shares quoted on the London Stock Exchange). 40

Fractal A geometric shape, each part of which resembles the whole. 168

Free cash flow Net cash from operations after deducting necessary investment. 108

Fundamental indices Market indices in which the weights of different securities are derived from economic indicators other than their market values. 244

Fundamental value The expected value of the cash flows generated by an asset. 56, 204

Futures The right to buy or sell a security or commodity at a fixed price on a future date. 158

General knowledge Publicly available information. 65, 170

Generally accepted accounting principles The principal US accounting standard. 100

Going concern basis The assumption (for valuation purposes) that a company will continue in business. 35

Gross redemption yield (GRY) The total return from a bond, including any decline or increase in capital value between the present and maturity. 43

Halo effects The tendency to give high ratings to all characteristics of a favoured item or individual. 158

Harmonised index of consumer prices (HICP *or* CPI) A European standard measure of inflation. Differs from UK Retail Prices Index mainly in its limited treatment of housing costs and technical details of construction. Generally increases more slowly than RPI. 31

Hedge An asset whose price is expected to move in the opposite direction from the price of the asset it hedges. 143

Hedge fund An adventurous, open-ended investment company charging high fees. 25, 181

High-net-worth Rich. 12

Hot hand Persistence of strong performance (*see* SERIAL CORRELATION). **159**

Independent Two variables are independent if their movements are unrelated. **144**

Independent financial adviser FCA category for adviser who is obliged to consider all products before making recommendations, and not just those of his employer or a restricted group of providers. **12, 264**

Index fund Fund whose value follows that of a benchmark. **199**

Index-linked stocks Securities on which interest and principal increase in line with inflation. **42**

Information asymmetry Characteristic of markets in which the seller knows more about the goods than the buyer. **65**

Initial public offering (IPO) The first offering of stock in a company to the public. **34, 194**

Insider trading Dealing by corporate executives or their advisers (or their agents) on the basis of information about the company not yet publicly disclosed. **60**

Insolvent A company or individual is insolvent when liabilities exceed assets. **48, 127**

Intangible assets Assets other than property, plant and investments: e.g., brands, patents, reputation. Sometimes called 'goodwill'. Figures for intangible assets reported in balance sheets mainly refer to overpayment for acquisitions and mean little. **112**

Intelligent investor Someone who defines their own investment strategy by reference to fundamental value, thinks total return and minds their portfolio. **222**

Interest rate risk The risk that a bond will fall in value due to interest rate rises. **41**

International financial reporting standards Accounting standards applied in most countries outside the United States. **100**

Investment banking Traditionally, banking focused on securities issuance and corporate advice (principally IPOs and acquisitions). Modern investment banks also undertake (principally undertake) market-making and asset management. Most are now part of financial conglomerates with corporate and retail banking operations. **85, 218**

Investment-grade The best-quality bonds, as defined by rating agencies. **46**

Investment trusts Closed-end funds quoted on a stock exchange. **51, 218**

ISA (individual savings account) A scheme that allows share and corporate bond holdings free of income or capital gains tax. 15, 208

Junk bonds Bonds below investment grade. 189

Know your customer The regulatory obligation on a financial adviser to base recommendations on specific knowledge of the investor's circumstances. 12

Lemons Goods that the seller, but not the buyer, knows to be of inferior quality. 66

Leverage The process of increasing risk and potential return on an asset through borrowing. 48

Life insurance Insurance policy which pays on the death of the insured. Often packaged with savings products – such a package is called life assurance. 18

Likelihood The degree of belief in a narrative. 78, 127

Long The opposite of short: a positive position in a security. 138, 181

Long end Bonds with long periods to run until redemption. 43

Long/short fund A fund that takes short positions as well as long. (A 130/30 fund will own shares worth 130 per cent of its value and have short positions equivalent to 30 per cent.) 191

Mark to market The practice of revaluing assets in line with current market values. 56, 94

Market capitalisation The total value of the shares of a company. 114

Market risk The risk profile created by general market movements. 145

Mean reversion A tendency for variables to return to their long-term average. 65

Mental accounting An inclination to compartmentalise a portfolio rather than to mind a portfolio as an aggregate. 178

Mergers The combination of two firms. 9, 102

Momentum (*See* SERIAL CORRELATION). The tendency for price movements to continue in the same direction. 64

Monoliners Financial services firms that specialise in a single product or product group. 16

Moral hazard The tendency for average product quality to deteriorate when there is information asymmetry. 68

Mortgage-backed security (MBS) An asset-backed security whose value is based on a pool of mortgages. 190

Mutual fund A US term for a European OEIC (*see* OPEN-END INVESTMENT COMPANY). 30

New issues The sale of new shares for cash by a company (*see* IPO). 9

Noise Short-term price movements not justified by changes in fundamental value. 37

Noise traders Frequent traders who act on noise (*see* DAY TRADERS). 37

Nominee account Holding securities through a bank rather than in one's own name. 208

Non-recurring items Costs that a company does not want to charge against profits. 105

Normal distribution The most common – bell-shaped – statistical distribution. 128

Open-end investment company (OEIC) A fund that creates or redeems shares or units in line with investor demand. 51

Option The right to buy or sell securities at a price agreed in advance. 184

Over-rented A property on which the current rent exceeds the market rent. 51

Overweight No longer the result of long City lunches! Holding a larger proportion of one's portfolio in a particular security than the share of that security in the relevant index. 90

Passive fund, passive investment A fund or investment strategy that tracks an index. 53

Passive management The opposite of ACTIVE MANAGEMENT. 53

Payment-in-kind securities Bonds on which the interest rate increases as the creditworthiness of the borrower declines. 140

Payment protection insurance Retail product which may meet loan repayments during sickness or unemployment. 19, 102

PE ratio The ratio of the market price of the share of a company to its earnings per share. 96

PEG ratio The ratio of the PE ratio and the growth rate of earnings. 98

Penny shares Shares whose value is only a few pence per share (even though there may be many millions of shares). Often issued to appeal to noise traders. 26

Personal pensions A scheme for long-term saving which may allow tax relief on contributions and tax-free accumulation. 13, 209

Personal probability (subjective probability) An estimate of the probability of a particularly outcome of a single event. 132

Pound cost averaging A scheme that reduces the average purchase cost of securities by regular investment. 242

Price:earnings ratio The ratio of the market price of a security to earnings per share after tax. 36, 96

Principal The amount outstanding on a loan. 41, 107

Private equity fund A fund that takes large stakes in unquoted companies. 194

Productive investment *See* FINANCIAL INVESTMENT.

Pro forma **earnings** The profits companies would like you to think they have earned. 105

Proprietary trading ('prop desks') The internal hedge funds of banks. 27

Protected equity A structured product which limits the risk of equity investment. 198

Put option An option to sell a security at a price agreed in advance. 184, 199

Quant Someone who specialises in mathematical modelling of investment questions. 6

Quantitative easing The purchase of debt securities by a central bank. 234

Random walk A process in which each change is independent of all previous changes. 58, 65

Rating agencies Companies (Moody's, Standard & Poors, Fitch) that evaluate and grade the quality of bonds. 45

Rational expectations The assumption that individual expectations reflect all potentially available information. 74

Real estate investment trusts (REITs) Closed-end funds which invest in property and enjoy a special tax regime. 51, 252

Real return Investment return after allowing for inflation. 31

Redemption date The date on which a loan will be repaid. 41

Reflexivity A characteristic of a process in which expected outcomes of a process affect the outcomes themselves. 88

Regression fallacy Mistaken attribution of mean reversion to a more fundamental cause. 163

Relative performance Investment performance relative to a benchmark. 32

Retail investor Someone who is not a professional investor or a market counterparty and therefore enjoys additional regulatory protections. 4, 188

Retail Prices Index (RPI) A UK consumer price index (*see* HARMONISED INDEX OF CONSUMER PRICES). 31

Retained profits Profits that are not distributed as dividends. 35

Revenue recognition Anticipation of revenues not yet received in cash. 101

Reversionary A property on which the market rent is below the current rent. 51

Risk-averse Disposed to value risks or gambles at less than their expected value. 141

Risk premium, equity risk premium The difference between the return on a risky asset and the yield on a safe one. 32, 108

Running yield The income yield on a bond whose market price differs from its redemption value (*see* GROSS REDEMPTION YIELD). 43

Scenario planning A mechanism for reviewing plans by positing several different scenarios of the future. 158

Secured loans Loans secured against specific assets. 20

Sell side The issue of securities and the provision of corporate advice (*see* BUY SIDE). 85

Serial correlation The relationship between price movements in successive time periods. Short-term positive serial correlation is when price movements continue in the same direction (momentum). Long-term negative serial correlation is the tendency for long-term movements to reverse (mean reversion). 64

Sharpe ratio The ratio of standard deviation (variability) to the return from an asset. 134

Short end Bonds with early maturities. 43

Short-term positive serial correlation (*See* MOMENTUM) The expectation that short-term price movements will be followed by other moves in a similar direction. 64, 238

Short sellers A negative position established to benefit from the fall in value of a share. 70, 182

SIPP (self-invested personal pension) A tax-advantaged scheme for long-term investors. 208

Sophisticated or high-net-worth investor Someone who under FCA rules may invest in a wider range of assets but loses certain regulatory protections. 15, 224

Specific risks Risks that are specific to the investment concerned and unrelated to movements in the general level of share prices. 144

Spread betting (*See* CONTRACT FOR DIFFERENCE) Betting on the rise and fall of a security or index. 182

Statistical arbitrage Computerised trading systems for exploiting short-term discrepancies between prices of similar securities. **191**

Stock options The right (often given to senior executives) to buy the company's shares at a future date at a favourable price. **92**

Strike price The price at which an option is granted. **184**

Strip A bond that has been divided into different components: e.g., one group of holders receives the interest, another repayment of principal. **189**

Structured product Security with complex relationship to the underlying assets and liabilities. The result of financial engineering. **198**

Subjective expected utility (SEU) A theory that individuals should or do approach risk by maximising the expected value of pay-offs using subjective (personal) probabilities. **125**

Subprime borrower, subprime mortgage Subprime borrowers have poor credit ratings, and the loans they take out in turn also attract the adjective subprime. **49, 158**

Survivor bias Misleading generalisation about performance based on analysis of a population from which poor performers have been removed. **163, 195**

Sustainable competitive advantage A competitive advantage that a business can successfully maintain over time. **114**

Swap, swap rates (generally of interest rates). A swap rate defines the terms on which fixed and variable rate obligations can be exchanged. The transaction is a swap. **17, 182**

Synergies Alleged benefits from mergers. **86**

Taleb distributions Processes in which frequent small gains are punctuated by occasional large losses. **78, 161, 192**

Technical analysis What chartists do. **79**

Time preference The 'exchange rate' between present and future consumption. **21**

Total expense ratio (TER) Management and related charges as a proportion of assets. Now superseded by ongoing charges ratio. **213, 251**

Total return Investment return as a percentage of assets, including both income and capital gain. **23, 220**

Tracking error A measure of how closely an index fund follows the benchmark index. **53**

Trading floor Traders in investment banks typically work at desks and screens in one trading room. **9**

Triple-A The highest grade of bonds. **46**

Underweight *See* OVERWEIGHT.

Unit trusts *See* OPEN-END INVESTMENT COMPANY.

Value at risk In risk modelling, the anticipated loss at some low percentile of the risk distribution. **129, 134**

Variability, volatility Measures of how much and how rapidly a security price goes up and down. **48, 133**

Winner's curse The tendency for assets to be bought by the person who makes the highest assessment of their value. **67**

With-profits insurance policy A form of investment product, linked to insurance, whose returns are determined, on opaque principles, by the company's actuaries. **29, 199**

Yield curve The relationship between interest rates and bond maturities. **43**

Bookshelves and Bookmarks

Do you want a small investment reference library? Both the *Financial Times* and *The Economist* offer guides that cover most investment topics – Glen Arnold's *Financial Times Guide to Investing* and Peter Stanyer and Mark Meadowes's *Guide to Investment Strategy*. A book like Dominic Connolly's *UK Trader's Bible* has more extensive coverage of the mechanics of markets and trading. And there are several guides to the broader context of personal finance. See, for example, the *Which?* guides from the Consumers' Association, particularly those on *Be Your Own Financial Adviser* and on taxation. If you plan to buy individual stocks, you should have a book on how to read accounting statements, such as Bob Parker's *Understanding Company Financial Statements*. The world of business and finance is notorious for writing that luxuriates in jargon and complexity. John Lanchester's *How to Speak Money* is an excellent antidote and guide.

Do you want a book that contains the secrets of how to be rich? I hope not. But you might want advice from Soros and Buffett. The most relevant of George Soros's several books is *The Alchemy of Finance*, while Lawrence Cunningham offers an entertaining collection of extracts from the essays Buffett writes in his annual reports to Berkshire Hathaway shareholders (which are available on the company's web site). *Snowball*, by Alice Schroeder, is an exhaustive biography of the sage of Omaha.

If you want a small shelf of books about the industry that are fun to read, you might consider: from the 1980s, Burrough and Helyar's *Barbarians at the Gate*, an account of the last days of RJR Nabisco, and *Liar's Poker*, by Michael Lewis, set in Salomon in its heyday; and John Cassidy's account of the New Economy bubble, *dot.com*, best read in parallel with J. K. Galbraith's *The Great Crash 1929*, which is beautifully written; its lessons are all still relevant.

The best narrative account of the global financial crisis is Andrew Ross

Sorkin's *Too Big to Fail;* Michael Lewis's *The Big Short* is a highly enter-taining account of one aspect of its origins, and the same author's more recent *Flash Boys* is an introduction to some of the issues raised by the absurd world of the high-frequency trader. I do not recommend the self-congratulatory memoirs of those who claim to have saved the world from the crisis for which they themselves were largely responsible; but Mervyn King's *The End of Alchemy* instead tries to draw lessons for finance and economics in relatively detached manner.

A comparison of Tom Wolfe's *The Bonfire of the Vanities* and Anthony Trollope's *The Way We Live Now* reveals that, while the actions and the instruments change, the fundamentals of financial follies do not.

Do you want another book like this one, which aims to provide practi-cal advice with a rigorous intellectual basis? (I'm not sure whether I would like you to answer yes or no to that question.) The model that was in my mind from the beginning is Burton Malkiel's *A Random Walk down Wall Street*, which has been for years what I recommended to the encouragingly numerous people who sought such a book. *Random Walk* has been through eleven editions since it was first published in 1973, but its age shows, and the institutions and products it considers are American. So are the jokes, which are not to European taste. Still, it remains a classic. The permanent classic is Benjamin Graham's *The Intelligent Investor.*

Other academics who have written popular books on investment are Jeremy Siegel, whose *Stocks for the Long Run* is an unashamed paean to the virtues of equity investment, and Robert Shiller, who had the good fortune to publish *Irrational Exuberance* just as the New Economy bubble was bursting. Similar books you might consider are William Bernstein's *Seven Pillars of Investing Wisdom* and either of David Swenson's volumes, *Pioneering Portfolio Management* and *Unconventional Success.* Swenson, Yale's much-fêted investment manager, adopts a rather similar approach to the one described here, but Swenson invests better than he writes.

There are many books written on corporate strategy and for investment analysts, but not many target readers of this book would want to finish them. Dick Rumelt's *Good Strategy, Bad Strategy* is witty and perceptive and has lessons for investors as well as corporate executives. I'm bound to recommend my own *The Hare and the Tortoise,* a distillation of *Founda-tions of Corporate Success.* Peter Bernstein's *Against the Gods,* on risk, is an exemplar of how to make complex concepts appear simple.

Do you want to pursue some of the more philosophical issues that have arisen in the course of this book? Quants and risk managers in the financial world make constant case of probabilities without much thought about what the numbers they readily deploy mean. Ian Hacking's *An Introduction to Probability and Inductive Logic* provides a good introduction to the underlying complexities. Questions about the nature of explanation – What does it mean to say a theory is illuminating but not true? – are at the heart of this book. People of a philosophical bent will appreciate the influence of Richard Rorty, whose related ideas are best set out in *Philosophy and the Mirror of Nature*. I found Wade Hands's *Reflections without Rules* an invaluable introduction to the central relevance of this sort of approach in modern economics.

Whatever books you put on your shelves, you will want to add some favourites to your computer. The internet gives you easy access both to products and information. But good web sites cost money to build and maintain, and, one way or another, he who pays the piper at least influences the tune. The fiercely independent Money Saving Expert has many useful financial tips, but unfortunately doesn't take you far into investment. You can access most financial services products through comparison sites such as Money Supermarket, though bear in mind that comparison sites are financed through commission. All financial services organisations use web sites to market and give access to their products, and competitive pressures ensure that most are easy to locate and use.

The internet also makes access to information much easier. Most companies have an investors relations section on their web site, from which you can obtain annual reports and other financial information. Your stockbroker's site will probably have a research section that summarises these data and gives you other data about the company. Pricing and trading information is available on the London Stock Exchange's own web site. This is one of several sources of regulatory news – companies are required to announce their results, large holdings and directors' dealings. Yahoo Finance is a good source of general equity market information, and Morningstar additionally provides information about funds; Trustnet is also useful here. Interactive Investor and ADVFN offer free access to information – and bulletin boards. While these are amusing, both the information and opinions should be treated with great caution.

Bibliography

Allais, M., 1953, Le Comportement de l'Homme Rationnel devant le Risque: Critique des Postulats et Axiomes de l'Ecole Americaine. *Econometrica*, v. 21, no. 4, p. 503, doi:10.2307/1907921.

Bachelier, L., trans. M. H. A. Davis and A. Etheridge, 2006, *Louis Bachelier's Theory of Speculation: The Origins of Modern Finance.* Princeton, NJ: Princeton University Press.

Bayes, M., and M. Price, 1763, An Essay towards Solving a Problem in the Doctrine of Chances. By the Late Rev. Mr. Bayes, F. R. S. Communicated by Mr. Price, in a Letter to John Canton, A. M. F. R. S. *Philosophical Transactions of the Royal Society of London*, v. 53, pp. 370–418, doi:10.1098/rstl.1763.0053.

Bernoulli, D., 1954, Exposition of a New Theory on the Measurement of Risk. *Econometrica*, v. 22, no. 1, p. 23, doi:10.2307/1909829.

Biggs, B., 2008, *Wealth, War, and Wisdom*. Hoboken, NJ: John Wiley & Sons.

Black, F., and M. Scholes, 1973, The Pricing of Options and Corporate Liabilities. *Journal of Political Economy*, v. 81, no. 3, pp. 637–54, doi:10.1086/260062.

Bowden, M., 2012, *The Finish: The Killing of Osama bin Laden*. New York: Atlantic Monthly Press.

Buffett, W., and L. A. Cunningham, 2002, The essays of Warren Buffett: lessons for investors and managers: Singapore; Chichester, Wiley.

Cunningham, L., 2002, *How to Think Like Benjamin Graham and Invest Like Warren Buffett*. London: McGraw-Hill Education.

Dimson, E., P. Marsh, and M. Staunton, 2002, *Triumph of the Optimists: 101 Years of Global Investment Returns*. Princeton, NJ: Princeton University Press.

Fama, E. F., and K. R. French, 1992, *The Cross-Section of Expected Stock Returns*. Chicago, IL: Center for Research in Security Prices, Graduate School of Business, the University of Chicago.

Friedman, M., and L. J. Savage, 1948, The Utility Analysis of Choices Involving Risk. *Journal of Political Economy*, v. 56, no. 4, pp. 279–304, doi:10.1086/256692.

Friedman, M., 1976, *Price Theory: A Provisional Text*. Chicago, IL: Aldine.

Graham, B., 1985, The intelligent investor: a book of practical counsel: New York, NY, Harper & Row.

Harrod, R. F., and J. R. Hicks, 1939, Value and Capital. *The Economic Journal*, v. 49, no. 194, p. 294, doi:10.2307/2225091.

Hicks, J., 1939, *Value and Capital; An Inquiry into Some Fundamental Principles of Economic Theory*. Oxford: Clarendon Press.

Kahnemann, D., P. Slovic, and A. Tversky, 1982, *Judgment under Uncertainty: Heuristics and Biases*. Cambridge: Cambridge University Press.

Kay, J., 2016, *The Long and the Short of It: A Guide to Finance and Investment for Normally Intelligent People Who Aren't in the Industry*. London, Profile Books.

Keynes, J. M., 1920, *The Economic Consequences of the Peace*. New York, Harcourt, Brace and Howe.

Knight, F. H., 1921, *Risk, Uncertainty and Profit*: Boston, MA: Houghton Mifflin.

Lo, A. and MacKinlay, A., 2002, *A Non-Random Walk Down Wall Street*. NJ: Princeton University Press.

M., H. W., and J. M. Keynes, 1933, Essays in Biography. *Journal of the Royal Statistical Society*, v. 96, no. 3, p. 512, doi:10.2307/2342137.

Malkiel, B., 1973, *A Random Walk down Wall Street*. New York: W.W. Norton.

Markowitz, H., 1952, Portfolio Selection. *The Journal of Finance*, v. 7, no. 1, p. 77, doi:10.2307/2975974.

Pigou, A. C., and J. M. Keynes, 1921, A Treatise on Probability. *The Economic Journal*, v. 31, no. 124, p. 507, doi:10.2307/2223083.

Selman, L., and Wright, J., (Hymans Robertson), 2014, LGPS structure analysis: December 2013, Department for Communities and Local Government, available at: https://www.gov.uk/government/uploads/system/uploads/attachment_data/file/307926/Hymans_Robertson_report.pdf

Sharpe, W. F., 1964, Capital Asset Prices: A Theory of Market Equilibrium under Conditions of Risk. *The Journal of Finance*, v. 19, no. 3, p. 425, doi:10.2307/2977928.

Shiller, R. J., 2000, *Irrational Exuberance*. Princeton, NJ: Princeton University Press.

Soros, G., 2003, *The Alchemy of Finance* (2nd edn). London: John Wiley and Sons Ltd.

Taleb, N. N., 2001, *Fooled by Randomness: The Hidden Role of Chance in the Markets and in Life*. New York: Texere.

Zuckerman, G., 2009, *The Greatest Trade Ever*. London: Penguin Books.

Zweig, J., 2008, *Your Money and Your Brain*. New York, Simon & Schuster.